The Evangel Dean Basic Training Manual

A Guide for Church Plant Movement Leaders to Equip Urban Church Planters

. . . .

Edited by
Rev. Dr. Hank Voss
Rev. Dr. Don L. Davis
Rev. Bob Engel

TUMI Press
3701 East Thirteenth Street North
Wichita, Kansas 67208

The Evangel Dean Basic Training Manual:
A Guide for Church Plant Movement Leaders to Equip Urban Church Planters

© 2019. The Urban Ministry Institute. All Rights Reserved.

The Urban Ministry Institute
3701 East 13th Street North
Wichita, KS 67208

ISBN: 978-1-62932-325-1

Published by TUMI Press
A division of World Impact, Inc.

The Urban Ministry Institute is a ministry of World Impact, Inc.

This manual is dedicated to

urban church planters around the world

the valiant men and women who have sacrificed personal ease and safety
to minister to those who are the voiceless, the broken,
and the most neglected in human society.

They have responded with open hearts and willing souls,
are willing to engage these communities with love and grace,
and are fearless in prophesying the deliverance of Christ and his Kingdom
to those who have been chosen to be rich in faith,
and heirs of the Kingdom (James 2.5).

For their courage and sacrifice,
for their burden and energy,
for their passion and perseverance,
we thank our Lord and God.
May their "beautiful feet" continue to walk the streets and alley-ways
of the neediest cities of this world,
never failing to publish peace, bringing Good News of happiness,
publishing to city dwellers God's salvation
and declaring without fear and shame that Jesus Christ is Lord,
to the glory of God.

~ Isaiah 52.7 ~

Table of Contents

Appendix

Additional Readings, Seminars, and Team Exercises

Evangel School Resource Pack Information

Welcome Letter

Greetings in the name of the One who is the Lord of the harvest.

We believe these are critical times. The harvest is plentiful and the workers continue to be few. As we consider the vast numbers of souls who are lost and without hope in Christ, we believe that church planting movements are needed to rapidly deploy called, gifted, and totally surrendered workers into every city, town, and village.

It is from this belief and from our missions calling to empower urban leaders and partner with local churches to reach their cities with the Gospel to the end that the Gospel of the Kingdom is proclaimed by the empowered urban poor to every people group through indigenous churches and movements. The Gospel continues to be the power of God for salvation; for hope in this world and the world to come.

If you: believe in the Church of the living God, no matter her size or resources, and that the keys of the Kingdom have been given to her; and you believe in the Gospel, that God in Christ is reconciling the world to himself; that the poor are rich in faith and co-laborers in God's kingdom advancement; and your heart breaks for the countless lost souls trapped in the bondage of the kingdom of darkness; then this handbook will refresh, challenge, and strengthen you to equip planters among the forgotten poor.

As you praise, pray, work, think, strategize, and laugh with your fellow deans-in-training, we hope you will be encouraged in what the Lord will do through your investment in learning about the Evangel Church Plant Schools.

Our prayer is that you would complete this training encouraged in the Lord and clear on your strategy for training church planters working among the urban poor.

Thank you for joining with us in seeking the beauty of the Lord displayed in new ways in the cities where God has called you to represent his Kingdom. Thank you for your unwavering and sacrificial service to the Lord of the harvest.

". . . Not of those who shrink back . . ." (Heb. 10.39)

Rev. Dr. Don Davis
Rev. Bob Engel

The Vision and Objectives of the Evangel Dean Training

Vision: Provide excellent equipping for church plant trainers working among the urban poor through the commissioning of deans certified to run Evangel Church Plant Schools in their own ministry context.

Objectives:

- Provide specialized, sustainable, and reproducible training for church planters working among the urban poor, especially bi-vocational church planters.
- Equip church plant teams within their ministry context by providing Evangel schools in urban centers across the United States and around the world.
- Create a network of skilled trainers who can host schools in multiple locations around the United States.
- Help urban church plant trainers to design their **ABC** system (Assessment, Boot Camp Training, Coaching).
- Partner with mission agencies, TUMI satellites, urban church associations, and denominations to host Evangel Schools across the country and around the world.

Evangel Dean Training Big Idea: Our team, upon completion of enlistment, basic training, and boot camp will be spiritually, strategically, and tactically ready to train urban church planters using *Ripe for Harvest: A Guidebook for Planting Healthy Churches in the City* in conjunction with Evangel Church Plant Schools.

World Impact, TUMI, and Evangel School of Urban Church Planting (History and Relation)

World Impact was founded in 1971. World Impact empowers urban leaders and partners with local churches to reach their cities with the Gospel to the end that the Gospel of the Kingdom is proclaimed by the empowered urban poor to every people group through indigenous churches and movements.

The Urban Ministry Institute (TUMI) was launched in 1995. As a national training arm for World Impact, the Institute equips leadership for the urban church, especially among the poor, in order to advance the Kingdom of God. We focus our investment on leaders who are called to evangelize, disciple, plant, pastor churches, and facilitate church planting movements especially among the poor. Our single passion and desire is to advance the Kingdom of God in America's inner cities and around the globe.

The Evangel School of Urban Church Planting was developed by The Urban Ministry Institute as one of several tools designed to equip urban church planters working among the poor. The Evangel Church Plant School operated between 2000 and 2006 during which time more than 40 church plant teams were commissioned.

In 2015, under the leadership of World Impact's then president, Rev. Efrem Smith, the Evangel School of Urban Church Planting was recommissioned. In its new format, Evangel now emphasizes training urban church planters within their own ministry context. The emphasis is on training urban church planters *from* and *for* the poor and on equipping them with the best resources and strategy possible.

While the first Evangel Church Planting School was held in 2000, 2016 marks the first time that TUMI is officially certifying other groups to run Evangel Church Plant Schools in their own ministry context. Those who intend to host an Evangel School will need to send at least two prospective deans for certification.

The Dean Training aims to provide excellent equipping for church plant trainers working among the urban poor through the commissioning of deans certified to run Evangel Church Plant Schools in their own ministry context.

Those who complete the training and are certified will be authorized to use Evangel's textbooks (e.g. *Ripe for Harvest: A Guidebook for Planting Healthy Churches in the City*; and *Planting Churches among the City's Poor: An Anthology of Urban Church Planting Resources, Vols. 1 and 2*), videos, PowerPoint presentations and other resources developed for Evangel Church Plant Schools in their own ministry contexts.

The Evangel Dean School Training focuses on two outcomes: 1) Dean teams will be spiritually, strategically, and tactically ready to train urban church planters using *Ripe for Harvest: A Guidebook for Planting Healthy Churches in the City* in conjunction with Evangel Church Plant Schools. 2) Dean teams will be inspired and challenged to implement the foundations of missions as church plant movement leaders.

Our Mission-Critical Perspectives

1. *The Calling of God*: We do all we do fully assured that God is at this very moment calling, gifting, and anointing men and women in the city to represent his interests there, and are convinced that these chosen city leaders will be the vessels through whom he advances his Kingdom.

2. *The Kingdom of God*: We are burdened to see the freedom, wholeness, and justice of the Kingdom of God embodied, celebrated, and proclaimed in church communities who show visibly what the "Rule of God" looks like when it is embraced by people who acknowledge Christ's lordship.

3. *The Centrality of the Church*: We hold deeply the conviction that effective ministry takes place in the Body of Christ, the agent of the Kingdom, where we facilitate the multiplication of healthy, reproducing urban churches, especially among the poor.

4. *The Power of Community*: We share a passion to employ innovative distance education programming to create and outfit a network of training centers in urban areas that provide excellent, affordable, and spiritually dynamic ministry education that is sensitive to urban culture.

5. *God's Election of the Humble*: We possess a certitude that God has chosen those who are poor in the eyes of this world to be rich in faith and to inherit the Kingdom which he promised to those who love him (James 2.5).

6. *The Standard of Excellence*: We are held by the consuming belief that all effective, credible leadership development demands the requisite formality and rigor of disciplined excellence, with a flat refusal to be remedial or second-class.

7. *The Explosiveness of Multiplication*: We are zealous to facilitate and empower urban church planting movements that share a common spirituality, express freedom in cultural expression, and strategically combine their resources to reach and transform the cities of America and the world.

Seminars

SEMINAR 1

The Evangel Church Plant School and TUMI's Vision

Rev. Dr. Don L. Davis

> As he reasoned of righteousness, temperance, and judgment to come, Felix trembled.
>
> ~ Acts 24.25
>
> We who rejoice in the blessings that have come to us through the Savior need to bear in mind that the gospel is not good news only!
>
> The message of the cross is good news indeed for the penitent, but to those who obey not the gospel, it carries an overtone of warning.
>
> The Spirit's ministry to the impenitent world is to tell of sin and righteousness and judgment. For sinners who want to cease being willful sinners and become obedient children of God, the gospel message is one of unqualified peace, but it is by its very nature also an arbiter of the future destinies of man.
>
> Actually, the message of the gospel may be received in either of two ways: in word only without power, or in word with power.
>
> The truth received in power shifts the bases of life from Adam to Christ – a new and different Spirit enters the personality and makes the believing man new in every department of his being!
>
> ~ A. W. Tozer

I. A Vision as Wide as the World

A. World Impact's Strategic Vision

1. *Purpose Statement*: Our purpose is to honor and glorify God and delight in Him among the unchurched urban poor by knowing God and making Him known.

2. *Mission Statement*: As a Christian missions organization, we are committed to facilitating church planting movements by evangelizing, equipping, and empowering America's urban poor.

3. We are committed to recruit, empower, and release urban leaders who will plant churches and launch indigenous church planting movements.

4. *Global Ends Statement*: The Gospel of the Kingdom proclaimed by the empowered urban poor to every people group through indigenous churches and movements.

5. *Our Tag Line*: Transforming Communities Together

6. Davis's reflections on the indigeneity of World Impact's language (three implications)

   a. To be truly missional is to discern our part in what God wants to do through us and others.

   b. God can do in and through any people whatever he desires; he can be as strong in them as he has been in us.

   c. All peoples deserve the right to engage in efforts to advance the Kingdom, and to fail as many times as we have!

B. The Institute's Purpose

   1. To equip leaders

   2. For the urban church

   3. Especially among the poor

   4. In order to advance the Kingdom of God

C. The Institute's Goal

   1. The Goal is Wisdom

   2. The Six Overall Objectives

II. Leadership as Representation and Our Mission-Critical Perspectives

A. The big idea in Christian leadership is representing Christ.

B. An official Evangel School requires an understanding and embrace of our Mission-Critical Perspectives.

1. *The Calling of God*: We do all we do fully assured that God is at this very moment calling, gifting, and anointing men and women in the city to represent his interests there, and are convinced that these chosen city leaders will be the vessels through whom he advances his Kingdom.

2. *The Kingdom of God*: We are burdened to see the freedom, wholeness, and justice of the Kingdom of God embodied, celebrated, and proclaimed in church communities who show visibly what the "Rule of God" looks like when it is embraced by people who acknowledge Christ's lordship.

3. *The Centrality of the Church*: We hold deeply the conviction that effective ministry takes place in the Body of Christ, the agent of the Kingdom, where we facilitate the multiplication of healthy, reproducing urban churches, especially among the poor.

4. *The Power of Community*: We share a passion to employ innovative distance education programming to create and outfit a network of training centers in urban areas that provide excellent, affordable, and spiritually dynamic ministry education that is sensitive to urban culture.

5. *God's Election of the Humble*: We possess a certitude that God has chosen those who are poor in the eyes of this world to be rich in faith and to inherit the Kingdom which he promised to those who love him (James 2.5).

6. *The Standard of Excellence*: We are held by the consuming belief that all effective, credible leadership development demands the requisite formality and rigor of disciplined excellence, with a flat refusal to be remedial or second-class.

7. *The Explosiveness of Multiplication*: We are zealous to facilitate and empower urban church planting movements that share a common spirituality, express freedom in cultural expression, and strategically combine their resources to reach and transform the cities of America and the world.

III. Evangel – What's in a Name?

A. Meanings and uses of the term "evangelism" (*evangelion*)

1. Evangelism as *content* (the testimony of God's salvation through the incarnation, death, and resurrection of Christ)

    a. *Evangelion* as "good message, good tidings" – This term refers in the NT to the salvation we possess through faith and trust in Jesus Christ, that same salvation which we all receive on the basis of our personal faith in the Lord Jesus, founded upon his expiatory death, his burial, resurrection, and ascension, cf. Acts 15.7; 20.24; 1 Pet. 4.17.

    b. Alternative meanings and nuances

        (1) The gospel of God (Mark 1.14; Rom. 1.1; 15.16; 1 Thess. 2.9; 1 Pet. 4.17)

        (2) The gospel of his Son (Rom. 1.9)

        (3) The gospel of Jesus Christ, the Son of God (Mark 1)

        (4) The gospel of our Lord Jesus (2 Thess. 1.8)

        (5) The gospel of the glory of Christ (2 Cor. 4.4)

        (6) The gospel of the grace of God (Acts 20.24)

        (7) The gospel of the glory of the blessed (1 Tim. 1.1)

        (8) The gospel of your salvation (Eph. 1.13)

        (9) The gospel of the Kingdom (Matt. 4.23; 9.35; 24.14)

2. Evangelism as *presentation* (verbs used in association with the content of the gospel)

    a. *kerusso* – to preach as a herald (Matt. 4.23; Gal. 2.2)

    b. *laleo* – to speak forth (1 Thess. 2.2)

    c. *diamarturomai* – to testify thoroughly (Acts 20.24)

    d. *evangelizo* – to preach (1 Cor. 15.1; 2 Cor. 11.7; Gal. 1.11)

    e. *pleroo* – to preach fully (Rom. 15.19)

3. Evangelism as *demonstration* (terms used in association with the presentation of the gospel)

    a. *Sunathleo en* – to labor with in (Phil. 4.3)

    b. *Sunkakopatheo* – to suffer hardship with (2 Tim. 1.8)

    c. To show forth the reality of the Kingdom message in word, life and deed

        (1) God's reign (Christ's ultimate authority)

        (2) God's righteousness (God's character and covenant)

        (3) God's realm (restoration/reconciliation of all things)

B. Jesus, Paul, and the Church (representative samples)

1. Jesus and the Evangel of the Kingdom: Mark 1.14-15 (the declaration of the Already/Not Yet Kingdom)

2. Paul and the Evangel: Rom. 1.16-17 (the apostolic testimony of God's offer of salvation to the nations, cf. Rom. 16.25-27; Col. 1.28-29; Eph. 3.3-10)

3. The Church, the Evangel, and the Kingdom: (the guardian of the Good News), 1 Tim. 3.14-16 – I hope to come to you soon, but I am writing these things to you so that, [15] if I delay, you may know how one ought to behave in the household of God, which is the church of the living God, a pillar and buttress of the truth. [16] Great indeed, we confess, is the mystery of godliness: He was manifested in the flesh, vindicated by the Spirit, seen by angels, proclaimed among the nations, believed on in the world, taken up in glory.

C. Gospel priority: we must keep the main thing the main thing

1. *Servants* of the Evangel: *We unconditionally lay down our lives for Christ and the gospel.* Mark 10.29-31 – Jesus said, "Truly, I say to you, there is no one who has left house or brothers or sisters or mother or father or children or lands, for my sake

and for the gospel, [30] who will not receive a hundredfold now in this time, houses and brothers and sisters and mothers and children and lands, with persecutions, and in the age to come eternal life. [31] But many who are first will be last, and the last first."

2. *Stewards* of the Evangel: *We faithfully defend and embody the Good News against dilution or change.* 1 Cor. 4.1-2 – This is how one should regard us, as servants of Christ and stewards of the mysteries of God. [2] Moreover, it is required of stewards that they be found faithful.

3. *Sowers* of the Evangel: *We unashamedly proclaim and demonstrate the power of the Good News to the nations.* Mark 16.15-18 – And he said to them, "Go into all the world and proclaim the gospel to the whole creation. [16] Whoever believes and is baptized will be saved, but whoever does not believe will be condemned. [17] And these signs will accompany those who believe: in my name they will cast out demons; they will speak in new tongues; [18] they will pick up serpents with their hands; and if they drink any deadly poison, it will not hurt them; they will lay their hands on the sick, and they will recover."

IV. Evangel's Roots

A. Rooted in the Love of Christ

1. Rooted in the work of Jesus, and our faith in him (Col. 2.7)

2. Rooted in Christ's Love (Eph. 3.17–19)

B. Rooted in the Gospel message itself (evangel)

1. The two wings of the Gospel: Rom. 1.16-17

a. No shame in our game: bold testimony of the Good News of Christ

b. Its *bold proclamation* through our words

c. Its *compelling demonstration* through our good works

2. The necessity of repentance[1]

    a. Repentance: *metanoia* (the movement of the convicted heart); redirection of the life under God's reign

       (1) Change of mind (Matt. 21.28-29; Luke 15.17-18; Acts 2.38)

       (2) Godly sorrow for sin (Ps. 38.18; Luke 18.9-14)

       (3) Confession and forsaking of sin (Luke 15.18; 18.13; Prov. 28.13; Isa. 55.7)

       (4) Turning to God in Christ (Acts 26.18; 1 Thess. 1.19)

       (5) Movement towards restitution and restoration (Luke 19.8-9)

    b. The saving power of faith

       (1) Faith: *pistis* (The medium of saving commitment); reorientation of one's life values and vision

       (2) Knowledge of the apostolic witness concerning Jesus of Nazareth (1 Cor. 15.1-4)

          (a) The incarnation

          (b) The passion

          (c) The death

          (d) The resurrection

          (e) The witness and the testimony

       (3) Confession of Jesus as Lord (Rom. 10.9)

       (4) Belief in God's resurrection of Jesus (Rom. 10.9)

---

1   Don L. Davis, *Evangelism and Spiritual Warfare*, Vol. 8, 16 vols. *Capstone Curriculum*. Wichita, KS: The Urban Ministry Institute, 2005.

C. Rooted in the Scriptures (The Authoritative Tradition)

1. Church Planters who love the Rabbi's Teaching (cf. John 8.31-32)

2. Discern the negotiable from the non-negotiable by relying on three levels of tradition

   a. The Authoritative Tradition (the principle of apostolicity), found in canonical Scripture

   b. The Great Tradition (the consensus embodied and defended in the historic orthodox Christian communion)

   c. Specific Church Traditions whose theology and practice testify consistently to the Great Tradition of the Church

D. Rooted in the Great Tradition: Sacred Roots

1. What has been believed everywhere, always, by all (Vincent of Lerins, 5th century)

2. As summarized in the Nicene Creed (AD 381)

   a. It summarizes the Story of God.[2]

   b. It is critical for establishing new believers and developing urban Christian leaders[3] [248–49].

   c. Its role in training urban church plant team leaders [249–52].

E. Rooted in a wide variety of specific church traditions (interdenominational)

1. Welcomes a wide variety of Nicene church traditions

---

2 Don Davis, *Sacred Roots: A Primer on Retrieving the Great Tradition*. Wichita, KS: The Urban Ministry Institute, 2010. p. 97–100.

3 Don L. Davis, ed., "Creedal Theology as a Blueprint for Discipleship and Leadership: A Time Tested Criterion for Equipping New Believers and Developing Indigenous Leaders," in *Planting Churches among the City's Poor: An Anthology of Urban Church Planting Resources, Vol. 1*. Wichita, KS: TUMI Press, 2015. pp. 241–52.

2. Embraces the freedom of the Holy Spirit as he leads specific church traditions into specific paths in specific contexts for specific times

V. Evangel's Practical Principles: Creating Kingdom Outposts through Church Planting among the Poor

A. Evangel seeks to provide a balance of *the big picture of God's working in the world* (seeing the conflict of the ages), a clear strategy of advancing God's reign (winning the war), and specific tactics to engage the enemy (winning the next battle).

B. Evangel anchors its theology and missiology in the *divinely authorized, canonical story of the Triune God*, as told in the Scriptures, which Jesus Christ effected by his saving work in the world, and which the early Church summarized in its Rules of Faith, and historic orthodoxy defended in its teaching and practice.

C. Evangel believes that no entity is as powerful as proclaiming and demonstrating the power of the Already/Not yet Kingdom in this world among the poorest of the poor as *a healthy, functioning local(e) church of believers* fleshing out their faith in the context of their neighbors and families.

D. Evangel is *more dialogical* (engagement with the Story and its implications) than material presented (dry theological and missiological data woodenly applied, without reference to audience or context).

E. Evangel is *team focused* not individual focused.

F. Evangel assumes *the Holy Spirit is raising up gifted and called leaders among the poor* who can benefit from training, coaching and wise practices.

G. Evangel assumes that all planning and ministry occurs in a *changing, turbulent context*, which demands that all participants learn to be open to new data and shifting situations, to discern God's will, and adapt plans and directions to be effective, under God's leadership.

H. Evangel operates with an affirmation of *spiritual enemies and their persistent interference to the church planting efforts*, and assumes that no ministry can operate without both understanding of the devil's tactics, and application of God's resources to counteract and overcome his machinations.

I. Evangel relies on God's ability to identify, equip, and deploy *godly indigenous leaders who will lead church planting movements* that complete the task of winning and discipling indigenous peoples, in their own context, under their own authority, and through the ongoing direction of the Holy Spirit.

Seminar 2
Evangel

Evangel is a global movement of networked churches committed to facilitating and resourcing movements to plant healthy, multiplying Christ-centered churches that honor and glorify God and delight in Him, especially from and for the poor. As a global movement of networked churches we commit to:

1) a common theology based on the guardianship and cross-cultural transference of the Great Tradition,

2) a common strategy based upon our missional engagement that is guided by our vision to recruit, empower and release urban leaders who will plant churches and launch indigenous church planting movements and our discipleship, church planting, and church planting movements as expressed in our P.L.A.N.T. acrostic, and

3) a common set of standard practices that are historic church practices to be implemented with cultural sensitivity and flexibility.

These common commitments are designed for movements by making it easy to train leaders and export to new churches. Church planters are freed from re-inventing the structures locally by plugging into the existing structures of our common commitments. (See *Evangel: That None Should Perish.*)

SEMINAR 3

Evangel Emphasizes Team

Rev. Dr. Don L. Davis

I. Why Does Evangel Use Teams?

A. Definitions: why we require teams at Evangel, not just lone Church Planters

1. Definition of team: "A number of persons forming one of the sides in a game or contest" as in a *football team*; "a number of persons associated in some joint action" as in a *team of advisers*

2. Definition of teamwork: "The cooperative or coordinated effort on the part of a group of persons acting together as a team or in the interests of a common cause"

B. Biblical and theological reasons

1. The example of Jesus the Church Planter

See points in "Building the Team for Success: Principles of Effective Team Play" (*Ripe for Harvest*, pp. 169–184; *Planting Churches among the City's Poor: An Anthology of Urban Church Planting Resources*, Vol. 2, pp. 79–93).

Jesus' use of the disciples, the seventy-two, and his sending out two by two (at least two; spouse key)

2. The example of Paul the Church Planter[1]

a. As a bi-vocational church planter Paul relied heavily on teams.

(1) More than eighty of his teammates are mentioned by name in Acts and Paul's letters. "Given the numerous and varied contributions of Paul's fellow ministers to his mission, it is clear they were an essential factor in

---

1   Don L. Davis, "Paul's Team Members: Companions, Laborers, and Fellow Workers," in *Planting Churches among the City's Poor: An Anthology of Urban Church Planting Resources, Vol. 1*. Wichita, KS: TUMI Press, 2015. pp. 260–262.

its accomplishments . . . these missioners indeed deserve the considered attention of students of Paul."[2]

(2) His commitment to team-members can also be seen in the language he often uses in his letters: "coworker" (20 different people), "brother or sister" (14 different people), "servant" (14 different people), "apostle" (9 different people), "fellow slave" (5 different people) "partner" (3 others), "toilers" (7 others), "fellow soldier" (four others), "fellow prisoner" (4 others).

b. Paul emphasized "body" and "family" when speaking about the church – both metaphors reveal the importance of team.

(1) Paul uses the metaphor of church as family more than any other. It is his most important metaphor for the church.[3]

(2) Paul also often uses the metaphor of the church as the body.[4]

3. No Lone Rangers: the contemporary evidence[5]

a. Steve Gray's Study of 112 church plants. 88% of the fast growing church plants used a team approach to church planting (60 churches).

---

2   E. E. Ellis, "Paul and His Coworkers," ed. Gerald F. Hawthorne, Ralph P. Martin, and Daniel G. Reid, *Dictionary of Paul and His Letters*. Downers Grove, IL: InterVarsity, 1993. pp. 183, 189.

3   Robert Banks, *Paul's Idea of Community: The Early House Churches in Their Historical Setting*. Grand Rapids: Eerdmans, 1980. pp. 52–61.

4   Ibid., 62–70.

5   Steve Gray, "No More Lone Rangers," *www.stephengray.org*, June 27, 2013, *http://www.stephengray.org/w/title/No-More-Lone-Rangers/id/62/blog.asp*. He also has a free e-book on assessment at this website.

b. 88.5 % of struggling church plant teams did NOT use a church plant team (52 struggling church plants).[6]

C. Why bring a church plant team to Evangel?

1. It affirms the obvious: "A leader leads if and only if followers are following" (assessment).

   a. If nobody is following, maybe you don't have a Team Leader.

   b. Interaction with team provides important input for assessment (Stress brings stuff out).

      (1) Can the Team Leader make decisions in stressful situations?

      (2) Can the Team Leader form consensus?

2. Helps the whole team embrace the vision and make a commitment to the task and to the whole team for the charter period

3. Provides an internal support and accountability system for the church planter

---

6 Cited in Ed Stetzer and Warren Bird, "The State of Church Planting in the United States: Research Overview and Qualitative Study of Primary Church Planting Entities" (*The Leadership Network*, 2007), 9–10, *www.christianitytoday.com/assets /10228.pdf.*

II. Two Types of Teams at Evangel

The Church Plant Team
Forming an Apostolic Band
Rev. Dr. Don L. Davis

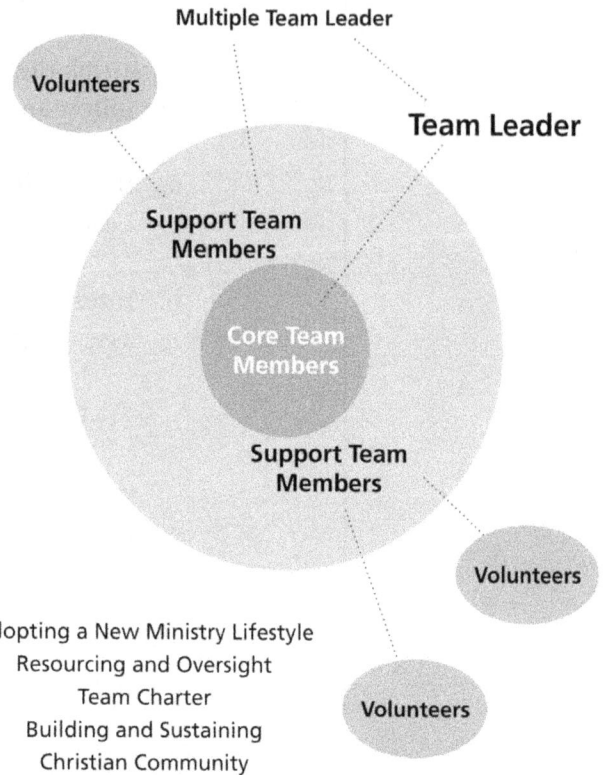

See *Planting Churches among the City's Poor: An Anthology of Urban Church Planting Resources, Vol. 2*, p. 94.

Multiple Team Leader

Team Leader

Volunteers

Support Team Members

Core Team Members

Support Team Members

Volunteers

Volunteers

Adopting a New Ministry Lifestyle
Resourcing and Oversight
Team Charter
Building and Sustaining
Christian Community

Spawning a Church Planting Movement Structure
Rev. Dr. Don L. Davis

A flexible structure that:
• Complements our vision
• Coordinates our particular initiatives
• Encourages cooperation at the grass-roots level
• Enables us to collaborate on shared projects

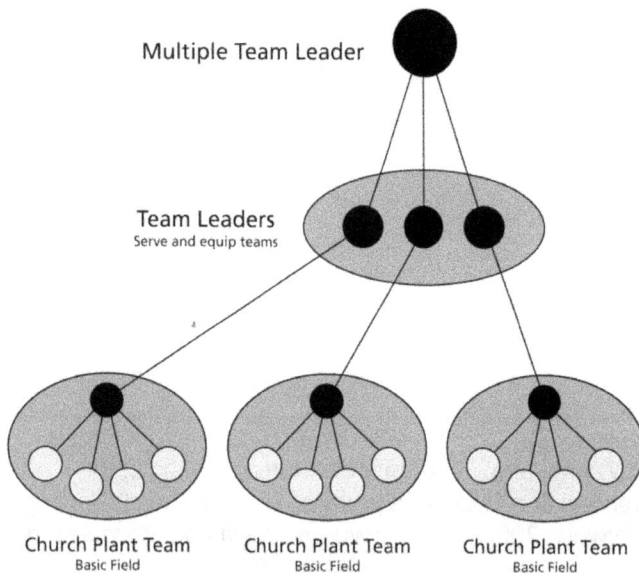

Multiple Team Leader

Team Leaders
Serve and equip teams

See *Planting Churches among the City's Poor: An Anthology of Urban Church Planting Resources, Vol. 2*, p. 24.

Church Plant Team
Basic Field

Church Plant Team
Basic Field

Church Plant Team
Basic Field

A. Toward a biblical theology of teamwork

   1. Team trumps solo acts, Eccles. 4.9-12

      a. Unity is pleasant, Ps. 133.1

      b. Each one is gifted and called, 1 Pet. 4.10

   2. Iron sharpens iron, Prov. 27.17

      a. We fall without guidance, Prov. 11.14

      b. God empowers us all, Ps. 127.1

   3. Diversity strengthens the team, 1 Cor. 12.20-25; Eph. 4.9-16; Rom. 12.3-8

      a. Each makes unique contribution, 1 Cor. 3.6-7

      b. Every one gifted by the Spirit, 1 Cor. 12.1-31

   4. Together we excel and win, Heb. 10.24-25

      a. We help each other endure, 2 Thess. 1.1-12

      b. The victory is ours, together, Phil. 2.1-11

B. Church plant teams at Evangel

   1. Role of a *Church Planter* (Team Leader)

   2. Role of a *Primary Team Member* (Core members)

   3. Role of a *Support Team Member* (Support members)

   4. Role of *Intercessors* (Prayer partners)

C. Evangel School Leadership Team

   1. Role of the *Deans*: Sponsors of the School

      a. Components of the job description

      b. Challenges

2. Role of the *Coaches*: mentoring, equipping, and overseeing church planters and their teams

   a. Components of the job description

   b. Challenges

3. Role of *Intercessors, Support, and Financial Sponsors*

   a. Intercessors *undergird* every person, practice, and phase of the church plant in constant, fervent, and believing prayer.

   b. Support members *provide targeted, specific aid* to the planter and team based on need, timing, and opportunity.

   c. Financial sponsors *give tangible resources and funds* to assist the team in gaining the resources and support they require at any particular phase of the team's work.

III. Contours of Effective Team Play: Ten Principles for Teams

Team building is perhaps the single most effective means to accomplish objectives. Regardless of the domain – whether in business, athletics, commerce, industry, music, science, politics, education, or the military – teamwork can be an integral force in shaping one's personal growth, as well as attaining group success. While there has been much written on the nature of teams, for our purposes we must look at the principles that undergird and support all effective team play. The following list of principles have been taken from my own reflection on the nature of effective team play, and are not considered to be an exhaustive list. In my mind, however, I consider these ten principles to be emblematic in the performance of all great teams, regardless of the task they face, and how they function together.

A. Persuasively articulate the vision for the team's association, actions, efforts: The Principle of ARTICULATION.

   1. Key Scripture: 1 Cor. 14.6-8

   2. Definition of the Concept

a. "To understand and embrace, at every level of team involvement, our mutually agreed-upon and clearly stated mission, purpose, and goal statement"

b. "To articulate in a team is to envision for the team the dream, end, and goal it is and will be pursuing throughout the 'season'"

3. The Principle Explained

a. This principle involves the vision that underlies the terms of the team's mutual association, i.e., "Why are we together, and what do we want?"

b. The content of articulation in a team context is its shared visions, convictions, beliefs, and values, along with its reciprocal determination to live these out together effectively as a unit.

c. The opposite of *Articulation* is silence or mumbling regarding the vision.

d. The result of no articulation is confusion among the members of the team.

4. The Golden Key: Let the leader blow a certain sound! (1 Cor. 14.8).

B. Welcome and involve every member as a full participant: The Principle of INCORPORATION.

1. Key Scripture: Rom. 15.4-7

2. Definition of the Concept

a. "To be received into a particular group of people who have intentionally bonded themselves together in order to embody and/or attain a common purpose or end"

b. When we incorporate a new member into our team, our first priority is:

(1) To unite, blend, or combine the person(s) into our already-existent structures in order to . . .

(2) Give them an immediate sense of security and significance, while at the same time . . .

(3) Helping them contribute to our team efforts so as to form an indistinguishable whole.

3. The Principle Explained

   a. To be incorporated is to be commissioned and called.

   b. All the privileges, rights, and responsibilities of the most veteran member is given to the greenest novice once we have embraced them within our team loyalties.

   c. Incorporation is the act of welcoming, receiving, and accepting another as a full, equal, and significant partner into the team.

   d. The opposite of *Incorporation* is the state of non-relation among members.

   e. The result of not incorporating new members is wasting team member resources.

4. The Golden Key: Find the right place for each member of the team as soon as possible.

C. Learn and express the power of shared responsibility: The Principle of COOPERATION.

1. Key Scripture: 1 Cor. 12.11-14

2. Definition of the Concept

   a. "To commit oneself and all one's capabilities, gifts, and resources to the work and the success of the team"

   b. Cooperation demands that each team member be willing to learn from others.

   c. It also demands a willingness to collaborate with other team members in order to reach our common goal.

3. The Principle Explained

    a. Cooperation produces synergy, and breaks down the possibility of conflict and antagonism.

    b. When members cooperate, they celebrate the importance of diversity within the team.

    c. Cooperation highlights the benefit of shared work, where each member is free to build upon their strengths and be supported in their limitations.

    d. Criteria needed

        (1) Special and unique gifting of each member

        (2) Spirit of cooperation to work together in order for team objectives

        (3) The opposite of *Cooperation* is divisive competition.

        (4) The result of no cooperation is individual action disconnected from team objectives.

4. The Golden Key: Celebrate diversity of gifting and burden among the team.

D. Discover and utilize the gifts, experience, and strengths of each member: The Principle of IDENTIFICATION.

  1. Key Scripture: Rom. 12.3-8

  2. Definition of the Concept

    a. "To assess and determine through careful analysis the gifts, abilities, and aptitudes of each team member to determine how they may best contribute to the team's efforts"

    b. Identification is the process where we design and facilitate the operation of each team member's role and function.

3. The Principle Explained

   a. Identification is concerned with the division of labor on an effective team.

   b. In identifying team members and their roles, we seek to help each member define her own special role on the team, and to find her "place" on the team which suits best her gifts, capabilities, and burdens.

   c. We facilitate identification by employing an array of methods and approaches designed to test and assess the overall gifts and aptitudes of the team member, and how such resources may be maximized within the team itself.

     (1) Interview

     (2) Experimentation

     (3) Assignment

   d. Its purpose: to take full advantage of each person's individual uniqueness and strengths in such a way that the team is enhanced and is found to lack nothing essential for its overall effectiveness.

   e. The opposite of *Identification* is haphazard placement.

   f. The result of not identifying individual gifts is frustration among members.

4. The Golden Key: Take individual difference seriously; help members discover their niche.

E. Strategically plan and arrange team action and movement: The Principle of ORGANIZATION.

1. Key Scripture: 1 Pet. 4.9-11

2. The Definition of the Concept

   a. "To determine the process by which the team will approach its tasks, manage its resources, and proceed toward its goal with as much efficiency and as little confusion as possible"

b. Team organization focuses on each member and team unit setting measurable and attainable goals in sync with the team's overall goal, and then developing plans and strategies in order to mobilize the team members around its overall "game plan."

3. The Principle Explained

   a. Organization occurs best within teams that recruit effective leadership, which functions to empower and facilitate the effectiveness of each member individually, and the team as a whole.

   b. Organization involves both procedural and structural elements.

      (1) Procedurally, it involves the process of setting goals, determining priorities, making strategic plans to carry out our goals, scheduling our lives and managing our resources together to attain them.

      (2) Structurally, it involves selecting leaders who have been delegated responsibility and authority to empower each team member to know his or her role, as well as to whom one reports, and for whom one is responsible.

      (3) Team organization arises from within many contexts, and takes place at all levels of responsibility of team play.

      (4) Organization is not the same as imprisonment to some particular strategy; rather, it involves managing our people, resources, monies, equipment, and facilities with wisdom and skill, proceeding towards our team goals with minimal waste, effort, and conflict.

      (5) The opposite of *Organization* is disorder and haphazardness.

      (6) The result of a lack of organization is gross inefficiency.

4. The Golden Key: Plan your effort and activity before you execute and act.

F. Train team members to maximize their gifts and strengths individually and together: The Principle of PREPARATION.

1. Key Scripture: Eph. 4.11-16

2. Definition of the Concept

    a. "To develop a sense of readiness and competence in each team member so they may be prepared for the various challenges and issues that will arise as they execute their roles"

    b. Preparation involves rigorous practice that aims to make each team member thoroughly prepared to execute their role effectively, regardless of the situation or circumstance encountered.

3. The Principle Explained

    a. Preparation focuses on readiness, and concentrates on efforts to enable team members to learn to anticipate "the future in advance" in order that the team may function without difficulty or confusion at the critical time.

    b. It is synonymous with training, the act, process, and art of imparting the requisite knowledge and skill to a person that empowers them to function in their role with competence and satisfaction.

    c. The opposite of *Preparation* is the state of being ill-equipped and untrained.

    d. The result of having no preparation is mediocrity and waste.

4. The Golden Key: Practice (and the right kind of practice) perfects what was practiced.

G. Execute your team strategies with excellence and enthusiasm: The Principle of IMPLEMENTATION.

1. Key Scripture: Col. 3.16-17

2. Definition of the Concept

   a. "To carry out the functions, requirements, and tasks attached to one's role with excellence and to an effective conclusion"

   b. To implement as a team member is to execute and perform, as individuals and a group, our assignments and tasks.

3. The Principle Explained

   a. Implementation focuses on criteria of acceptable and excellent performance.

   b. It is connected to delegation of authority, and to the accountability given team members as they carry out their responsibilities and functions.

   c. In executing their task, team members follow through on their agreed-upon regimens and schedules, performing their tasks in all contexts.

   d. What it demands

      (1) Open and honest communication between the team members

      (2) On-the-spot feedback, encouragement, instruction, and suggestions from both leaders and other team members

      (3) Clear sense of the task and ability to carry it out

   e. The opposite of *Implementation* is poor performance.

   f. The result of not implementing strategies is no accomplishment of team goals.

4. The Golden Key: Empower each member to do their job, and hold them accountable to do it.

H. Provide leadership and oversight to every dimension of team effort: The Principle of COORDINATION.

1. Key Scripture: 1 Cor. 12.15-27

2. Definition of the Concept

    a. "To bring the efforts of the various team members into a synchronized, purposeful, and harmonized movement through mutual support and careful oversight"

    b. Coordination is the act where members learn to function and operate their particular roles alone and together in such a way that the entire team prospers and succeeds.

3. The Principle Explained

    a. This is synonymous with a kind of coaching that orchestrates (not dominates) the activities and efforts of the team towards its predetermined goals.

    b. Coordination is coaching, and as such, it helps to establish and maintain the team members in both mutual and reciprocal relation.

    c. As a function of leadership, coordination attempts to keep all team activities in essential relation to each other lest team members operate separately as unattached units.

    d. How it functions

        (1) On-the-spot feedback and instruction, not only to individuals, but also to pairs and units within the team which relate directly to one another

        (2) Detailed plans of how and when members must interact

    e. The opposite of *Coordination* is individualized, uncoordinated action.

    f. The result of a lack of coordination is team confusion and poor performance.

4. The Golden Key: The purpose of team leadership is to coordinate the strengths of the members in a united plan that enables it to reach its goal.

I. Critically assess the processes and impacts of the team's efforts: The Principle of EVALUATION.

1. Key Scripture: 1 Cor. 9.23-27

2. Definition of the Concept

   a. "To carefully analyze and make judgments regarding both the overall effort and impact of team play, both individually and as a team"

   b. Evaluation measures critically but sympathetically our team and individual performance in order to gain information about how we might build upon our strengths and compensate for our limitations.

3. The Principle Explained

   a. Evaluation involves reviewing our actual deeds against our expectations.

   b. This is for the purpose of gaining wisdom into team performance, not assessing blame or guilt.

   c. Evaluation, from both leaders and members, requires a sympathetic but careful look at each team member's performance against their goals and the role's job description or criteria.

   d. Purpose and timing

      (1) To improve performance, not censure or berate.

      (2) To critique and give feedback; to praise, develop, train, and improve our individual and team actions for greater success for the entire team.

      (3) Evaluation of performance ought to be encouraged throughout every phase of team play, during practice and game play.

e. The opposite of *Evaluation* is providing no feedback on performance or progress.

f. The result of having no evaluation is little or no improvement in performance or team play.

4. The Golden Key: Offer feedback generously to all members individually, and as a whole.

J. Modify your team strategy and performance based on your analysis of the situation: The Principle of ADAPTATION.

1. Key Scripture: 2 Tim. 3.16-17

2. Definition of the Concept

a. "To be sensitive toward and responsive to new and/or changing circumstances, environments, or contexts"

b. To be adaptable is to be willing to "audible," i.e., to be open to adjust one's plans in response to new situations, and a readiness to modify or tailor the team's actions according to the needs of the current, particular setting and population.

3. The Principle Explained

a. Adaptation is openness to change.

b. It produces a fluidity and dynamism that slavish commitment to plan or past may inhibit and overshadow.

c. To adapt means that you are willing to give up loyalty to bad strategy, and allows for maximum ability to change for the sake of wiser, more effective action.

d. What Adaptation suggests and demands

(1) Wide range of modification in team action, from a modest adjustment of a particular play, to a wholesale change in strategy and game plan

(2) Either wholesale or modest change, depending on what is determined to be of critical importance

(3) In order to adapt, members must be able to change, and be given the freedom and authority to innovate (within certain bounds).

    e. The opposite of *Adaptation* is conformity to tradition and past methodologies.

    f. The result of not adapting is prolonged failure in a familiar course of action.

    4. The Golden Key: Grant team leaders and members the authority and right to adapt their methods and directions in order to increase team effectiveness.

The Final Binding Result: When the following principles are employed consistently, you can enable the team to INTEGRATE its efforts together, both individually and corporately. This is the highest goal of all effective team play.

- To facilitate each team member and units of team members' function together as significant parts of a single, unified whole.
- To Integrate something involves joining, combining, and adapting a system of parts in order to attain a particular effect together as a whole.

This is the culmination of all the other principles in operation, which results in a team where each individual element links up to form an effective, working unit, blending their several and individual efforts into a single, functioning, and unified whole. More than anything, integration demands that all members adopt as its primary perspective and mindset that team objectives, success, and victory is primary, and that personal prominence will be a welcomed and yet entirely secondary product of our overall team victory. To be integrated is to be synchronized in such a way that each member knows their role, executes their role with excellence, and supports their fellow team members.

IV. Practical Implications of Team Play

    A. Summary of the Principles of Team Play

        1. Persuasively articulate the vision for the team's association, actions, and efforts: The Principle of ARTICULATION

2. Welcome and involve every member as a full participant: The Principle of INCORPORATION

3. Learn the power of shared responsibility: The Principle of COOPERATION

4. Discover and utilize the strengths of each member: The Principle of IDENTIFICATION

5. Strategically plan and arrange your team's actions and movements: The Principle of ORGANIZATION

6. Train team members to maximize their gifts and strengths individually and together: The Principle of PREPARATION

7. Execute your team strategies with excellence and enthusiasm: The Principle of IMPLEMENTATION

8. Provide leadership and oversight to every dimension of team effort: The Principle of COORDINATION

9. Critically assess the processes and impacts of the team's efforts: The Principle of EVALUATION

10. Modify your team strategy and performance based on your analysis of the situation: The Principle of ADAPTATION

B. How to use the principles in team development: PWR review (e.g., SEER, "scanning, evaluating, engaging, responding")

1. Use the principles as a yardstick to measure your team's culture and practice.

2. Use the principles as a lens to discern the quality of your current team functionality.

3. Use the principles as a benchmark to develop effective team goals, plans, and direction.

4. Team evaluations should be:

a. Regular: take time every week to evaluate the quality of your team's life and practice together.

b. Holistic: evaluate your team according to all of the principles listed.

c. Forward thinking: the purpose of team evaluation should neither be punitive nor shame producing. Concentrate on better coordination for maximum results.

C. Be prepared to adapt (Bruce Tuckman's Model of Team/Group Development, 1965 ["Adjourning" added in 1977])

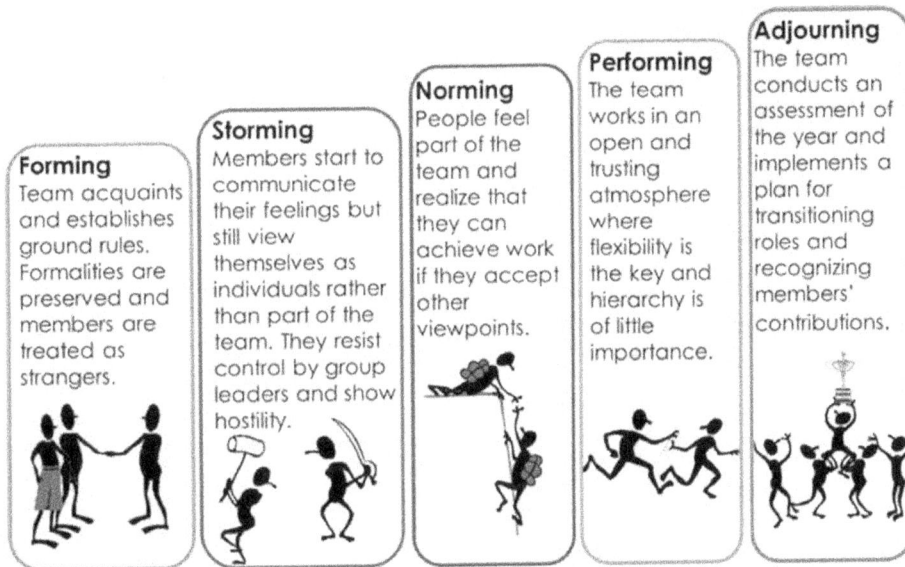

Forming
Team acquaints and establishes ground rules. Formalities are preserved and members are treated as strangers.

Storming
Members start to communicate their feelings but still view themselves as individuals rather than part of the team. They resist control by group leaders and show hostility.

Norming
People feel part of the team and realize that they can achieve work if they accept other viewpoints.

Performing
The team works in an open and trusting atmosphere where flexibility is the key and hierarchy is of little importance.

Adjourning
The team conducts an assessment of the year and implements a plan for transitioning roles and recognizing members' contributions.

1. Discern the underlying cause of the conflict

a. Is it team-related (immaturity)? (Incompetent leadership? Egotistical individual team members?)

b. Is it strategy-related (tactical flaws)? (Bad planning? Horrible execution?)

c. Is it enemy-related (evil sabotage)? (Is he sowing doubt? Is he stirring division? Is he causing discouragement? Is he suggesting inevitable defeat?)

2. Do a situation analysis (Sit-rep) and act

   a. Get the latest and best intel on the situation. (Get the whole picture, with good, latest data.)

   b. Analyze the info's weight and meaning. (Weigh the information for importance, relevance; look for patterns in the bits you collect.)

   c. Draft possible plans of attack. (Think of "scenarios" and "options"; run simulations: use the whiteboard.)

   d. Decide your next course of action.

   e. Assign fresh team roles based on new course.

Equipping the Church Plant Team Member
Developing Workable Training Strategies
Rev. Dr. Don L. Davis

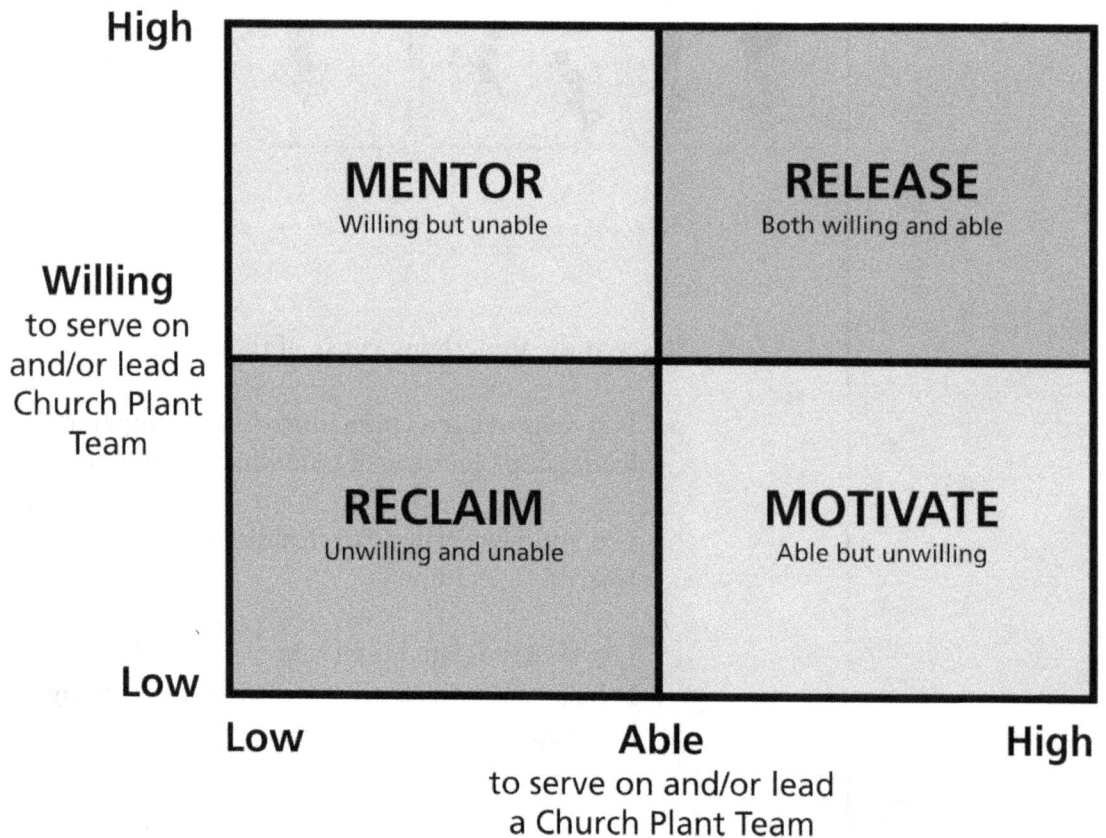

High

MENTOR
Willing but unable

RELEASE
Both willing and able

Willing
to serve on
and/or lead a
Church Plant
Team

RECLAIM
Unwilling and unable

MOTIVATE
Able but unwilling

Low

Low   **Able**   **High**

to serve on and/or lead
a Church Plant Team

See *Planting Churches among the City's Poor: An Anthology of Urban Church Planting Resources, Vol. 2*, p. 78.

V. Additional Resources on Team

A. Don L. Davis. "Coordinating Your Team's Strengths" in *The Power of Team: TUMI Satellite Summit 2015*. Wichita, KS: TUMI Press, 2015. pp. 25-33.

B. Don L. Davis. *Dealing with Team Conflict: From Difficult People to Disbanded Teams*. TUMI Satellite Summit 2015, workshop. *www.tumi.org/summit*.

C. *If only one book*: Paul H. Hersey, Kenneth H. Blanchard, Dewey E. Johnson, *Management of Organizational Behavior*. 10th edition. Upper Saddle River, New Jersey: Pearson Education, 2013.

D. An abridged bibliography on teams and teamwork:

1. Bennis, Warren and Burt Nanus. *Leaders: The Strategies for Taking Charge*. New York: Harper & Row, 1985.

2. Blake, Robert R., Jane Mouton, and Robert Allen. *Spectacular Teamwork*. John Wiley.

3. Blanchard, Kenneth; Donald Carew, and Eunice Parisi-Carew. *The One Minute Manager Builds High Performing Teams*. New York: William Morrow, 1990.

4. Buchholz, Steve, and Thomas Roth. *Creating the High-Performance Team*. John Wiley & Sons, 1987.

5. Cohen, Alphie. *No Contest: The Case Against Competition*. Englewood Cliffs, New Jersey: Prentice-Hall, 1985.

6. Daniels, Aubrey. *Performance Management*. 3rd Ed. Tucker, GA: Performance Management Publications, 1989.

7. Dee, David. *Make Your Team a Winner*. Chicago: Dartnell, 1990.

8. Douglass, Merrill E. and Donna N. Douglass. *Time Management for Teams*. New York: American Management Assn., 1992.

9. Francis, Dave and Don Young. *Improving Work Groups: A Practical Manual for Team Building*. San Diego: Pheiffer & Co., 1992.

10. Hackman, J. Richard, ed. *Groups That Work (and Those That Don't)*. San Francisco: Jossey-Bass, 1990.

11. Hastings, Colin. et. al. *The Superteam Solution: Successful Teamworking in Organisations*. San Diego: University Associates, 1987.

12. Hersey, Paul, and Kenneth H. Blanchard. *Management of Organizational Behavior*, 10th Ed. Upper Saddle River, NJ: Pearson Education, Inc., 2013.

13. Katzenbach, Jon R. and Douglas K. Smith. "The Discipline of Teams: A Mindbook-Workbook for Delivering Small Group Performance." *Harvard Business Review*. March-April 93: 111.

14. ———. *The Wisdom of Teams: Creating the High-Performance Organization*. Boston: Harvard Business School Press, 1993.

15. Larson, Carl E. and Frank LaFasto. *Teamwork: What Must Go Right, What Can Go Wrong*. Newbury Park, California: Sage Publications, 1989.

16. Maddox, Robert B. *Team Building: An Exercise in Leadership*. Menlo Park: Crisp Publications, 1992.

17. Maxwell, J. C. *The 17 Indisputable Laws of Teamwork: Embrace Them and Empower Your Team*. Thomas Nelson, 2001.

18. ———. *The 17 Essential Qualities of a Team Player: Becoming the Kind of Person Every Team Wants*. Thomas Nelson, 2006.

19. ———. *Teamwork 101: What Every Leader Needs to Know*. Thomas Nelson, 2009.

20. Orsburn, Jack D. et. al. *Self-Directed Work Teams: The New American Challenge*. Burr Ridge, Ill: Business One Irwin, 1992.

21. Parker, Glen M. *Team Players and Teamwork*. San Francisco, CA: Jossey-Bass, 1990.

22. Sanborn, Mark. *Teambuilt: Making Teamwork Work*. Mastermedia: New York, 1994.

23. Schein, Edgar H. *Organizational Culture and Leadership*. 2nd Ed. San Francisco, CA: Jossey-Bass, 1992.

24. Scholtes, Peter. *The Team Handbook*. Madison WI: Joiner, 1988.

25. Senge, Peter M. *The Fifth Discipline*. New York: Doubleday Currency, 1990.

26. Shonk, James H. *Working in Teams: A Practical Manual for Improving Work Groups*. NY: AMACOM, 1982.

27. West, M. A. 2003. *Effective Teamwork: Practical Lessons from Organizational Research*. Blackwell Publishing.

E. "Defining the Leaders and Members of a Church Plant Team" (See next page.)

This chart was taken from our earlier church plant school documents. Although the terminology has changed, we have maintained the same functions for the positions. In previous materials, the term used for the church planting supervisor or mentor to whom the team leader reported or received input from was called a *Multiple Team Leader* or *MTL*. All references to *MTL* or *Multiple Team Leader* in this chart should now be understood as *Field Coach*. The term *Team Leader* for the person in charge of the church plant team and church plant effort is now referred to as the *Church Planter*. And, the term *City Director* or *Supervisor* is now *Commissioning Pastor* or *Ministry Supervisor*.

Defining the Leaders and Members of a Church Plant Team

World Impact, Inc.

SA - Spiritual Authority   TL - Team Leader   FC - Field Coach   CPT - Church Plant Team

	Church Plant Team Member	Church Plant Team Leader	Field Coach
Definition	Member of cross-cultural church planting team	Leader of cross-cultural church planting team	Facilitator and coordinator of multiple church planting teams
Responsibility	To employ gifts to enhance the ministry of the team as it plants a viable church	To facilitate and manage the effective operation of the team in order to plant a church	To provide counsel, resources, and support to all teams in a given area
Training	Church Plant School, initial training, ongoing team input (John Mark Curriculum	Specialized training curriculum, personal mentoring and TUMI	TUMI course work, regional training, and specialized input
Accountable to Whom?	Team Leader	Spiritual Authority (support from FC)	Spiritual Authority
Time Commitments	Accredited to plant for specified period of charter as primary or support member	Throughout the duration of the church plant's charter	Regular review and substantive ministry assessment at end of CPT Time
Resources	Church Plant School, Team members and leaders, CPT "kit"	Team members, ministry budget, access to Field Coach and Spiritual Authority	Transportation to CPTs, access to Spiritual Authority
Authority	To pursue those steps necessary to evangelize, disciple, and plant	To lead the team in all of its operations as it seeks to plant a church in a given period of time	To support the team during its charter, and decide whether at the end the plant warrants further time and effort
Assignment	By SA and TL for particular time and role	By SA for duration of the church plant	By Spiritual Authority as they determine necessary
Composition	Primary members, support members, and/or volunteers	Individual or co-leaders	Individual selected by Spiritual Authority

Hosting Your Own Evangel School of Urban Church Planting
The Process from A to Z

Lorna Rasmussen

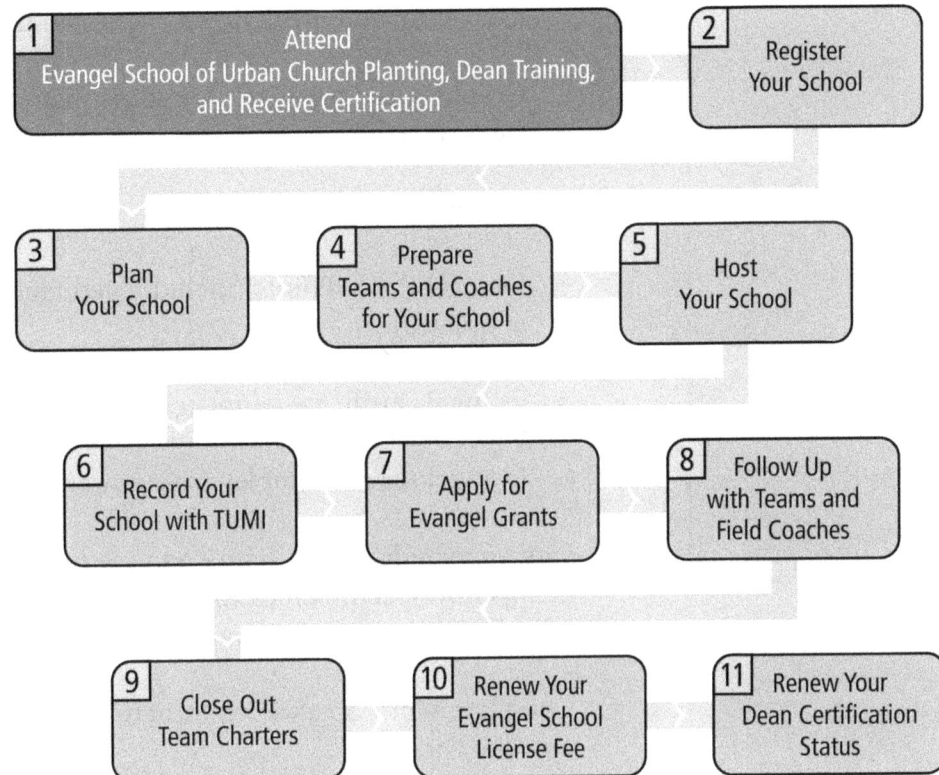

I. **Register Your School – *www.tumi.org/evangel***

A. "Register Your Upcoming School" (at least 60 days prior to the date school scheduled)

B. You will need to list the two Deans who are hosting the school

C. Dates of the school, school contact info, etc.

D. Registration link (if you have one that you want us to share on our website)

II. Plan Your School

A. Gather Project Team and review available resources (Evangel School Resource Pack) for your school (see *Evangel School Resource Pack Overview* in the Appendix)

1. Project planning templates (including editable minute by minute schedules, at a glance schedule for teams, shopping list, set up and break down suggested lists)

2. Graphics and templates for shirts, banners, name tags, team signs, etc.

3. Evangel videos

4. Evangel PowerPoints (including editable announcement templates)

5. Evangel certificate templates

6. Evangel service templates: Communion, Commissioning

B. Plan your budget (see "Three Sample Evangel School Budgets" in appendix), school location, and support staff needed for your school

C. Complete Work Breakdown Structure (WBS) – assigning tasks and due dates

D. Prepare for your school following your project WBS (aka Project Task Chart) checking in with your team at milestone dates

E. Purchase Resources – *www.tumistore.org* (Evangel Resources)

1. *Ripe for Harvest: A Guidebook for Planting Healthy Churches in the City* and *Planting Churches among the City's Poor: Vols. 1 and 2* for every Field Coach and Team Leader

2. *Ripe for Harvest: A Guidebook for Planting Healthy Churches in the City*, *Front Matters: Prerequisite Readings for the Evangel School of Urban Church Planting*, and *Evangel: That None Should Perish* for every delegate of each school.

F. Set up for school at location, ensuring all things ready to go at start of school

III. Prepare Teams and Coaches for Your School

A. Recruit potential church planters: work with sponsoring churches, associations and networks

B. Interview potential church planter (see Appendix: "Evangel Church Planter Assessment")

C. Initiate Church Planter Assessment – *www.tumi.org/evangel*

1. Church Planter Assessment

2. World Impact Planter Profile and Assessment (WIPPA) 360 review

   a. Church Planter Self Evaluation

   b. Church Planter Evaluation by Pastor

   c. Church Planter Evaluation by Spouse

D. Receive applicant's pastor's approval

1. Submit and receive Pastor's Reference Form to/from the applicant's pastor

2. Interview pastor

E. Secure and Orient Coaches

1. Coaches for Evangel School (see Appendix, "How Will We Coach")

2. Field Coaches for teams (see Appendix, "Field Coaches" and "Key Principles and Other Tools for Evangel Field Coaches and Assessor Coaches")

   a. PWR Process

   b. Quarterly Reports – *www.tumi.org/evangel* (Coaches)

F. Order and send Prerequisite Readings to each registrant for the school with instructions to be read prior to attending the school.

IV. Host Your School

A. Host your school following your planned schedule (minute by minute), adjusting as needed, all the while staying as close to your schedule as possible (refer to the Evangel Session Summary in the Appendix).

B. Commission Teams

1. The formal commissioning of each team is a key part of the school.

2. Feel free to open this up to others to come and celebrate with the teams for this service.

C. Evangel Assessor Coaches complete charters, and Field Coaches (if present) and Deans sign off on charters (see "Evangel Church Plant Charter Form" in the Appendix)

V. Record Your School with TUMI – *www.tumi.org/evangel*

A. "Submit Evangel School Reports"

B. Register how many church plant teams attended, along with each Church Plant Team name, team leader name, team target area, and what group they are a part of

C. List the Evangel Coaches for each team, as well as the Field Coach for each team.

D. Upload final team charter and picture for each team.

VI. Apply for Any Available Evangel Grants – *www.tumi.org/evangel*

A. Complete grant application, Deans

B. Receive award letter if approved, Deans

C. Notify Church Plant Team Leaders of grant award with details.

D. Complete process to ensure teams receive grant awards, Dean responsibility

E. Follow up with National Director of Church Planting regarding team grant

VII. Follow Up With Teams and Field Coaches

A. E-mail approved charters to Field Coach for each team.

B. Field Coach sets up and hosts quarterly meetings (3 month, 6 month, 9 month) with team; completing the quarterly report – *www.tumi.org/evangel*

1. "Coaching" – Field Coach Quarterly Report Form

2. The Evangel Field Coach Quarterly Report is a form that guides the Field Coach in their quarterly review of their Church Plant Team.

VIII. Close Out Team Charters

A. Field Coach meets with team at end of year for wrap up and presents Antioch blessing.

B. Field Coach submits 12-month wrap up report and send to Evangel Dean.

C. Evangel Dean forwards on to National Director of Church Planting for approval.

D. National Director of Church Planting approves and closes off Charter.

IX. Renew Your Evangel School License Fee Annually (September 15)

A. *Tumistore.org* (Evangel Resources | Evangel Dean Team Annual License Fee)

B. Annual fees must be kept up to date in order to maintain approved Evangel School status with The Urban Ministry Institute.

C. Registration fees for the Dean School cover your first full year license fee.

X. Renew Your Dean Certification Status (every 3 years)

A. Attend an Evangel Dean School

B. By approval from National Director of Church Planting and your pastor or spiritual authority (reference required), attend TUMI Summit Church Planting Track

Evangel's Prepare, Launch, Assemble, Nurture, and Transition Phases

Dr. Hank Voss

> Freedom is not one element in the Christian life. . . . It is the Christian life.
>
> ~ Jacques Ellul. *The Ethics of Freedom*.

I. Evangel's Core Content

A. Five Major Sessions

Session Theme	Block
Session 1 See the Big Picture	Articulate theological and biblical themes for the church's advance of the kingdom in the world. Name three expressions of the church especially important for planting churches among the poor. Explain the five phases of PLANT and their relation to the apostolic mission outlined in the New Testament. Describe the vision and values of your church plant and the particular community demographics of the area your team is called to serve. Explain how wisdom is developed through the PWR process.
Session 2 Prepare	Articulate basic themes of the preparation phase of church planting. Explain why freedom in Christ is important in cross-cultural church planting. Describe the basic components of a biblical theology of the poor. Define the basic characteristics of team as they relate to church planting. Outline the standard practices of your church plant and the church plant expression you will use.

Session Theme	Block
Session 3 Launch and Assemble	Articulate key principles for evangelism and follow-up. Explain the significance of *oikos* for evangelism. Describe how the theme of "To Christ the Victory" can shape your church's worship, discipleship, and evangelism. Describe how your church plant will complete projects. Outline your plan for preaching, follow up, baptism, and discipleship.
Session 4 Nurture and Transition	Articulate key themes for nurturing believers through discipleship, preaching, teaching, and leadership development. State basic principles for effective Bible preaching and teaching. Identify criteria for transitioning from church planter to pastor or from church planter to indigenous leadership.
Session 5 Bringing It All Together	Articulate the need for a rhythm of sustained review. Identify how changes and challenges require us to adapt if we want to win. Identify when you and your team will take the necessary time to review church plant progress in order to adapt to win. Complete a church plant charter with vision, values, authority lines, field coach, goal deadlines, review times, and church expression.

B. Session Activities

1. Worship and Devotionals (five devotionals)

2. Seminar Teachings (fourteen seminars)

3. Team Exercises (eight Team Exercises)

4. Team Presentations (five Team Presentations)

5. Chartering and Commissioning Service

II. Session Mechanics

A. Worship and Devotionals (five Devotionals)

   1. Worship in song

   2. Nicene Creed

   3. Teaching

B. Summary of Seminar Teachings

   1. Fourteen seminars

   2. Seminars are twenty-five minutes long

   3. Evangel seminar summary

C. Team Exercises

   1. Eight team exercises

   2. Most involve reading assignments, team discussions, team worksheets, and team prayer

   3. Required prerequisite assignments for Evangel Church Plant School

   It is required that you ask Church Planters, Church Plant Team Members, and Field Coaches to complete reading assignments prior to Evangel School. These are found in *Front Matters: Prerequisite Readings for the Evangel School of Urban Church Planting*. These are listed in conjunction with the sessions in the Appendix entitled *Evangel Session Summary*.

D. Team Presentations

   1. Teams will make five team presentations to the Evangel Deans and Assessor Coaches

   2. Opportunity for assessment

3. Opportunity for encouragement

4. Opportunity for peer learning

E. Chartering and Commissioning Service

1. Assessor Coaches and Deans will need to decide which teams will be chartered prior to commissioning service.

2. Ideally this decision will be made by the end of session four and will be mutual between Team Leader, Assessor Coaches, and Deans.

3. Teams that are not chartered can still participate in ceremony and be commended for courage and hard work.

III. School Structures

A. Evangel School time budget

Item	Time per Event	Total Time
5 Devotionals	45 min each	3 hrs, 45 min
13 Seminars	30 min each	6 hrs, 30 min
8 Exercises	1.5 hrs each	12 hrs
5 Presentations	1 hr	5 hrs
Commissioning Service	1 hr	1 hr
Total		28 hrs, 15 min ≈ 29 hrs

B. Evangel formats

1. Weekend format: 29 hours of content time in 2.5 day format

Item	Thursday	Friday	Saturday	Sunday
7:00	Travel	Breakfast	Breakfast	Breakfast
8:00		Block 2	Block 6	Block 10
9:00				
10:00				
11:00				
12:00		Lunch	Lunch	Lunch
1:00		Block 3 and 4	Block 7 and 8	Travel
2:00				
3:00				
4:00	Registration Open			
5:00	Dinner	Dinner	Dinner	
6:00	Block 1	Block 5	Block 9	
7:00				
8:00				
9:00	Free Time	Free Time	Free Time	

2. Six-Saturday format

   a. 8:00-1:00 for six Saturdays = 30 hours

   b. Could be done one Saturday a month (six months)

   c. Could be done every other month (one year)

3. Four-Saturday format

   a. One month

   b. 8:00 to 5:00 for four Saturdays (one month – 36 hours)

4. Sixteen evenings

   a. Two-hour blocks for sixteen evenings (32 hours)

   b. Could be any night of the week

5. One-on-One with an Assessor Coach and a church plant team

Seminar 6

Assessment and Church Planters For/From the Urban Poor

Dr. Hank Voss

> Listen, my beloved brothers, has not God chosen those who are poor in the world to be rich in faith and heirs of the kingdom, which he has promised to those who love him?
>
> ~ James 2.5

> Only, they asked us to remember the poor, the very thing I was eager to do.
>
> ~ Galatians 2.10

> Far from us, say the Christians, be any man possessed of any culture, or wisdom or judgment; their aim is to convince only worthless and contemptible people, idiots, slaves, poor women and children. . . . They would not dare to address an audience of intelligent men. . . but if they see a group of young people or slaves or rough folk, there they push themselves in and seek to win the admiration of the crowd.
>
> ~ Celsus, 3rd century AD

I. The "A" in the ABCs: Church Planter Assessments

A. Biblical foundations for church planter assessment

1. Qualifications for church leaders

    a. Church leader qualifications (1 Tim. 3.6; cf. 3.1–13)

    b. Church planter qualifications (Titus 1.5; cf. 1.5–11)

2. Paul's warning to the Ephesian church leaders (Acts 20.28–31)

3. Importance of counting the cost (Luke 14.26-33)

B. Recent practical research on church planter assessments

1. Thomas Graham was one of the first in North America to Develop a Formal Assessment Center for Church Planters (1983).[1]

2. *How to Select Church Planters* (1988) became a foundational assessment resource used in North America (by Charles Ridley). It identified thirteen characteristics of "successful" church planters.

The Ridley Categories
(*Focus on Reproduction*, Capstone Module 12, p. 30-31)

1	*Visionizing Capacity* is the ability to imagine the future, to persuade other persons to become involved in that dream, and to bring the vision into reality.
2	*Intrinsically Motivated* means that one approaches ministry as a self-starter, and commits to excellence through hard work and determination.
3	*Creates Ownership of Ministry* suggests that one instills in others a sense of personal responsibility for the growth and success of the ministry and trains leaders to reproduce other leaders.
4	*One Who Relates to the Unchurched* develops rapport and breaks through barriers with unchurched people, encouraging them to examine and to commit themselves to a personal walk with God. As an additional outcome, new believers become able to lead others to salvation in Jesus Christ.
5	*Spousal Cooperation* describes a marital partnership by which church planting couples agree on ministry priorities, each partner's role and involvement, and the integration and balance of ministry with family life.
6	*Effectively Builds Relationships* is the skill to take initiative in meeting people and deepen relationships as a basis for more effective ministry.

---

1   Ed Stetzer and Warren Bird, "The State of Church Planting in the United States: Research Overview and Qualitative Study of Primary Church Planting Entities" (The Leadership Network, 2007), 12, *www.christianitytoday.com/assets /10228.pdf.*

7	***Starters Committed to Church Growth*** value congregational development as a means for increasing the number and quality of disciples. Through this commitment they increase numerical growth in the context of spiritual and relational growth.
8	***Responsiveness to the Community*** describes abilities to adapt one's ministry to the culture and needs of the target area residents.
9	***One who Utilizes Giftedness of Others*** equips and releases other people to minister on the basis of their spiritual giftedness.
10	***A Starter Who Is Flexible and Adaptable*** can adjust to change and ambiguity, shift priorities when necessary, and handle multiple tasks at the same time. This leader can adapt to surprises and emergencies.
11	***Builds Group Cohesiveness*** describes one who enables the group to work collaboratively toward common goals, and who skillfully manages divisiveness and disunifying elements.
12	***A Starter Who Demonstrates Resilience*** shows the ability to sustain himself or herself emotionally, spiritually, and physically through setbacks, losses, disappointments, and failures.
13	***One Who Exercises Faith*** translates personal convictions into personal and ministry decisions and resulting actions.

3. In the last twenty-five years more than one hundred assessments have been developed by various church planting denominations, church planting networks, agencies, and churches.

    a. S.H.A.P.E.[2]

        (1) Spiritual gifts

        (2) Heart or passion

        (3) Abilities

        (4) Personality type

        (5) Experiences

---

2   Ed Stetzer, *Planting Missional Churches*, First Ed. Nashville, TN: B&H Academic, 2006, pp. 81–82.

    b. Look for an apostolic gift[3]

        (1) Great faith

        (2) Prayer warrior

        (3) Apostolic call (heart, evangelist, mentor)

C. Benefits of assessment

    1. Realistic vision for church planters

        a. Assessments help provide a realistic vision of self

        b. Assessments help provide a realistic vision of the church planting task

        c. One study of 1,000 church planters conducted by the North American Missions Board of the Southern Baptist Church determined that church plants where the church planter had a realistic vision of the church planting task were 400% more likely to survive than those that did not. [4]

    2. The separation of shepherds from wolves

    3. Good stewardship (Matt. 25.14–30)

        a. People

        b. Time

        c. Money

---

3   Mark Hammond and Don Overstreet, *God's Call to the City.* Bloomington, IN: Crossbooks, 2011. pp. 157–82.

4   Stetzer and Bird, "The State of Church Planting in the United States: Research Overview and Qualitative Study of Primary Church Planting Entities," 6–7.

II. Church Planting *From* and *For* the Urban Poor

A. The distinctive mark of Evangel's Church Plant Schools is its commitment to equipping church planters *from* and *for* the urban poor.[5]

1. God has chosen the poor (James 2.5; 1 Cor. 1.27–29).

   a. In prioritizing the poor we are "working with the grain of the universe."

   b. *eklegomai* – "it involves preference and selection from among many choices."

2. Who are the poor?

   a. The poor are a major theme in Scripture.

   b. They are "those whose need makes them desperate enough to rely on God alone."

   c. They are "those who have been denied God's shalom."

3. Four fundamental responses

   a. Respect (as demonstrated by Paul with Onesimus)

   b. Love, compassion, and justice

   c. Preach the Gospel

   d. Expect great things: the principle of divine irony in leadership selection

      (1) The Vision of TUMI and Evangel (*Multiplying Laborers*, 31-32)

      (2) How Capstone got its name (Ps. 118.22–23)

---

5 Don Davis, "Our Distinctive: Advancing the Kingdom among the Urban Poor," in *Multiplying Laborers for the Urban Harvest: Shifting the Paradigm for Servant Leadership Education*, 15th ed. Wichita, KS: The Urban Ministry Institute, 2013. pp. 23–29.

B. More resources on mission and the poor

1. From TUMI

a. "Christian Mission and the Poor"[6]

b. "Jesus and the Poor," in Foundations of Christian Mission[7]

c. "On World Impact's 'Empowering the Urban Poor'"[8]

d. "The Theology of the Poor for Church Planters"[9]

e. "Upside down Ethics" (*Planting Churches among the City's Poor: An Anthology of Urban Church Planting Resources*, Vol. 1, p. 109)

2. Other resources

a. The poor in biblical theology: Craig Blomberg's *Neither Poverty Nor Riches* [10]

b. The poor in the Great Tradition. Tom Oden's *The Good Work's Reader*[11]

---

6   Don L. Davis, *Focus on Reproduction*, vol. 12, *The Capstone Curriculum.* Wichita, KS: The Urban Ministry Institute, 2005. pp. 175–226.

7   Ibid., 12:251–56.

8   Don Davis, "On World Impact's 'Empowering the Urban Poor,'" in *Ripe for Harvest: A Guidebook for Planting Healthy Churches in the City*, ed. Don Allsman, Don L. Davis, and Hank Voss. Wichita, KS: TUMI Press, 2015. pp. 195–200.

9   Terry Cornett, "The Theology of the Poor for Church Planters," in *Ripe for Harvest: A Guidebook for Planting Healthy Churches in the City*, ed. Don Allsman, Don L. Davis, and Hank Voss. Wichita, KS: TUMI Press, 2015. pp. 155–168.

10   Craig Blomberg, *Neither Poverty nor Riches: A Biblical Theology of Material Possessions*, NSBT. Grand Rapids: Eerdmans, 1999.

11   Thomas C. Oden, *The Good Works Reader.* Grand Rapids: Eerdmans, 2007.

III. **Assessment and the Urban Poor: A Narrow Way Between Two Cliffs**

   A. Asking David to wear Saul's armor

      1. 1 Samuel 17.38–40

      2. Expecting too much or adding unnecessary burdens

   B. Missing the Holy Spirit's gifts and callings at work

      1. Acts 4.13

      2. Expecting too little from the "uneducated, common people" and patronizing them.

IV. **Assumptions about Assessing Church Planters from and for the Urban Poor**

   A. God is the one who will raise up the workers for his harvest fields.

      1. The Father raises up the workers (Matt. 9.38).

      2. The story of Gideon's 300 warriors

   B. Church plant assessors must be biblically normed, theologically formed, and culturally shorn.

      1. Biblically normed: submissive to the authoritative tradition

      2. Theologically formed: attentive to the Great Tradition

      3. Culturally shorn: carefully avoidant of hegemony and respectful of the church planter's target culture

   C. "In Context" assessment provides an invaluable resource to church plant field coaches and sending agencies.

      1. Local church endorsement is a prerequisite to the process.

      2. Local and regional emphasis help field coaches and deans take advantage of site visits and "ministry projects."

D. Not all church planters are the same: be prepared to assess both calling and gifting.

1. Recognize and support different church planter callings: St. Paul and St. Thomas or a St. John?

   a. *Apostolic calling of the church planting missionary* (the "Pauline" perspective, e.g. "Paul and Timothy in Philippians 1.1)

      (1) The Pauline or apostolic perspective approaches church planting from the perspective of one who has an "overwhelming passion to go to those who had never heard the good news of Christ."[12]

      (2) Values apostolic mission and confidence in the Holy Spirit's work of raising up leaders who are self-governing, self-supporting, and self-propagating (e.g. Hector Cedillo, David Garrison).[13] Apostolic church planters can work within their own culture or be cross cultural church planters.

      (3) The sub-category of an Apostolic church planter working cross-culturally requires a high degree of cultural competence. This cross-cultural apostolic call is illustrated by Thomas who tradition records traveled outside the Roman Empire to preach the gospel all the way to India.

   b. *Church planting pastor* (The "Local Church Leader" perspective, e.g. "overseers and deacons" in Philippians 1.1 or the Apostle John in Ephesus)

---

12 Don L. Davis, *Vision for Mission: Nurturing an Apostolic Heart.* Wichita, KS: TUMI Press, 2000. p. 10.

13 Don L. Davis, ed., *Planting Churches among the City's Poor: An Anthology of Urban Church Planting Resources, Vol. 2.* Wichita, KS: TUMI Press, 2015. pp. 401, 419; David Garrison, *Church Planting Movements: How God Is Redeeming a Lost World.* Midlothian, VA: WIGTake, 2004.

(1) The Church Planting Pastor seeks to create a strong congregation that will be a sending center and nurturing headquarters for new church plants.[14] Rev. Eric Mason describes his rationale for embracing this role: "I found that with inner-city ministry, you have to be in it for the long haul because these are extremely relational communities. When you're actively involved in an inner-city neighborhood, you develop a 'trust capital' that provides a pipeline for ministry. Building that trust takes time. . . . The inner city is based on social capital. . . . When someone transitions out of ministry in the community, it impacts the momentum of the work there."[15]

(2) Values the ancient Christian practice of "stability" (e.g. St. Benedict, Eugene Peterson)[16]

2. Recognize and support different gifting.

   a. Some necessary gifts, skills, and training are necessary for all church plant team leaders.

   b. Some necessary gifts, skills, and training are different for church planters planting a small church, community church, or a hub church. Assessors must remain aware of this diversity in the body of Christ.

---

14 The Church Planting Pastor combines elements of the "founding pastor model" and the "Beachhead Model" as discussed in Dr. Davis' "Church Plant Models" in Don Allsman, Don L. Davis, and Hank Voss, eds., *Ripe for Harvest: A Guidebook for Planting Healthy Churches in the City.* Wichita, KS: TUMI Press, 2015. p. 87.

15 Jessi Strong, "Rooted in the City of Brotherly Love," *Bible Study Magazine,* November 2014, *http://www.biblestudymagazine.com/eric-mason#sthash. goHTyLV9.dpuf.* See also church website at *epiphanyfellowship.org.*

16 Eugene H. Peterson, *Under the Unpredictable Plant: An Exploration in Vocational Holiness.* Grand Rapids, MI: Eerdmans, 1994. p. 18–24.

V. Evangel Church Planter Assessment

A. Enlistment: Steps to accepting a potential church plant team at your Evangel School

1. Host interview with Potential Church Planter.

2. Complete Evangel Church Planter Assessment.

3. Submit and receive Pastor's Reference form to/from the applicant's pastor.

4. Interview the Pastor on the applicant.

5. Send link to "The Call to an Ancient-Evangelical Future" to Team Leader, and ask them to sign.

6. Send link to Team Leader to purchase and read *Sacred Roots: A Primer on Retrieving the Great Tradition*.

7. Forward Evangel Application to Team Leader.

B. Evangel School Basic Training

C. Visit *www.tumi.org/evangel*

Seminar 7

The Coaches and the Church Plant Team at Evangel

Rev. Dr. Don L. Davis

> No one presumes to teach an art that he has not first mastered through study. How foolish it is therefore for the inexperienced to assume pastoral authority when the care of souls is the art of arts.
>
> ~ Gregory the Great. *The Book of Pastoral Rule*, 1.1.

I. The Recent Popularity of the "Coach" in our Culture

II. Biblical and Historical Examples of a Coach

A. Biblical examples of coaching

Coaching is not yelling, shaming, or simply offering information. Rather, coaching involves the formation of people for excellence through clear command and edifying direction.

1. The LORD God. Through careful teaching, open ended questions, and constant feedback God directed his leaders in their ministries

   a. *Moses.* Quibbling with God regarding his command to lead Israel out of bondage. Exod. 4.14 – Then the anger of the LORD was kindled against Moses and he said, "Is there not Aaron, your brother, the Levite? I know that he can speak well. Behold, he is coming out to meet you, and when he sees you, he will be glad in his heart."

   b. *Joshua.* When Joshua believed that the Amorites might overcome the Israelites. Josh. 7.10-13 – "Get up! Why have you fallen on your face? [11] Israel has sinned; they have transgressed my covenant that I commanded them; they have taken some of the devoted things; they have stolen and lied and put them among their own belongings. [12] Therefore the people of Israel cannot stand before their enemies. They turn their backs before their enemies, because they have become devoted for destruction. I will be with you no more, unless you destroy the devoted things from among you. [13] Get up! Consecrate the people and say, 'Consecrate yourselves for tomorrow; for thus says the LORD, God of Israel, "There are devoted things in your midst, O Israel. You cannot stand before your enemies until you take away the devoted things from among you."'"

c. *Samuel*. Continued mourning over Saul. 1 Sam. 16.1 – The LORD said to Samuel, "How long will you grieve over Saul, since I have rejected him from being king over Israel? Fill your horn with oil, and go. I will send you to Jesse the Bethlehemite, for I have provided for myself a king among his sons."

d. *David*. When Nathan indirectly confronted David with the meaning of his actions with Bathsheba and Uriah, 2 Sam. 12.

e. *Isaiah*. Volunteering to represent God to his people. Isa. 6.8 – And I heard the voice of the Lord saying, "Whom shall I send, and who will go for us?" Then I said, "Here I am! Send me."

f. *Jeremiah*. When he was waffling at God's call to be his prophet. Jer. 1.11 – And the word of the LORD came to me, saying, "Jeremiah, what do you see?" And I said, "I see an almond branch."

2. Our Lord Jesus Christ: *providing both command and provision*

a. Calling the apostles, Mark 3:13-15

b. Rebuking Peter at Phillipi Caesarea, Matt. 16.15-23

c. Commanding the Great Commission, Matt. 28.18-20

3. Paul, *employing authority and example*, 1 Cor. 11.1; 2 Tim. 2.2

a. Coaching is like *good parenting*, 1 Thess. 2.10-12 – You are witnesses, and God also, how holy and righteous and blameless was our conduct toward you believers. [11] For you know how, like a father with his children, [12] we exhorted each one of you and encouraged you and charged you to walk in a manner worthy of God, who calls you into his own kingdom and glory.

b. Speak the truth and let no one disregard your role, Titus 2.15 – Declare these things; exhort and rebuke with all authority. Let no one disregard you.

B. Biblical principles for those who mentor and coach

1. A solid mentor *examines himself/herself,* and does not impose standards on others s/he is unwilling to keep! Matt. 23.1-3 – Then Jesus said to the crowds and to his disciples, [2] "The scribes and the Pharisees sit on Moses' seat, [3] so do and observe whatever they tell you, but not the works they do. For they preach, but do not practice."

2. A solid mentor *speaks the truth in love,* Eph. 4.9-15.

3. A solid mentor "flies out front;" they *lead by example,* Phil. 4.9.

4. A solid mentor *constantly reads the conditions and context* affecting those whom they lead and coach.

   a. They look ahead, foreseeing trouble and danger ahead, Prov. 22.3 – The prudent sees danger and hides himself, but the simple go on and suffer for it.

   b. They plan their work, and work a plan, Prov. 21.5 – The plans of the diligent lead surely to abundance, but everyone who is hasty comes only to poverty.

   c. They hold their plans loosely, counting on God's editing and re-direction.

      (1) Prov. 16.9 – The heart of man plans his way, but the LORD establishes his steps.

      (2) Jer. 10.23 – I know, O LORD, that the way of man is not in himself, that it is not in man who walks to direct his steps.

      (3) Ps. 37.23 – The steps of a man are established by the LORD, when he delights in his way.

5. A solid mentor *adapts quickly to changing situations;* they do not insist on reliance on strategies which are failing to produce results, Acts 16.6-10 – And they went through the region of Phrygia and Galatia, having been forbidden by the

Holy Spirit to speak the word in Asia. [7] And when they had come up to Mysia, they attempted to go into Bithynia, but the Spirit of Jesus did not allow them. [8] So, passing by Mysia, they went down to Troas. [9] And a vision appeared to Paul in the night: a man of Macedonia was standing there, urging him and saying, "Come over to Macedonia and help us." [10] And when Paul had seen the vision, immediately we sought to go on into Macedonia, concluding that God had called us to preach the gospel to them.

6. A solid mentor *diagnoses accurately*; they respond to the needs of those who they lead, 1 Thess. 5.12-14 – We ask you, brothers, to respect those who labor among you and are over you in the Lord and admonish you, [13] and to esteem them very highly in love because of their work. Be at peace among yourselves. [14] And we urge you, brothers, admonish the idle, encourage the fainthearted, help the weak, be patient with them all.

7. A solid mentor is *patient; they respect the time-tags that must be paid* in order for those whom they lead to learn and grow, 2 Tim. 4.1-2 – I charge you in the presence of God and of Christ Jesus, who is to judge the living and the dead, and by his appearing and his kingdom: [2] preach the word; be ready in season and out of season; reprove, rebuke, and exhort, with complete patience and teaching.

III. Characteristics of Excellent Coaches

A. The need for *humility*, James 3.1 – Not many of you should become teachers, my brothers, for you know that we who teach will be judged with greater strictness.

B. The need for *quality example*, 1 Cor. 11.1 – Be imitators of me, as I am of Christ.

C. The need for *leveraging insight and proven experience*, 2 Cor. 8.22-23 – And with them we are sending our brother whom we have often tested and found earnest in many matters, but who is now more earnest than ever because of his great confidence in you. [23] As for Titus, he is my partner and fellow worker for your benefit. And as for our brothers, they are messengers of the churches, the glory of Christ.

D. The need for *plain, compelling instruction and command*, 1 Tim. 4.10-15 – For to this end we toil and strive, because we have our hope set on the living God, who is the Savior of all people, especially of those who believe. [11] Command and teach these things. [12] Let no one despise you for your youth, but set the believers an example in speech, in conduct, in love, in faith, in purity. [13] Until I come, devote yourself to the public reading of Scripture, to exhortation, to teaching. [14] Do not neglect the gift you have, which was given you by prophecy when the council of elders laid their hands on you. [15] Practice these things, immerse yourself in them, so that all may see your progress.

E. Tested Guidance from Great Coaches

1. "Seek opportunities to show you care. The smallest gestures often make the biggest difference" (John Wooden).

2. "Things that aren't important, that have nothing to do with winning and losing, don't have to be a rule" (Peter Richmond, *Badasses: The Legend of Snake, Foo, Dr. Death, and John Madden's Oakland Raiders*).

3. "Every leader is different. Every bench is different. Every business is different. So while the complexities change, the work of coaching stays the same – keep your clients at the center of the work, push them to use their strengths more and to temper their weaknesses, and illuminate blind spots because these are what really get in the way" (Stacy Feiner, *Talent Mindset*).

4. "I think what coaching is all about, is taking players and analyzing their ability, put them in a position where they can excel within the framework of the team winning. And I hope that I've done that in my 33 years as a head coach" (Don Shula).

5. "To have long term success as a coach or in any position of leadership, you have to be obsessed in some way" (Pat Riley).

6. "Football is such a team sport, so no one individual does it. No one coach or no one assistant coach or no one player, it's a great team sport, so I don't get carried away with a bunch of accolades" (Jimmy Johnson).

7. "If you win a Super Bowl before you're fired, you're a genius, and everyone listens to you. But, a coach is just a guy whose best class in grammar school was recess and whose best class in high school was P.E. I never thought I was anything but a guy whose best class was P.E." (John Madden).

8. "I feel that a great coach is one that has a vision, sets a plan in place, has the right people in place to execute that plan and then accepts the responsibility if that plan is not carried out" (Mike Singletary).

9. "I'm sure that had I not been a coach, I would have been some form of a teacher" (John Madden).

10. "I didn't have a thing to do with picking a coach, and didn't want to. But I didn't think they'd pick one I didn't like" (Bear Bryant).

11. "A coach is someone who can give correction without causing resentment" (John Wooden).

IV. The Evangel Coaches

A. Responsibilities of Assessor Coach

1. Evaluation of Leader and Team (See "Team Evaluation Form for Assessor Coach," the last page of this seminar.)

2. Formal feedback to Team Leader (See *Planting Churches among the City's Poor: An Anthology of Urban Church Planting Resources*, Vol. 2, pp. 179-80.)

B. Responsibilities of Field Coach

1. Communication (contact, content, and connection [to the larger vision])

    a. With church planter

    b. With church plant team

    c. With Church Planter's spiritual authority.

2. Assessment (church planting is a war; church plant activities are series of battles and operations)

3. Feedback (if desired, and if possible)

Team Evaluation Form for Assessor Coach
World Impact

Coach: _____ Team: _____

	Criteria/Question	Not Ready	Some Reservations	Equipped	Exceptional
1	How are their relationships with each other?				
2	How is their communication? Do they listen to each other? Is everyone being heard?				
3	Is there sufficient consensus within the team?				
4	Are they able to resolve issues as they come up?				
5	Do they understand the PWR process? Are they showing indication that they will be able to flex and adjust their plan at a later time?				
6	Is the team leader functioning with strength?				
7	Have they considered all the relevant points?				
8	Will they be able to implement their plans?				
9	Are they open and teachable?				
10	Did they understand the exercises and complete them satisfactorily?				

Comments:

Things that need follow-up:

SEMINAR 8

How to Jump Start a Dead Spiritual Battery:
Rediscovering Our Calls as the Stewards of God

Don L. Davis

- It involves all we are and own; it is not a matter of money alone.

- It reflects the heart of God's nature as creator, owner, sustainer, and consummator of all things.

- It reveals the level of spiritual vision we have as sojourners and pilgrims in this "already/not yet" kingdom dimension.

I. **God Is Maker, Sustainer, and Ultimate *Telos* of All Things; He Alone Is the Owner and Purpose of the Universe.**

Ps. 24.1-2 (NASB) – The earth is the LORD's and the fullness thereof, the world and those who dwell therein, [2] for he has founded it upon the seas and established it upon the rivers.

1 Chron. 29.11-12 (NASB) – Yours, O LORD, is the greatness and the power and the glory and the victory and the majesty, for all that is in the heavens and in the earth is yours. Yours is the kingdom, O LORD, and you are exalted as head above all. [12] Both riches and honor come from you, and you rule over all. In your hand are power and might, and in your hand it is to make great and to give strength to all.

Ps. 50.12 (NASB) – If I were hungry, I would not tell you, for the world and its fullness are mine.

A. All things were created by God, all things are sustained by him, and all things exist for his ultimate praise and glory.

B. From a biblical perspective, ownership is singular concept: all things belong to him.

C. All things are answerable to him.

Implication: Because God is our owner, we ought not ever think of ministry in terms of our own efforts or energy. From A to Z, all that takes place in our lives is superintended by God as Source and End of all things that affect us.

> When the Possessor of heaven and earth brought you into being and placed you in this world, He placed you here not as an owner but as a steward – as such He entrusted you for a season with goods of various kinds – but the sole property of these still rests in Him, nor can ever be alienated from Him. As you are not your own but His, such is likewise all you enjoy.
>
> ~ John Wesley
>
> Dennis the Menace was walking out of church with his dad and mom. As they approached the pastor, Dennis asked, much to the embarrassment of his father, "What are you going to do with my dad's quarter?"
>
> "Whatever your lot in life, God expects you to build something on it."

II. As Loving Father and Wise Sovereign, God Has Entrusted His Rich Resources into the Care of His Servants and His People.

James 1.17 (NASB) – Every good gift and every perfect gift is from above, coming down from the Father of lights, with whom there is no variation or shadow due to change.

Exod. 19.5 (NASB) – Now therefore, if you will indeed obey my voice and keep my covenant, you shall be my treasured possession among all peoples, for all the earth is mine.

1 Chron. 29.14-16 (NASB) – But who am I, and what is my people, that we should be able thus to offer willingly? For all things come from you, and of your own have we given you. [15] For we are strangers before you and sojourners, as all our fathers were. Our days on the earth are like a shadow, and there is no abiding. [16] O LORD our God, all this abundance that we have provided for building you a house for your holy name comes from your hand and is all your own.

A. Entrustment and representation are the two primary concepts of serving God: as servants of the Lord Most High, each of us has been provided with a share of his wealth, a specific set of relationships and opportunities determined by the Lord.

B. We each have unique opportunities and possibilities to employ the relationships and resources he has entrusted to us as disciples of the Kingdom to come.

C. Relationships and resources are God's entrustments, never to become our idols or our focus.

Implication 1: God has entrusted to us as his servants his most valuable possessions and most significant mandate.

Stewards of the mysteries of God, 1 Cor. 4.1-2 – This is how one should regard us, as servants of Christ and stewards of the mysteries of God. [2] Moreover, it is required of stewards that they be found faithful.

The Treasure of the Spirit within us, 2 Cor. 4.6-7 – For God, who said, "Let light shine out of darkness," has shone in our hearts to give the light of the knowledge of the glory of God in the face of Jesus Christ. [7] But we have this treasure in jars of clay, to show that the surpassing power belongs to God and not to us.

Implication 2: The heart of spiritual renewal is the affirmation that our lives have their source in God, who called us, supplies us with his power, who leads us, who works in our lives, and gives to us all we need for life and godliness. No minister of the gospel should pretend that any part of their life or ministry is based on their own power and ingenuity. "It is not by power nor by might but by My Spirit, says the Lord" (Zech. 4.6).

No man was ever honored for what he received. Honor is the reward for what he gave.

If your outgo exceeds your income then your upkeep will be your downfall.

We make a living by what we get out of life but we make a life by what we give.

III. As Stewards of the Lord's Mysteries and Resources, We Are Called to Invest Them Ambitiously, Courageously, and Ingeniously in Order That His Purposes May Be Fulfilled through Us.

Luke 21.1-4 (NASB) – Jesus looked up and saw the rich putting their gifts into the offering box, [2] and he saw a poor widow put in two small copper coins. [3] And he said, "Truly, I tell you, this poor widow has put in more than all of them. [4] For they all contributed out of their abundance, but she out of her poverty put in all she had to live on."

2 Cor. 9.6-12 (NASB) – The point is this: whoever sows sparingly will also reap sparingly, and whoever sows bountifully will also reap bountifully.

[7] Each one must give as he has decided in his heart, not reluctantly or under compulsion, for God loves a cheerful giver. [8] And God is able to make all grace abound to you, so that having all sufficiency in all things at all times, you may abound in every good work. [9] As it is written, "He has distributed freely, he has given to the poor; his righteousness endures forever." [10] He who supplies seed to the sower and bread for food will supply and multiply your seed for sowing and increase the harvest of your righteousness. [11] You will be enriched in every way to be generous in every way, which through us will produce thanksgiving to God. [12] For the ministry of this service is not only supplying the needs of the saints but is also overflowing in many thanksgivings to God.

Matt. 25.14-30 – "For it will be like a man going on a journey, who called his servants and entrusted to them his property. [15] To one he gave five talents, to another two, to another one, to each according to his ability. Then he went away. [16] He who had received the five talents went at once and traded with them, and he made five talents more. [17] So also he who had the two talents made two talents more. [18] But he who had received the one talent went and dug in the ground and hid his master's money. [19] Now after a long time the master of those servants came and settled accounts with them. [20] And he who had received the five talents came forward, bringing five talents more, saying, 'Master, you delivered to me five talents; here, I have made five talents more.' [21] His master said to him, 'Well done, good and faithful servant. You have been faithful over a little; I will set you over much. Enter into the joy of your master.' [22] And he also who had the two talents came forward, saying, 'Master, you delivered to me two talents; here, I have made two talents more.' [23] His master said to him, 'Well done, good and faithful servant. You have been faithful over a little; I will set you over much. Enter into the joy of your master.' [24] He also who had received the one talent came forward, saying, 'Master, I knew you to be a hard man, reaping where you did not sow, and gathering where you scattered no seed, [25] so I was afraid, and I went and hid your talent in the ground. Here, you have what is yours.' [26] But his master answered him, 'You wicked and slothful servant! You knew that I reap where I have not sown and gather where I scattered no seed? [27] Then you ought to have invested my money with the bankers, and at my coming I should have received what was my own with interest. [28] So take the talent from him and give it to him who has the ten talents. [29] For to everyone who has will more be given, and he will have an abundance. But from the one who has not, even what he has will be taken away. [30] And cast the worthless servant into the outer darkness. In that place there will be weeping and gnashing of teeth.'"

A. Stewardship involves courage and sacrifice of an extreme kind; We are called to engage His work wholeheartedly but not in a self-dependent fashion; playing it safe is the sure way to lose what you have been given.

B. He expects us to invest, to discipline ourselves to enjoy and employ his resources in such a way as to glorify him in every dimension of our stewardship.

C. The over-zealous minister may think that everything depends on his or her efforts, but this is the height of selfish preoccupation and blatant pride; ultimately, only God can ensure fruit or transformation in anyone's life.

Ps. 127.1 – Unless the LORD builds the house, those who build it labor in vain. Unless the LORD watches over the city, the watchman stays awake in vain.

Ps. 33.16-20 – The king is not saved by his great army; a warrior is not delivered by his great strength. [17] The war horse is a false hope for salvation, and by its great might it cannot rescue. [18] Behold, the eye of the LORD is on those who fear him, on those who hope in his steadfast love, [19] that he may deliver their soul from death and keep them alive in famine. [20] Our soul waits for the LORD; he is our help and our shield.

The stewardship axiom: God never calls his person or his people to do anything without also making provision for them to possess everything they may need in order to accomplish his will.

Phil. 4.11-13 (NASB) – Not that I am speaking of being in need, for I have learned in whatever situation I am to be content. [12] I know how to be brought low, and I know how to abound. In any and every circumstance, I have learned the secret of facing plenty and hunger, abundance and need. [13] I can do all things through him who strengthens me.

This principle will allow you to . . .

- Chill hard with the Lord, even in the midst of the most difficult situations
- Not overestimate your significance or importance as you serve Christ

- Relax as you engage in the various dimensions of ministry that God has given, and

- Confidently expect God to work for his glory, even if his manner, method, and timing are dramatically different than yours

If I Had My Life to Live Over

I'd dare to make more mistakes next time,
I'd relax, I would limber up, I would be sillier than I have been this trip,
I would take fewer things seriously, I would take more chances,
I would climb more mountains and swim more rivers,
I would eat more ice cream and less beans,
I would perhaps have more actual troubles,
But I'd have fewer imaginary ones.
You see, I'm one of those people who live
Sensibly and sanely hour after hour, day after day.
Oh, I've had my moments, and if I had it to do over again,
I'd have more of them. In fact, I'd try to do nothing else,
Just moments, one after the other instead of
living so many years ahead of time.
I've been one of those persons who never go anywhere
without a thermometer, hot water bottle, rain coat and parachute.
If I had to do it again, I would travel lighter than I have.
If I had my life to live over, I would start barefoot earlier in the spring,
And stay that way later in the fall,
I would go to more dinners,
I would ride more merry-go-rounds,
I would pick more daisies.

IV. Finally, God Has Promised to Reward Us According to the Quality and Scope of Our Investments towards His Great Purposes.

1 Cor. 4.2 (NASB) – Moreover, it is required of stewards that they be found faithful.

Gal. 6.7-9 (NASB) – Do not be deceived: God is not mocked, for whatever one sows, that will he also reap. [8] For the one who sows to his own flesh will from the flesh reap corruption, but the one who sows to the Spirit will from the Spirit reap eternal life. [9] And let us not grow weary of doing good, for in due season we will reap, if we do not give up.

1 Cor 3.10-15 (NASB) – According to the grace of God given to me, like a skilled master builder I laid a foundation, and someone else is building upon it. Let each one take care how he builds upon it. [11] For no one can lay a foundation other than that which is laid, which is Jesus Christ. [12] Now if anyone builds on the foundation with gold, silver, precious stones, wood, hay, straw—[13] each one's work will become manifest, for the Day will disclose it, because it will be revealed by fire, and the fire will test what sort of work each one has done. [14] If the work that anyone has built on the foundation survives, he will receive a reward. [15] If anyone's work is burned up, he will suffer loss, though he himself will be saved, but only as through fire.

A. Smart investments in God's purposes pay real tangible dividends in the quality of life, relationships, and ministry that he has given to us.

B. The promise of God is categorical regarding sowing and reaping; if we sow wisely, we will reap a harvest of return if we persevere and do not give up.

C. Ultimately, Christ himself will reward our faithfulness to him, which goes beyond anything that our family, church, denomination, or religion can muster or comprehend.

Remember . . .

Nothing sacrificed or stewarded for the Lord Jesus will be in vain!

1 Cor. 15.58 (NASB) – Therefore, my beloved brothers, be steadfast, immovable, always abounding in the work of the Lord, knowing that in the Lord your labor is not in vain.

The story is told by the chief accountant for one of the wealthiest men who ever lived – John D. Rockefeller, Sr. Someone asked the accountant one day, "How much did John D. leave? We know he was an immensely wealthy man." Without a moment's hesitation, the accountant answered, "Everything!"

SEMINAR 9

Publicizing and Funding Your Evangel School

Rev. Bob Engel

I. Ownership of Your Evangel School: Five Keys to Seeking Resources

A. Your Vision

B. Plan to steward/give

C. Relationships

D. Prayer

E. It's the Lord's resources

II. Registering Your School

A. Sixty days prior to hosting (form found at *www.tumi.org/evangel*)

B. TUMI website to publicize (*www.tumi.org/evangel* and social media)

III. Publicity Options

IV. Support Raising Options

SEMINAR 10

Evangel Support and Resources

Rev. Bob Engel

I. **Ripe for Harvest: A Guidebook for Planting Healthy Churches in the City**

II. **Planting Churches among the City's Poor: An Anthology of Urban Church Planting Resources**

   A. *Volume 1: Theological and Missiological Perspectives for Church Planters*

   B. *Volume 2: Resources and Tools for Coaches and Teams*

III. **Front Matters: Prerequisite Readings for the Evangel School of Urban Church Planting**

IV. **Church Planter's Tool Kit**

   A. *Church Planter's Tool Kit* for each Dean Team

   B. Display table at your Evangel School

V. **Evangel School Resource Pack (see Appendix for full detail of contents in pack)**

VI. **Evangel Grant**

   A. Depends on funds for coming year

   B. Evangel Dean recommendation

Assignments and Dean Exercises

ASSIGNMENT 1

Read and Respond: Readings on the Poor

Note: Please use the form available in the training module for this assignment.

Instructions

Read the following articles on the poor and answer the questions below:

- *Our Distinctive: Advancing the Kingdom among the Urban Poor*
- *On World Impact's "Empowering the Urban Poor"*
- *Responding to God's Call to the Poor*

Answer the following questions about these articles (1-3 pages total):

1. What challenged you in these readings?

2. What changes do you need to make, if any?

3. What are the implications these readings have for your Evangel School?

ASSIGNMENT

ASSIGNMENT 2

Read and Respond:
Sacred Roots: A Primer on
Retrieving the Great Tradition

Note: Please use the form available in the training module for this assignment.

Instructions

1. Read *Sacred Roots: A Primer on Retrieving the Great Tradition.*

2. Write a precis (concise summary) of its main point, as you see it, summarizing its major theme and argument. (Articulate its argument in a respectful way whether you agree with the author or not.) Then, give your concise evaluation of what you read. (Respond as to why you agree or disagree with the thesis.) This practice helps strengthen your ability to engage different opinions in a respectful way and learn to listen to others and respond with clarity and respect. In this way, you learn to dialog with and discuss with others whose beliefs are different than your own.

ASSIGNMENT 3

Read and Respond:
Get Your Pretense On!

Note: Please use the form available in the training module for this assignment.

Instructions

1. Read *Get Your Pretense On!*

2. Write a precis (concise summary) of its main point, as you see it, summarizing its major theme and argument. (Articulate its argument in a respectful way whether you agree with the author or not.) Then, give your concise evaluation of what you read. (Respond as to why you agree or disagree with the thesis.) This practice helps strengthen your ability to engage different opinions in a respectful way and learn to listen to others and respond with clarity and respect. In this way, you learn to dialog with and discuss with others whose beliefs are different than your own.

ASSIGNMENT 4

Watch and Respond:
The Centrality of the Church

Note: Please use the form available in the training module for this assignment.

Instructions

1. Watch *The Centrality of the Church* (Crowns of Beauty, Dr. Davis).

2. Write a precis (concise summary) of its main point, as you see it, summarizing its major theme and argument. (Articulate its argument in a respectful way whether you agree with the author or not.) Then, give your concise evaluation of what you read. (Respond as to why you agree or disagree with the thesis.) This practice helps strengthen your ability to engage different opinions in a respectful way and learn to listen to others and respond with clarity and respect. In this way, you learn to dialog with and discuss with others whose beliefs are different than your own.

ASSIGNMENT 5

Read and Respond: What Is a Church?

Note: Please use the form available in the training module for this assignment.

Instructions

1. Read *What Is a Church?*

2. Write a precis (concise summary) of its main point, as you see it, summarizing its major theme and argument. (Articulate its argument in a respectful way whether you agree with the author or not.) Then, give your concise evaluation of what you read. (Respond as to why you agree or disagree with the thesis.) This practice helps strengthen your ability to engage different opinions in a respectful way and learn to listen to others and respond with clarity and respect. In this way, you learn to dialog with and discuss with others whose beliefs are different than your own.

DEAN EXERCISE 1

How Will Evangel Help New Church Plants Embrace the Church and the World?

One hour

Note: Please use the form available in the training module for this Dean Exercise.

It is essential that new church plants possess a theology of the Kingdom that leads to a unified partnership with other churches for the sake of witness to the world. In this exercise you will discuss how church plants from your school will embrace both a specific family of churches and pursue shared kingdom witness with other "embassies" in their locale.

Exercise Instructions

1. Open in prayer, committing your time to the Lord and seeking his wisdom (5 min).

2. Discuss your Dean Team's experience with denominations, church associations, and locale expressions of the church (10 min).

   a. What church family (tradition) were you a member of when you were baptized? What church family do you belong to now?

   b. What has been your involvement with church associations or networks that especially focused on church planting or church planting movements?

   c. What barriers have you seen to local churches working together in kingdom partnerships? What benefits have you seen to local churches partnering with other churches for the sake of Kingdom witness to the world?

3. Discuss the following questions:

   a. What church family or families (tradition/s) will your Evangel school partner with to plant churches among the poor?

   b. How will you ensure that church plants from your school have locale relationships with other local churches committed to the task of church planting and kingdom compassion ministries (pursuing shalom together)?

  c. Are there paths to licensing and ordination open to the church planters you are working with among the poor?

  d. What level of licensing or ordination will you require of church planters before they come to Evangel?

  e. How will you ensure that church plants sent out from your school will be committed to the ongoing pursuit of church plant movements?

4. Set SMART (Specific, Measurable, Achievable, Relevant, Time-bound) goals to ensure that church planters from your school are plugged into Urban Church Associations. If there is not a clear path to licensing and ordination for church planters attending your school, set goals to ensure that progress is made on this issue during the next six months in relation to your Evangel School. At the Dean School you will add these goals to your project schedule.

5. Appoint a spokesperson who will present your visual schedule and school charter.

Dean Exercise 2

Seeing the Big Picture: Establishing Context

Note: Please use the form available in the training module for this Dean Exercise.

This dean's exercise is an adaptation of the Evangel School exercise found on pages 79–82 in *Ripe for Harvest: A Guidebook for Planting Healthy Churches in the City*. After reviewing the Exercise Guidelines and Instructions, please complete with your Evangel Dean Team.

Exercise Instructions

1. Discuss "A Call to an Ancient Evangelical Future," in *Ripe for Harvest*, pp. 83–86, and "Church Planting Models," pp. 87–89.

2. Complete a one-page history of your team.

   - How our team was formed
   - Expressions of the church our Evangel School will pursue
   - Resources available to us
   - Why does this Dean Team want to host an Evangel School?
   - Describe the gifts of your Dean Team.

3. Conduct a SWOT (Strengths, Weaknesses, Opportunities, Threats) Analysis for your church plant school.

   - Internal Strengths
   - Internal Weaknesses
   - External Opportunities
   - External Threats

4. Over lunch today, please sit with the members of your Dean Team, and discuss answers to the following personal team questions.

   a. Where were you born, and what was life like for you growing up?

   b. How were you "reborn," i.e., how did you come to Christ, and what has it been like for you "growing up" spiritually?

DEAN EXERCISE 3

Seeing the Big Picture
Establishing Values and Vision of Your Evangel School
One hour, ten minutes

Note: Please use the form available in the training module for this Dean Exercise.

Your Dean Team will need to be able to clearly articulate the vision and the values that guide your training of urban church plant teams. This dean's exercise is an adaptation of the Evangel School exercise found on pages 95–103 in *Ripe for Harvest: A Guidebook for Planting Healthy Churches in the City.*

Exercise Instructions

1. Open in prayer (5 min).

2. To understand how "values and vision" are defined for this exercise, review *Ripe for Harvest*, page 65 ("Using Wisdom in Ministry") and pages 95-103 ("Seeing the Big Picture: Defining Values and Vision") (10 min).

3. Discuss our Mission-Critical Perspectives (found on page 13 of this book). Determine three to five values you will draw upon to help you make decisions. Remember, these values are guiding principles, assumptions, or driving forces that will guide you to a decision when you face uncertainty as to which way to go. ("Wisdom is choosing what is best between viable truths.") You can draw upon these shared values when you get to the heat of battle (25 min).

   a. Which values do you resonate with the most?

   b. Are there values important to your team in addition to these seven?

   c. If you had to choose the five most important values for your team, what would they be?

4. Craft a two-to-three sentence vision statement for your Evangel School for the next three to five years. [Enter your vision statement in the place provided at the end of this exercise.] (30 min)

   a. *Crafting* a Vision Statement

      (1) Who, what, when, where, and how

      (2) Customized, detailed, distinctive

      (3) Distinguishes you from others who are doing the same thing

      (4) Identifies the target audience (e.g. ethnicity, geographic, economic, personality)

      (5) Emphasizes aggressive, futuristic action

      (6) Quantitative

      (7) Should not change after a year or two

      (8) Has a focused "main thing" (in this case, establishing your Evangel School)

      (9) Limited to two-to-three sentences

      (10) Has longer than two-year horizon

   b. Questions for Reflection

      (1) How long will we take?

      (2) What geographical boundaries will we target?

      (3) What ethnic or unreached people group(s) will we target? [*A people group is considered unreached (UPG) when there isn't an indigenous church in that people group (a church that looks like the people and is led by the people of the culture).*]

      (4) What unengaged and unreached people group(s) will we target (if applicable)? [*Unreached people groups are unengaged (UUPG) when there is no one strategizing to reach that group, i.e., there is no tangible intent of targeting that people group with the Gospel.*]

(5) What distinguishes us from other church planting efforts?

(6) What will our general approach be to reach the vision?

Our Evangel School Vision is as follows (2-3 sentences):

Our Mission-Critical Perspectives are as follows:

5. Appoint a spokesperson who will present your school's values and vision.

Dean Exercise 4

Evaluating Team Effectiveness

Note: Please use the form available in the training module for this Dean Exercise.

Your Dean Team will need to work together to access, train, and coach urban church plant teams. This exercise will help you evaluate how ready you are to work together as a team. The exercise helps you evaluate and track the ten areas of team effectiveness discussed in the Seminar *Evangel Emphasizes Team*.

Exercise Instructions

1. Take team effectiveness test individually (10 minutes; you do not need to average team results for this exercise).

2. Discuss results as a team

   a. Do our results generally agree, or are there large differences of opinion?

   b. Do we seem balanced in these ten areas or do we have obvious strengths and weaknesses?

   c. What areas most need improvement?

   d. What areas of strength can we build upon as we plan our strategy?

   e. Have we been focusing our prayer in the right areas?

3. Discuss who potential team mates might be for various roles on your Dean Team (Deans, Coaches, Support Personnel, Intercessors, Donors).

4. What are the various roles and responsibilities of our current team members? What roles or skills do we lack, and how will we fill those positions, or get those roles done?

5. Of all the ten essential elements of effective teams, what do you think is the most important characteristic of a good team member? How would you rate yourself on that trait right now? Be specific.

6. How will we continue to assess the effectiveness of our team as we move forward? What tools will we use to do so?

7. Choose a spokesperson who will be prepared to present on the strengths and weaknesses of your team as well as who will be filling the roles of Deans, Coaches, Support Personnel, and Intercessors for your Evangel School of Urban Church Planting.

Principles of Team Effectiveness Diagnostic Chart

One way of tracking growth in these principles is by using the attached diagnostic chart. Once a quarter ask team members to evaluate how the team is doing in each of the ten areas of Team Effectiveness using the Rating Chart on the next page. (The Rating Chart asks each member to assign the team's performance on each characteristic a number from 1-10 with 10 being the best and 1 being the worst.)

After each team member (including the team leader) has rated the team in each area, collect the results and find the average rating for each characteristic. (Example: On the characteristic of articulation Team Member #1 assigned it a 6, Member #2 a 7, Member #3 a 4 and Member #4 a 7. When the four scores are added together and divided by the number of team members the average score for the characteristic of articulation is 6.)

Then plot the number 6 on the Team Effectiveness Evaluation Chart under the characteristic of articulation. After each characteristic has been plotted on the chart, connect the points with a line. The chart will help the team see how it perceives itself.

Questions that should be asked are:

- Do we seem balanced in each of these areas or do we have obvious strengths and weaknesses?

- What areas most need improvement and how are they affecting our effectiveness? Are there any immediate changes we should make?

- What areas of strength should we build on as we plan our strategy?

- Have we been focusing our prayer in the right areas?

Team Effectiveness Rating Chart

Please rate your team on each of the following characteristics of team effectiveness. For each characteristic, 1 represents a poor performance, 5 an average performance, and 10 an excellent performance. (Please use the form available in the training module.)

ARTICULATION

1   2   3   4   5   6   7   8   9   10

INCORPORATION

1   2   3   4   5   6   7   8   9   10

COOPERATION

1   2   3   4   5   6   7   8   9   10

IDENTIFICATION

1   2   3   4   5   6   7   8   9   10

ORGANIZATION

1   2   3   4   5   6   7   8   9   10

PREPARATION

1   2   3   4   5   6   7   8   9   10

IMPLEMENTATION

1   2   3   4   5   6   7   8   9   10

COORDINATION

1   2   3   4   5   6   7   8   9   10

EVALUATION

1   2   3   4   5   6   7   8   9   10

ADAPTATION

1   2   3   4   5   6   7   8   9   10

Team Effectiveness Evaluation Chart

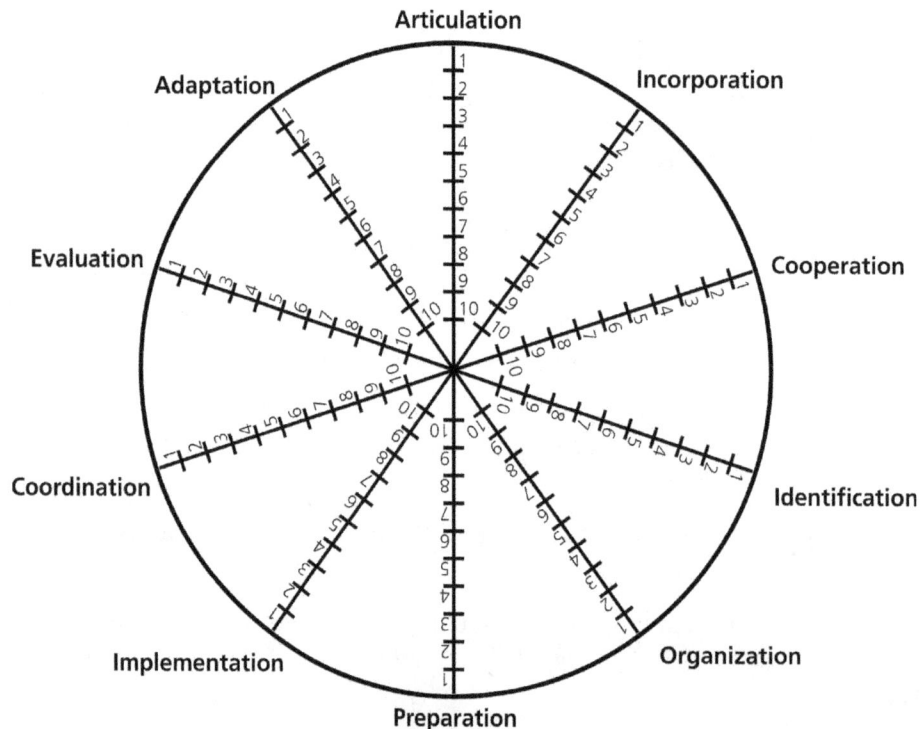

DEAN EXERCISE 5

Using Wisdom in Ministry
The PWR Process

Note: Please use the form available in the training module for this Dean Exercise.

Exercise Instructions

Read pages 62-73 in *Ripe for Harvest* (Seminar 3: *Using Wisdom in Ministry*). Then, discuss the following with your team:

1. Why is biblical wisdom and its application so critical in all our attempts to accomplish credible ministry and mission in God's name?

2. What are the basic elements of PWR?

3. What particular ideas in the PWR framework can help us organize our efforts as we approach the challenge/call of planting a church among an unreached people group in the city?

4. What pitfalls must we avoid as we move forward in implementing a PWR strategy in planting a church?

DEAN EXERCISE 6

How Will Evangel Recruit and Assess Church Planters For and From the Poor?

One hour

Note: Please use the form available in the training module for this Dean Exercise.

Your Dean Team will need to recruit potential candidates for your Evangel School of Urban Church Planting. In this exercise you will identify your initial recruitment plan for church plant team leaders.

Exercise Instructions

1. Open in prayer, committing your time to the Lord and seeking his wisdom (5 min).

2. Reflect on today's seminar about assessment, the urban poor, and the vision for Evangel Schools of Urban Church Planting. What one or two big ideas stand out to you (5 min)?

3. Complete the Recruiting Church Planters Chart (on your form in the training module):

Recruiting Church Planters
Pools we will recruit from:
Who will we deputize to recruit for Evangel?
What strategies will we pursue for recruitment?

4. As you reflect on your own Evangel Vision and Values, what goals do you need to set for the next six months in the area of recruiting church planters? Set at least one SMART (Specific, Measurable, Achievable, Relevant, Time-bound) goal for each category from the Recruiting Church Planters Chart. It is okay to postpone making a decision as long as you establish a goal for when you will make the decision (e.g. Make decision on who to deputize by January 1, 2018).

DEAN EXERCISE 7

How Will We Coach At and After Evangel?

One hour

Note: Please use the form available in the training module for this Dean Exercise.

Coaching is the "C" in the ABCs of Urban Church Planting. In this exercise you will identify key elements of your school's approach to coaching.

Exercise Instructions

1. Open in prayer, committing your time to the Lord and seeking his wisdom (5 min).

2. Discuss your Dean Team's experience with coaching (10 min).

   a. What has been your experience with coaching in general, and coaching church plant teams in particular?

   b. Who is a coach you respect and have learned from?

   c. What resources have you found helpful for coaching?

   d. What was one thing that stood out to you from the seminars on coaching?

3. Complete Recruiting Assessor Coaches and Recruiting Field Coaches Chart (on your form in the training module):

Recruiting Assessor Coaches	Recruiting Field Coaches
How will our school recruit Assessor Coaches?	How will our school recruit Field Coaches?
What qualifications will we require of our Assessor Coaches?	What qualifications will we require of our Field Coaches?
What training will we provide for our Assessor Coaches?	What training will we provide for our Field Coaches?

Recruiting Assessor Coaches	Recruiting Field Coaches
How will our Assessor Coaches take advantage of TUMI's resources for church planters and urban churches? What other resources are available to our Assessor Coaches?	How will our Field Coaches take advantage of TUMI's resources for church planters and urban churches? What other resources are available to our Field Coaches?
How will we communicate with our Assessor Coach Network?	How will we communicate with our Field Coach Network?
How will we keep our Assessor Coaches accountable to the commitments they make at Evangel?	How will we keep our Field Coaches accountable to the commitments they make at Evangel?

4. As you reflect on your own Evangel Vision and Values, what goals do you need to set for the next six months in the area of recruiting Assessor and Field Coaches? Set at least one SMART (Specific, Measurable, Achievable, Relevant, Time-bound) goal for each category from the Recruiting Assessor and Field Coaches Chart. It is okay to postpone making a decision as long as you establish a goal for when you will make the decision.

5. Transfer your goals to your Project Management Form.

DEAN EXERCISE 8

Why Is It Both Prudent and Necessary to Develop a Team Charter?

Note: Please use the form available in the training module for this Dean Exercise.

The *Team Charter* is both a summary and culmination of the team's strategic process, and equips the team to approach its ministry with unity and wisdom.

Instructions
Review and discuss the points below, and initial each item.

Developing a Team Charter makes good sense because:

_____ • It offers the team a *clear ministry plan*.

_____ • It builds *clarity and confidence* in the Church Plant Team as they communicate their vision to partners, supporters, volunteers and the emerging church.

_____ • It provides World Impact and its partners with a *strategic way to oversee* church plants.

_____ • It enables *ongoing feedback* as reviews are made according to time-specific checkpoints.

_____ • It can help the team *eliminate waste* through the non-strategic expenditures of time and effort.

_____ • It prevents *open-ended failure* and instills in the team a *sense of urgency*.

_____ • It makes the team *semi-autonomous* allowing the team to carry out its own vision without micro-management.

DEAN EXERCISE 9
Study of Charters

Note: Please use the form available in the training module for this Dean Exercise.

Instructions
Contrast and compare the charters in *Planting Churches among the City's Poor, Volume 2*, pages 135-136. Record your thoughts on the form available in the training module.

Evangel School Training Deans' Certification Form

Note: Please use the form available in the training module for this task.

Name of your Evangel School: _____

Date: _____

Dean: _____   **Dean:** _____

Dean: _____   **Dean:** _____

Dean: _____   **Dean:** _____

Church Expressions Endorsed (Check all that apply):

_____ Small (House) Church [approximately 20-50]

_____ Community Church [approximately 50-150]

_____ Hub (Mother) Church [200+]

Denominational Affiliation: _____

Field Coaches and length of commitment:

Target Area: _____

Ethnicity and/or unreached people group(s):
[A people group is considered unreached (UPG) when there isn't an indigenous church in that people group (a church that looks like the people and is led by the people of the culture.]

Unengaged and unreached people group (if applicable):
[Unreached people groups are unengaged (UUPG) when there is no one strategizing to reach that group, i.e., there is no tangible intent of targeting that people group with the Gospel.]

School Values

School Vision Statement

School Goals

6 months: _____

1 year: _____

2 years: _____

3 years: _____

National Evangel Dean Approval:_____ **Date:** _____

National Evangel Dean Approval:_____ **Date:** _____

National Evangel Dean Approval:_____ **Date:** _____

By the grace of God we will work our goals with excellence and under the logo of Evangel School of Urban Church Planting.

_____ **Date:** _____
Dean's Signature

Signed on behalf of

_____
Name of Team

DEAN EXERCISE 10
How Will Deans Fund and Publicize Their Evangel School of Urban Church Planting?
One hour

Note: Please use the form available in the training module for this Dean Exercise.

Your Dean Team will need to fund and publicize your Evangel School of Urban Church Planting. In this exercise you will think through funding options and ways in which to publicize your School.

Exercise Instructions

1. Open in prayer, committing your time to the Lord and seeking his wisdom (5 min).

2. Complete Funding and Publicity Chart (on your form in the training module):

Funding	Publicity
Pools we will seek funding from:	Avenues we can publicize:
Who will we deputize to raise funds for Evangel?	Who will we deputize to publicize for Evangel?
What strategies will we pursue for funding?	What strategies will we pursue to publicize Evangel?

3. As you reflect on your own Evangel Vision and Values, what goals do you need to set for the next six months in the areas of publicity and funding? Set at least one S.M.A.R.T. (Specific, Measurable, Achievable, Relevant, Time-bound) goal for each category from the Publicity and Funding chart. It is okay to postpone making a decision as long as you establish a goal for when you will make the decision.

4. Transfer your goals to your Project Management Form.

Appendix

The Nicene Creed with Biblical Support

The Urban Ministry Institute

We believe in one God, *(Deut. 6.4-5; Mark 12.29; 1 Cor. 8.6)*
    the Father Almighty, *(Gen. 17.1; Dan. 4.35; Matt. 6.9; Eph. 4.6; Rev. 1.8)*
    Maker of heaven and earth *(Gen. 1.1; Isa. 40.28; Rev. 10.6)*
    and of all things visible and invisible. *(Ps. 148; Rom. 11.36; Rev. 4.11)*

We believe in one Lord Jesus Christ, the only Begotten Son of God, begotten of the Father
    before all ages, God from God, Light from Light, True God from True God, begotten not
    created, of the same essence as the Father,
        (John 1.1-2; 3.18; 8.58; 14.9-10; 20.28; Col. 1.15, 17; Heb. 1.3-6)
    through whom all things were made. *(John 1.3; Col. 1.16)*

Who for us men and for our salvation came down from heaven and was incarnate by the Holy
    Spirit and the Virgin Mary and became human.
        (Matt. 1.20-23; John 1.14; 6.38; Luke 19.10)
    Who for us too, was crucified under Pontius Pilate, suffered and was buried.
        (Matt. 27.1-2; Mark 15.24-39, 43-47; Acts 13.29; Rom. 5.8; Heb. 2.10; 13.12)
    The third day he rose again according to the Scriptures,
        (Mark 16.5-7; Luke 24.6-8; Acts 1.3; Rom. 6.9; 10.9; 2 Tim. 2.8)
    ascended into heaven, and is seated at the right hand of the Father.
        (Mark 16.19; Eph. 1.19-20)
    He will come again in glory to judge the living and the dead, and his Kingdom will have
    no end. *(Isa. 9.7; Matt. 24.30; John 5.22; Acts 1.11; 17.31; Rom. 14.9; 2 Cor. 5.10; 2 Tim. 4.1)*

We believe in the Holy Spirit, the Lord and life-giver, *(Gen. 1.1-2; Job 33.4; Ps. 104.30; 139.7-8;*
    Luke 4.18-19; John 3.5-6; Acts 1.1-2; 1 Cor. 2.11; Rev. 3.22)
    who proceeds from the Father and the Son, *(John 14.16-18, 26; 15.26; 20.22)*
    who together with the Father and Son is worshiped and glorified,
        (Isa. 6.3; Matt. 28.19; 2 Cor. 13.14; Rev. 4.8)
    who spoke by the prophets. *(Num. 11.29; Mic. 3.8; Acts 2.17-18; 2 Pet. 1.21)*

We believe in one holy, catholic, and apostolic Church.
    (Matt. 16.18; Eph. 5.25-28; 1 Cor. 1.2; 10.17; 1 Tim. 3.15; Rev. 7.9)

We acknowledge one baptism for the forgiveness of sin, *(Acts 22.16; 1 Pet. 3.21; Eph. 4.4-5)*
    And we look for the resurrection of the dead and the life of the age to come.
    (Isa. 11.6-10; Mic. 4.1-7; Luke 18.29-30; Rev. 21.1-5; 21.22-22.5)
    Amen.

The Nicene Creed with Biblical Support – Memory Verses

Below are suggested memory verses, one for each section of the Creed.

The Father
Rev. 4.11 – Worthy are you, our Lord and God, to receive glory and honor and power, for you created all things, and by your will they existed and were created.

The Son
John 1.1 – In the beginning was the Word, and the Word was with God, and the Word was God.

The Son's Mission
1 Cor. 15.3-5 – For what I received I passed on to you as of first importance: that Christ died for our sins according to the Scriptures, that he was buried, that he was raised on the third day according to the Scriptures, and that he appeared to Peter, and then to the Twelve.

The Holy Spirit
Rom. 8.11 – If the Spirit of him who raised Jesus from the dead dwells in you, he who raised Christ Jesus from the dead will also give life to your mortal bodies through his Spirit who dwells in you.

The Church
1 Pet. 2.9 – But you are a chosen race, a royal priesthood, a holy nation, a people for his own possession, that you may proclaim the excellencies of him who called you out of darkness into his marvelous light.

Our Hope
1 Thess. 4.16-17 – For the Lord himself will descend from heaven with a cry of command, with the voice of an archangel, and with the sound of the trumpet of God. And the dead in Christ will rise first. Then we who are alive, who are left, will be caught up together with them in the clouds to meet the Lord in the air, and so we will always be with the Lord.

World Impact Affirmation of Faith

World Impact

There is one living and true God, infinitely perfect in glory, wisdom, holiness, justice, power and love, one in His essence but eternally existing in three persons: God the Father, God the Son and God the Holy Spirit. God sovereignly created the world out of nothing, so that His creation, while wholly dependent upon Him, neither comprises part of God, nor conditions His essential perfection.

The books which form the canon of the Old and New Testaments are verbally inspired by God, inerrant in the original writings, the only infallible rule of faith and practice.

God created man in His own image, in a state of original righteousness, from which humankind subsequently fell by a voluntary revolt, and consequently is guilty, inherently corrupt and subject to divine wrath.

Jesus Christ, the eternal Son, became man without ceasing to be God by uniting to His divine nature a true human nature in His incarnation, and so continues to be both God and man, in two distinct natures and one person, forever. He was conceived by the Holy Spirit, born of the virgin Mary, exhibited His deity by manifold miracles, fulfilled the requirements of the Law by His sinless life, shed His blood as a vicarious and propitiatory atonement for humankind's sin, was resurrected from the dead in the same body, now glorified. He ascended into heaven and now intercedes in glory for His redeemed as our great high priest and advocate, and as the Head of the Church and Lord of the individual believer.

The Holy Spirit convicts the world of sin, righteousness and judgment, through the ministry of regeneration and sanctification applies salvation and places believers into the Church, guides and comforts God's children, indwells, directs, gifts and empowers the Church in godly living and service in order to fulfill the Great Commission, and seals and keeps the believer until Christ returns.

Every person, regardless of race or rank, who receives the Lord Jesus Christ by faith is born into the family of God and receives eternal life. This occurs solely because of the grace of God and has no ground in human merit.

The Holy Church is the one institution specifically ordained of God to function in the furthering of the Kingdom until Christ comes again. It consists of all those regenerated by the Spirit of God, in mystical union and communion both with Christ, the head of the Body, and with fellow believers. Neighborhood congregations are the local manifestation of the Church universal. In obedience to the command of Christ, these congregations preach the Word of God, equip God's people for the work of ministry, and administer the Lord's Supper and Baptism.

The Lord Jesus Christ will return bodily, visibly and personally to receive His own, to conform believers to His own image and to establish His millennial kingdom. He will judge the quick and the dead and will effect a final separation of the redeemed and the lost, assigning unbelievers to eternal punishment and believers to eternal glory, enjoying conscious fellowship with Him.

Humankind's chief end in life is to honor and glorify Almighty God. Personal salvation is a means to this end.

Let God Arise! Prayer Concert

Adoration, Admission and Availability

ADORATION

- Delight and Enjoyment in God; Overwhelming Gratefulness;
- Acknowledging God in His Person and Works

ADMISSION

- Powerlessness; Helplessness
- Awareness of One's Desperate Need for God

AVAILABILITY

- Dying to preoccupation with self and love of the world; No confidence in fleshly wisdom, resources, or method
- Consecrating ourselves as living sacrifices to God

Awakening and Advancement

AWAKENING

- Refreshment: outpouring of the Holy Spirit on God's people; Renewal: Obedience to the Great Commandment – Loving God and neighbor
- Revolution: Radical new orientation to Christ as Lord

ADVANCEMENT

- Movements: outreaches to unreached, pioneer regions; Mobilization: of every assembly to fulfill the Great Commission
- Military mindset: Adopting a warfare mentality to suffer and endure hardness in spiritual warfare

Affirmation and Acknowledgement

AFFIRMATION

- Giving Testimony over what the Lord has done
- Challenging one another by speaking the truth in Love

ACKNOWLEDGMENT

- Waiting patiently on God to act by His timing and methods; Living confidently as though God is answering our petitions
- Acting as if God will do precisely what He says He will do

Our Distinctive
Advancing the Kingdom among the Urban Poor

God Has Chosen the Poor

One does not have to read many pages into the New Testament to discover where the early Church got the idea that the poor were specially chosen by God to receive the Gospel and spread it throughout the earth. Jesus, himself, had announced publicly that he was intentionally preaching the Gospel to the poor (Luke 4.18, Luke 6.20) and even suggested that this action helped demonstrate that he was, indeed, the Messiah (Matt. 11.2-6).

Building on Jesus' teaching, it is not unusual to find very explicit statements in the Epistles about God's choice of, and expectations for, those who are without power, resources, or money. For example, James teaches:

> Listen, my dear brothers: Has not God chosen those who are poor in the eyes of the world to be rich in faith and to inherit the kingdom he promised those who love him?
>
> ~ James 2.5

In a similar manner, Paul writes:

> But God chose the foolish things of the world to shame the wise; God chose the weak things of the world to shame the strong. He chose the lowly things of this world and the despised things-and the things that are not-to nullify the things that are, so that no one may boast before him.
>
> ~ 1 Corinthians 1.27-29

These ideas are not a new theme introduced by the New Testament writers. Instead, they faithfully reflect the Old Testament teachings about how God relates to the poor. One scholar summarizes the Old Testament teaching about the poor in three principles.

1. God has a particular concern for the poor.

2. God's people must manifest a similar concern [for the poor].

3. The poor are frequently identified with the pious and the righteous.

The words "chose" and "chosen" in James 2 and 1 Corinthians 1 come from the Greek word eklégomai which means "giving favor to the chosen subject. . . It involves preference and selection from among many choices." In other contexts, it is used to describe God's choice of the "elect" (Mark 13.20) and Jesus' choosing of his disciples (Luke 6.13).

Douglas J. Moo, James, *Tyndale Old Testament Commentary Series,* Gen. Ed. Leon Morris. Leicester, England-Grand Rapids, MI: IVP-Eerdmans, 1985. pp. 53-54.

Who Are the Poor?

> In the teaching of Jesus, material possessions are not regarded as evil, but as dangerous. The poor are often shown to be happier than the rich, because it is easier for them to have an attitude of dependence upon God.
>
> ~ R.E. Nixon. "Poverty." *The Illustrated Bible Dictionary*. eds. J.D. Douglas, et al. Leicester, England: IVP, 1980. p. 1255.

To understand God's choice of the poor it is necessary to understand who the "poor" are. The way that Scripture uses the term "poor" is both alike and different from the way we often use the term.

1. The Greek word used in the New Testament means essentially the same thing as our English word "poor." It describes someone who is economically deprived, someone who doesn't have enough money or resources. However, when this word is used by the New Testament writers, they seem to also rely on the Old Testament understandings of the word "poor." Thus, in the New Testament, the poor are both "those who don't have enough money" (Greek understanding) plus "something else" (the Hebrew understanding).

2. This "something else" was an understanding developed over time in the Hebrew Scriptures. In the Old Testament, "the poor" are those who are so powerless and dependent that they are vulnerable to being misused by those who have influence in the society. The emphasis is on *being on the wrong end of a relationship* with those in power. Therefore, in the Old Testament, the poor came to mean those people who were characterized by three things:

    a. They lack the money and resources they need,

    b. They are taken advantage of by those who do have money and resources, and

    c. The result is that they must humbly turn to God as their only source of protection.

3. Therefore, from a theological point of view, we could say that Scripture defines "the poor" as:

Those whose need makes them desperate enough to rely on God alone.

Biblical scholar Robert A. Guelich makes exactly these points when he writes about the development of the term "poor" in the Old Testament.

> The most common of these words [for the poor], *'ny* and its later relative, *'nw*, have a much broader scope than simply to denote a socioeconomic status. . . . The *'ny* refers to one so powerless and dependent as to be vulnerable to exploitation by those who have the power base. Thus the accent falls on a socioeconomic relationship rather than on material possessions as such. Yet this powerless and dependent relationship caused one to rely upon God for one's needs and vindication. This humble posture of the poor devoid of pretension before God reflects the religious dimension and comes out frequently in the Psalms. . . . But the religious dimension is never exclusive of the socioeconomic. Both elements are integral to *'ny*. . . . .In summary, the poor in Judaism referred to those in desperate need (socioeconomic element) whose helplessness drove them to a dependent relationship with God (religious element) for the supplying of their needs and their vindication.
>
> ~ Robert A. Guelich. *The Sermon on the Mount.*
> Waco: Word Books, 1982. pp. 68-69.

This understanding helps us perceive how Luke can record Jesus' teaching as "Blessed are *the poor* for yours is the Kingdom of God" (Luke 6.20); while Matthew records "Blessed are the *poor in spirit* for theirs is the Kingdom of heaven" (Matt. 5.3). In both accounts the point is the same: blessed are those who have become desperate enough to rely on God alone. Only people who are willing to acknowledge their helplessness can receive this help from God. As Clarence Jordan points out:

> When one says 'I don't need to be poor in things; I'm poor in spirit,' and another says, 'I don't need to be poor in spirit; I'm poor in things,' both are justifying themselves as they are, and are saying in unison, 'I don't need.' With that cry on his lips, no man can repent.
>
> ~ Clarence Jordan. *Sermon on the Mount*, Rev. ed.
> Valley Forge: Koinonia-Judson Press, 1980. p. 20.

Obviously, people who are not poor can come to this point of being desperate enough to rely on God alone. (The Bible records many examples, such as Zaccheus or Joseph of Arimathea, to make this

What are some life experiences besides poverty that often help people realize their desperate need for God?

apparent.) *It is also clear that many poor people may refuse to acknowledge their need before God.* However, Jesus and the apostles consistently teach that it is even more difficult for the affluent to acknowledge their need for God (Matt. 19.24; Mark 10.23; James 2.6-7) and that the poor should be expected to respond with faith. This confidence in God's choice of the poor is so profound that one scholar can say: "In the New Testament the poor replace Israel as the focus of the gospel" (C.M.N. Sugden, "Poverty and Wealth," *New Dictionary of Theology*, eds. Sinclair B. Ferguson, et al. [Downers Grove: InterVarsity Press, 1988], p. 524).

Four Fundamental Responses

> To live in radical obedience to Jesus Christ means to be identified with the poor and oppressed. If that is not clear in the New Testament, then nothing is.
>
> ~ Jim Wallis. *Agenda for Biblical People.*
> New York: Harper & Row, 1976. p. 94.

When we recognize that the Scriptures treat the poor as a group with theological significance, it forces us to consider what our response will be. Both as Christians, and as missionaries, there are at least four responses that we should make.

1. Respect

God's choice of the poor fundamentally challenges the normal way that people respond to the poor. Within society, people avoid the poor, disdain their ways, and expect little from them in any area. Certainly they are not seen as the natural place to search for leaders.

God, however, identifies himself with the poor. The Scriptures say that to oppress the poor is to show contempt to God himself (Prov. 14.31). God's identification with the poor and God's choice of the poor (James 2.5) should make a profound difference to anyone who acknowledges Christ as Lord. Simply put:

- If we respect God, we will respect the poor.

- If we obey God, we will identify with the poor.

- If we believe God, we will see the poor as the potential leaders of his Church.

Sadly, many people look at those who are poor and see them primarily as objects of benevolence. Such people view the poor only as those who need their help. While it is certainly right to help the poor (see point two below), such help will create dependence and a loss of dignity if it is not firmly coupled with deep respect for the poor as those that God has chosen. We believe it is not a sacrifice, but rather, a privilege and delight to be called to make disciples among the unreached urban poor.

2. Love, Compassion, and Justice

Christians are called to respond to others with love, compassion and justice. This response to the poor is the same response that Christians give to all people everywhere. What makes it unique is that the world system mitigates against applying this concern to the poor. Theologian Thomas C. Oden says:

> Although Christian charity is due everyone, the poor are Christ's particular concern, precisely because they are the neediest.
>
> ~ Thomas C. Oden. *Pastoral Theology: Essentials of Ministry*. San Francisco: Harper & Row, 1983. p. 268.

God emphasizes our response to the poor, not to play favorites, but because otherwise they would be overlooked.

> One of the ways that St. Francis described his relationship with the poor (and others) was through the word "cortesia." We use the word 'courtesy' to mean manners. Originally, it meant the behavior and etiquette expected of one who served at a noble court . . . . For St. Francis . . . cortesia was a way of seeing and acting towards others.
>
> ~ Lawrence Cunningham. *St. Francis of Assisi*. San Francisco: Harper & Row, 1981.

The Scriptures constantly underscore the responsibility of God's people to share with the poor and help them escape from the grinding effects of poverty. God's Word places responsibility on us to work for justice for the poor. Working for shalom (peace, fullness, abundance, wholeness) means that we will never be content to leave the poor to their poverty while any of us have the means to affect change.

3. Preach the Gospel

Out of all our responses to the poor, none is more important than preaching the Gospel. It is exactly what Jesus himself did. Nothing is more revolutionary in liberating the poor than bringing them into relationship with God through Christ.

No project or program can ever achieve what salvation does for the poor. In coming to acknowledge Jesus as Lord and Savior, the poor experience radical liberation through the acquisition of an entirely new identity.

- They move from being at the bottom of the social structure to being an adopted child of the King of kings.
- God's favor, protection, and resources are made available through Christ.
- They are given authority over sin, hell, and death, and every evil thing that would seek to destroy them.
- They are incorporated into a new community (the Church) which offers equality, respect, love, sharing, fellowship, and the opportunity to exercise their gifts and calling from God.

Salvation means that the presence of the living God is active among the poor bringing freedom, wholeness, and justice. It means that they are now part of a "royal priesthood," "members of a holy nation," in which they serve as "Christ's ambassadors" announcing hope and reconciliation to those around them who have not yet experienced liberation.

4. Expect Great Things

There is, perhaps, no more surprising statement that comes from Jesus' lips than the word he gives to his disciples in John 14.12-14:

> I tell you the truth, anyone who has faith in me will do what I have been doing. He will do even greater things than these, because I am going to the Father. And I will do whatever you ask in my name, so that the Son may bring glory to the Father. You may ask for anything in my name, and I will do it.

> The intercession of a poor man is acceptable and influential with God.
>
> ~ The Pastor of Hermas. Bk. 3. *Ante-Nicene Fathers*, Vol. 2.
> Eds. A. Roberts and J. Donaldson.
> Peabody: Hendrickson, 1995. p. 32.

On the surface, the idea of accomplishing greater things than Jesus seems absurd. And yet, in just a few short years the Book of Acts records more conversions than ever happened within the life and ministry of Jesus.

Two principles underlie this amazing statement. First, Jesus said discipleship reproduces students who are like him (Luke 6.40). Second, when Jesus returned to the Father and sent the Holy Spirit (John 14.16; Acts 2.38), he made his power universally available to all who believe (John 14.14).

It would be easy to expect little from the poor because of their lack of resources. However, when Scripture disciplines our thinking, a new dynamic emerges. We expect congregations of the urban poor to do greater works than Jesus did on earth because they enter into a discipling relationship with Jesus who freely gives them his Holy Spirit.

As we plant churches we must:

- *Encourage the poor to believe in the calling, gifts, and abilities that God has given them* (both individually and corporately). We must have faith in what God will do through them even before they believe it themselves.

- *Set high standards.* The only acceptable goal for any Christian is to become like Jesus. Being poor is never an excuse for ignoring God's commands or shirking the responsibilities he gives every believer.

- *Teach people to rely on Jesus, not on us.* Missionary resources are limited. God's resources are unlimited.

- *Instill a passion for reproduction* (evangelism, follow-up, discipleship, and church planting). "You did not choose me, but I chose you to go and bear fruit – fruit that will last. Then the Father will give you whatever you ask in my name" (John 15.16).

One veteran missionary, who has served in both U.S. and Brazilian cities, describes successful churches among the urban poor in this manner:

> Churches . . . that used a "we-help-you-in-your-need" methodology were not winning the lower, working class. People were helped but the spiritual direction of their lives did not change . . . . [whereas] churches that lacked financial and earthly resources were filled with poor people, were led by barely literate lay preachers, and made hard demands on people. New members were expected to be faithful tithers, to wear clothes that conformed to a rigid dress code, to carry their Bibles to church, and to dedicate a large amount of time to worship services, healing services, home prayer meetings, street meetings, and outreach visitation. The churches that gave the most and expected the least were not growing, but those that gave the least material benefit and demanded the most were growing fastest. They demanded conversion from sin and preached that Christ had the power to make it happen, and that this power could be received though faith and prayer.
>
> ~ Charles D. Uken. "Discipling White, Blue-Collar Workers and Their Families."
> *Discipling the City: A Comprehensive Approach to Urban Mission*, 2nd ed.
> Ed. Roger S. Greenway.
> Grand Rapids: Baker Book House, 1992. p. 180.

We honor both God and the poor when we respect them enough to believe that they will function as full-fledged disciples of Jesus Christ.

Overview of TUMI's Resources From and For the Urban Poor

The Urban Ministry Institute (TUMI) has developed more than seven hundred resources for equipping church leaders to engage in urban ministry and mission. Currently these resources are being used in hundreds of churches and urban ministries around the globe. The resources fall into three categories: Church Planting, Spiritual Formation and Discipleship, and Leadership Development.

I. Church Planting

A. What are the two most important practical tools for Church Plant Team Leaders and Field Coaches?

1. Don Allsman, Don L. Davis, and Hank Voss, eds., *Ripe for Harvest: A Guidebook for Planting Healthy Churches in the City*. Wichita, KS: TUMI Press, 2015.

2. Evangel School Resource Pack

B. What are the two most important theological books for Church Planters?

1. Davis, Don. *Sacred Roots: A Primer on Retrieving the Great Tradition*. Wichita, KS: The Urban Ministry Institute, 2010.

2. Ladd, George Eldon. *A Theology of the New Testament*. Grand Rapids: Eerdmans, 1993.

C. What is the most important supplementary resource produced by TUMI for urban church planters and field coaches?

1. Don L. Davis, ed., *Planting Churches among the City's Poor: An Anthology of Urban Church Planting Resources, Volume 1: Theological and Missiological Perspectives for Church Planters*. Wichita, KS: TUMI Press, 2015.

2. Don L. Davis, ed., *Planting Churches among the City's Poor: An Anthology of Urban Church Planting Resources, Volume 2: Resources and Tools for Coaches and Teams*. Wichita, KS: TUMI Press, 2015.

3. This two-volume set (with nearly 1,000 pages of resources) is an anthology of much of our research, dialogue, and insight gleaned over the past two decades of church planting among the poor. It is a comprehensive collection of diverse materials, covering numerous topics and issues, all designed to help you better understand the theological, missiological, cultural, and anthropological roots of valid church planting work in the city. For those interested in church planting among the city's neediest population, this set is an absolute must.

D. How many courses are available from TUMI on Church Planting?

   1. *Focus on Reproduction*

      a. One of four Capstone Curriculum Urban Missions Courses, this eight segment course covers the foundational principles of church planting.

      b. This is the most important course available for WI Church Planters.

   2. *Winning the World*

      a. The focus of the course is on Church Plant Movements.

      b. This course can be downloaded and taken for free at *www.biblicaltraining.org.*

   3. *Vision for Mission: Nurturing an Apostolic Heart*

      a. A TUMI Foundations Class.

      b. Significantly impacted numerous World Impact missionaries to pursue church planting. *http://www. tumistore.org/foundations-nurturing-an-apostolic-heart-course/*

E. What is Evangel School of Urban Church Planting, Dean Training?

The Evangel Dean School of Urban Church Planting equips church plant trainers (Deans) to host an Evangel School of Urban Church Planting in their city. Dean Teams who enlist and complete our church plant "Basic Training" will be qualified to attend our "Boot Camp," i.e., The Evangel Dean School of Urban Church Planting. At Boot Camp, Dean Teams who successfully complete our spiritual, strategic, and tactical training will be certified to train urban church planters and their team to plant healthy, multiplying churches among the poor.

F. What is the Evangel School of Urban Church Planting?

Our Evangel School of Urban Church Planting trains church planters to plant healthy churches from and for the city's poor, applying biblical wisdom in order to effectively evangelize, equip, and empower unreached city folk to respond to the love of Christ, and take their place in representing Christ's Kingdom where they live and work. *Ripe for Harvest: A Guidebook for Planting Healthy Churches in the City*, the official text of the Evangel School, outlines a process of church planting that respects the unique cultures, environments, communities, and situations reflected in urban America. The PLANT approach outlined here provides practically wise and spiritually vital instruction for urban church planting teams. Filled with devotionals, seminars, exercises, and worksheets, with dozens of graphics, diagrams, and articles, this rich resource will empower church planting teams to design a strategy consistent with the vision God has given them – the kind of strategy that results in the creation of healthy, Kingdom-declaring churches, and the launch of reproducing church planting movements.

G. For more church planting resources from TUMI go to: *www.tumi.org/churchplanting*.

II. Spiritual Formation and Discipleship

  A. Sermons and preaching resources

    1. A plethora of sermons, lectures, and conference presentations are available for free download at two TUMI websites:

      a. Sermons available for download at *https://soundcloud.com/tumimedia/sets*

      b. At *http://www.tumimedia.org*

        (1) Sermons, lectures and conference presentations

        (2) Topics can be searched easily using topical search tool

    2. What kind of series are available for free download?

      a. Revised Common Lectionary Year A, B, and C sermons

      b. Courses (e.g. Effective Worship Leading) and sermon series (e.g. Revelation) and many more.

  B. Songs and Worship Resources

    1. Dr. Davis has written more than 1,500 songs, many of which are available for free. (As of October 10, 2014 there are 44 songs and soundtracks available for free download at *https://soundcloud.com/tumimedia/sets.*)

    2. Listen to the twelve-session course on *Effective Worship Leading* at *www.tumimedia.org*. See also the TUMI's technical resource for learning the guitar entitled *Making Joyful Noises.*

  C. Spiritual discipline resources

    1. TUMI Annual (*http://www.tumistore.org/church-resources/*)

      a. A devotional guide to prayer and reading Scripture, published every year by TUMI

      b. Each year focuses on a different theme.

2. TUMI Calendar (*http://www.tumistore.org/church-resources/*)

   a. TUMI's Scripture texts for the preaching, reading, and prayer taken from the RCL each year

   b. Each year redesigned with new artwork

3. Master the Bible (*http://www.tumistore.org/master-the-bible/*)

   a. Four-year plan to memorize more than 800 scripture passages. See a review at *http://www.tumi.org/forum/showthread.php?t=80*

   b. Resource for churches to plan how to help their people memorize Scripture. Includes, book, dvds, bookmarks, posters

4. Prayer Resources

   a. Prayer Mountain! Free Retreat Center at World Impact's Oaks Conference Center for all church planters taking a personal spiritual retreat

   b. Let God Arise Prayer Network Resources

     (1) Don Davis, *Let God Arise* (TUMI, 2000)

     (2) *www.letgodarise.com*

D. Discipleship Resources

1. *Fight the Good Fight: Playing Your Part in God's Unfolding Drama* is now available (Jan 1, 2015). It is a new believers follow-up curriculum based on the book of Ephesians and can be purchased at *http://www.tumistore.org/fight-the-good-fight/*.

2. *Fit to Represent: Vision for Discipleship Seminar* is available now at *http://www.tumistore.org/fit-to-represent-vision-for-discipleship-seminar/*.

E. What are the best Men's and Women's Discipleship tools developed by TUMI and World Impact to date? (*http://www.tumi.org/siafu*)

    1. Don Davis. *The SIAFU Network Guidebook: Standing Together for Christ in the City.* TUMI, 2013.

    2. Don Davis. *The SIAFU Chapter Meeting Guide.* TUMI, 2013.

F. More than 700 resources developed for urban churches and leaders engaged in urban ministry available at *www.tumistore.org* and at *http://www.cafepress.com/tumi.*

    1. Resources include artwork, videos, clothing, books, etc.

    2. More than 30 resources available in Spanish

III. Leadership Development

A. Books

    1. Don Davis. *Sacred Roots: A Primer on Retrieving the Great Tradition.* Wichita, KS: The Urban Ministry Institute, 2010.

    2. Don Allsman. *Jesus Cropped from the Picture: Why Christians Get Bored and How to Restore Them to Vibrant Faith.* Wichita, KS: The Urban Ministry Institute, 2010.

    3. Efrem Smith. *The Post-Black and Post-White Church: Becoming the Beloved Community in a Multi-Ethnic World.* Vol. 59, Jossey-Bass Leadership Network Series. San Francisco: Jossey-Bass, 2012.

B. Leadership Development Classes

    1. The Urban Ministry Institute Satellite (TUMI) Network

        a. Currently more than 180 urban ministries, churches, and denominations have launched TUMI leadership training institutes for training leaders in their ministry context.

      b. Learn how to start a satellite at your ministry by visiting *www.tumi.org/satellite*.

  2. The Capstone Curriculum

      a. TUMI's premier leadership training program. Sixteen classes usually taken over a four year period with courses in four subject areas: Biblical Studies; Christian Ministry; Urban Mission; and Christian Theology.

      b. The Capstone Courses can be transferred to several accredited colleges and universities for those interested in continuing their education. For more information on Capstone, visit *www.tumi.org/capstone*.

  3. Foundations courses (13 currently available)

      a. Sample courses include *Church Matters*. A course that covers the major periods of the church and emphasizes how evangelical churches can be renewed by a retrieval of the Great Tradition and the pursuit of a shared spirituality. *http://www.tumistore.org/foundations-church-matters-course/*

      b. Sample Courses include *Marking Time: Forming Spirituality through the Christian Year*. This course introduces evangelicals to a theology of time rooted in the practice of the Christian Year. The course looks at the way a shared spirituality can equip churches working among the poor with vital resources for discipleship, preaching, and worship. *http://www.tumistore.org/foundations-marking-time-course/*

C. Conferences

  1. Annual TUMI Summit. More than two hundred leaders from around the globe who are involved with urban leadership development through the TUMI satellite network. Find more information at *www.tumi.org/satellite*.

  2. Men's and Women's SIAFU Conferences. Regional men's and women's conferences to encourage missional outreach in the cities. See *http://www.tumi.org/siafu* for more information.

The History of The Urban Ministry Institute

TÚMI

The Urban Ministry Institute is a non-denominational, evangelical training center devoted to equipping servant leadership for the urban church, especially among the poor.

Reaching the cities of the world is among the greatest missionary challenges facing the Church today. Cities are growing rapidly, becoming more diverse, more divided, and increasingly unreached by the Gospel.

- The number of city dwellers has grown rapidly, from 13% of all people in 1900 to 50% of all people today.

- Ethnics in America communicate in 157 distinct languages. Numbering over 60 million (25% of the population), they are increasingly drawn to the city.

- Of the more than 60 million people who live in America's inner cities, 16 million are in poverty and over 90% are unchurched.

- Traditional theological education is often inaccessible to emerging urban Christian leaders because it is:

  ~ Too expensive
  ~ Unavailable to leaders who have not completed high school or college
  ~ Irrelevant to the cultural experience of many inner-city churches

World Impact has been sharing the Gospel in the inner cities of America since 1971. As a Christian missions organization, World Impact evangelizes and disciples the unreached urban poor, helping them form dynamic congregations which minister Christ's love in the city.

The Urban Ministry Institute is an important part of the way in which leaders from these and other churches can receive quality biblical training and be equipped for the task of ministry. The Urban Ministry Institute is led by experienced faculty who combine many years of missionary field experience with formal theological credentialing.

Rev. Dr. Don L. Davis (B.A., Wheaton College; M.A., Wheaton Graduate School; Ph.D., University of Iowa) is the Director of The Urban Ministry Institute.

Bob Stevenson (A.A., Pasadena City College; B.A., San Diego State University) is the Satellite Director of The Urban Ministry Institute.

In the summer of 1995, Don Davis and his family moved to Wichita, Kansas to start The Urban Ministry Institute. The Institute opened in

The Institute opened in the spring of 1996 and currently holds classes, hosts colloquia, and sponsors seminars for laypersons and pastors who minister in the city.

the spring of 1996 and currently holds classes, hosts colloquia, and sponsors seminars for laypersons and pastors who minister in the city. Our mission is to equip leadership for the urban church, especially among the poor, to advance the Kingdom of God in the city. We provide biblical and theological training that is both inexpensive and accessible to Christian leaders among the underprivileged in the city.

Our sincere conviction is that God has selected the poor to be rich in faith and heirs of the Kingdom of God. We believe without equivocation that some of the finest disciples and missionaries of our time will arise from the rank and file in the churches of the urban poor. We have dedicated ourselves to do everything we can to raise up qualified spiritual laborers for Christ and his Kingdom among the poorest of the poor in America's inner cities. All of our programming, teaching and sponsorships are to this end.

Overview of The Urban Ministry Institute's Structure and Strategy

The Urban Ministry Institute exists to equip leadership for new, emerging, and existing urban churches, especially among the poor, to advance the Kingdom of God.

Our focus is on providing missionaries, lay pastors, ministers in training, and urban church leadership with the necessary resources to do effective urban ministry.

Our Structure

The Urban Ministry Institute is a ministry of World Impact, an interdenominational Christian missions organization dedicated to sharing God's love in the inner cities of America. As a missions organization, World Impact seeks to evangelize the urban poor, disciple them in the Word of God, and plant churches cross-culturally in urban neighborhoods where no evangelical church exists. The Urban Ministry Institute, as a training arm of this unique ministry, exists to equip leadership for new, emerging, and existing urban churches, especially among the poor, to advance the Kingdom of God.

While traditional theological education and seminaries have been the mainstays of most Christian leadership development, the urban poor are often overlooked or completely ignored in their programs. As successful as traditional seminaries have been in raising up qualified leaders for churches, traditional theological education is simply too cumbersome for the development of leaders among the urban poor. Its programming is too expensive, usually offered far from the context of urban need, tends to be inaccessible to the poor because of academic qualifications, and, in large part, remains culturally distant from their experience and work.

Since 1995, The Urban Ministry Institute (TUMI) has served both the national ministry of World Impact as well as Wichita area Christian workers, pastors, and urban missionaries by providing inexpensive and excellent theological and ministry training geared to the specific needs and context of city dwellers. Since our inception, we have taught more than one hundred seminary-level courses, conferred our academic Certificates and Diplomas upon graduating classes of local students, and provided ongoing resources across the country to Christian leaders involved in urban outreach and ministry. We seek to make these resources as affordable and culturally sensitive as possible. Moreover, all of our courses, conferences, seminars, and workshops are facilitated by our experienced TUMI faculty, ordained Christian academics with many years in pastoral care and urban ministry.

Our Strategy

The staff and faculty of The Urban Ministry Institute wholeheartedly believe that God is raising up in significant numbers men and women among the urban poor who serve his Kingdom in extraordinary ways, all across the nation. We desire to provide the most excellent, affordable, and accessible training that will result in a new generation of equipped men and women, able to disciple and build Christian community in Wichita and around the world, all for God's glory. Because of this vision, our focus is on providing missionaries, lay pastors, ministers in training, and urban church leaders with the necessary resources to do effective urban ministry.

While we do give considerable attention to providing resources to urban churches to help them ground new and growing Christians in Christ, the heart of our vision is to equip leaders for the urban church. This entails two things: 1) providing new and emerging Christian leaders and workers in urban churches with the essential theological resources and support necessary for effective urban ministry, and 2) to provide ongoing investment for seasoned urban church leaders who intend to both sharpen their own ministries and train others for ministry as well (please see the following appendices for our structure and strategy).

Why Develop Extension Centers for Theological Education?

Do Christian leaders from among the urban poor deserve access to formalized and excellent theological input? To those of us that would answer "Yes," the immediate questions are *"How will this happen?"* and *"What would it look like?"*

For the urban poor, only rarely will such education take the form of traditional seminary education. Although often excellent and thorough in their training, traditional seminaries are too expensive, too culturally distant and too removed from the immediate issues which dominate the theological concerns of the poor to be the primary answer for their theological education.* Instead, innovative extension centers for theological education need to be established that:

- are located in the urban church context,
- prioritize the needs of people already in ministry, and
- address themselves to the cultural and socioeconomic realities of inner-city Christian leaders.

We believe that such innovative new approaches stand squarely in the evangelical tradition, provide a unique educational opportunity for quality investment, and are an essential response to the challenges of the urban setting.

An Evangelical Tradition

The evangelical impulse at the heart of the Church has always had a sense of urgency about the task of mission and the unreached. This urgency has prompted Christian educators to identify and prepare those called to leadership for their mission and ministry.

---

*   Robert E. Freeman offers a helpful perspective when he says: "The traditional U.S. Protestant seminary has in the past sixty or seventy years become prominently two things: a) a community of scholars carrying on research as professional academicians (which is sorely needed to deal with the many complex issues of today), and b) a place where candidates for the ordained ministry (and Christian scholarship) are trained. The extension seminary . . . does in no way intend to replace or play down the first crucial function, but it does intend to operate parallel to the latter by a new method which allows a wider, and perhaps superior, selection of students since it allows proven leaders to participate . . . . The task of the seminary is not to make leaders, the calling of the seminary is to train the leaders that God has already made" (Freeman, 1999, p. 2).

Evangelical missiologist Ralph Winter has written extensively about how many of the monastic missionary orders in medieval Catholicism emerged as a specific response to "home" and "foreign" mission. He reminds us that in these orders:

> There weren't just monks who were celibate but they had secondary and tertiary orders as well as all kinds of laymen . . . . After the barbarian invasions swirled through what is modern Spain, France, and Italy for a couple of hundred years . . . . there may have been 2,000 to 3,000 students from the continent studying the Bible in these . . . [Irish] monasteries (Winter, 1969, p. 300).

In the American experience of the early 1900's, the evangelical church found that it could not train leaders rapidly enough to respond to the groundswell of new converts among the urban poor at home or to the emerging opportunities among new mission fields abroad. The new "Bible Institutes" were created in order that "leaders might be equipped for better service in their churches, and in the slums and destitute places of our great cities (Cook 1930, 1) as well as to become a source of training for the emerging interdenominational foreign missions movement (see Carpenter, 1990, 92-132). What began with an emphasis on equipping primarily the laity for service quickly shifted to also being a new means of "training men and women for 'full-time' Christian service as pastors or missionaries" (Daniel 1980, 333).

Since the 1950's, the evangelical church has recognized that the traditional seminaries which serve established churches and denominations so well often are not fully capable of meeting the same needs for emerging missions churches or for movements among those who culturally or economically stand at the margins of a society. Theological Education by Extension (TEE) emerged as an innovative means of educating leaders for ministry and mission in these contexts. TEE can be defined as:

> A form of theological education which is characterized by these three essential elements: self-study materials, practical work in the student's own congregation, and regular encounters or seminars with students and professors (Ross Kinsler).

Or more broadly:

> TEE is theological leadership training, using any method that accomplishes established objectives, which reaches people in the geographical area (close proximity) with minimal cultural disruption (Ralph Porter).

In missionary situations throughout the world, tens of thousands of church leaders have been trained using innovative methods in theological education that allow people to access formal theological training without leaving their jobs, their churches, their culture, or their social networks.

Today, as the missionary task has been transformed from the old distinctives of "Home" and "Foreign" to a model that is "from everywhere to everywhere" the need for innovative theological education that combines the best of the old (seminaries, Bible Institutes, TEE) with new forms of distance education has never been more important. The urgency of reaching those who have not heard in every nation compels us to find new ways to invest in all those whom God has called to lead his Church, especially among those who are at the margins of any society.

An Educational Opportunity

Perhaps the most important educational argument for innovation in theological training is a growing awareness that learning happens best when a person can move back and forth between theory and practice.

> Learning is best facilitated in an environment where there is dialectic tension and conflict between immediate concrete experience and analytic detachment (Kolb, 1984, p. 9).

The best education happens when a learner stays "in context" so that the concepts and skills learned in the classroom can immediately be applied and tested in the real world of practical ministry.

Robert E. Freeman observes that:

> Being absent or extracted from active church involvement in ministry puts the learner in a learning about or for situation rather than a learning in or of situation (Freeman, 1999).

The extension seminary model offers "field-based" education to learners who are already doing ministry, not merely preparing for it. Thus, doing theological education using extension models "is not an attempt to make the best of a bad situation. It is part of a world-wide trend based upon substantial research about how people learn" (Ward and Rowen, 1972).

Adult learners learn best when they can make a direct application of their knowledge.

> When they are able to put something to use immediately, that learning experience stays with them. . . Christian service [is] a vital component in the [theological education by extension] learning process. Each subsequent class gives opportunity for feedback and discussion on the experiences in Christian service that week. Every new insight gained can be applied immediately. What the adult student did and how it worked out become important discussion matters (Snook, 1992, p. 16-17).

Investing in those already involved in Christian leadership while they remain in their ministry situation not only makes formal theological education possible for many, it also makes it better.

An Essential Response

The rapid expansion of the urban poor around the world today presents the church with a great challenge and a remarkable opportunity. As missionary outreach among the poor continues to bear fruit, innovative approaches to leadership development are of vital significance. In developing nations, non-traditional extension seminaries are an accepted part of leadership training models and can be accessible to the poor, though they often need to be refocused to serve a predominantly urban rather than rural clientele.

In the affluent Western countries, however, much less attention has been given to the poor as a pool of potential leaders for the Church. (Their marginalized status in society has often translated into a marginalized status within an affluent and well-resourced Western church.) Even where concern for the urban poor as leaders has emerged, the questions have often centered around access to existing models of traditional seminary education. Only infrequently has the usefulness of the traditional seminary model for the urban poor of North America been examined critically and churches have been slow to develop the kind of in-context, extension models which have proved so useful in other settings.

Emerging Christian leaders from among the urban poor in North America provide a set of challenges which theological educators must respond to:

- They are already "in ministry" and are often bi-vocational, so theological education must accommodate itself to their time schedules and to the fact that they often must limit their course loads and pursue their theological education non-sequentially. Theological education must come in "bite- sized" chunks and find a way to teach core themes across the curriculum rather than depending on extensive prerequisite courses.

- Christian leaders from the same church groups may range from functionally illiterate, to semiliterate, to very literate. Theological education must find a way to both strengthen literacy and provide ways of accessing information that do not make reading skills the critical factor.

- Affordability is a key issue in obtaining theological education. There must be a conviction that poverty cannot be allowed to stand between functioning church leaders and the theological resources they need for more effective ministry.

- Differences in culture, class, and ethnicity must be taken seriously in the theological curriculum. The problems that are faced, the thinking styles that predominate, the theological themes that are prioritized, and the languages that are used may all be significantly different from mainstream culture. Contextualization of theological education is imperative.

- Leadership in the Christian community has been earned based on the living out of God's call and gifting in practical experience. Acceptance into a program of theological education must be based on these criteria rather than on purely educational prerequisites. Theological education must be for those (whether lay or ordained) who are already doing ministry.

- Leadership development is taking place in a context of mission and outreach. Special emphasis should be placed on evangelism and the incorporation of new believers into the church.

- Leadership development is taking place in a context of human need. Theological education should provide a way of understanding poverty, justice, development, and the role of the Church in holistic ministry.

It is essential that the Church in North America create innovative models of theological education to respond to these challenges. Practically, the evangelization of our urban cities depends on it. Theologically, faithfulness to God's choosing of the poor as key leaders of faith (James 2.5) demands it.

The Urban Ministry Institute

The Urban Ministry Institute exists as a way of resourcing the vision of theological educators who are committed to finding new models for investing in the urban poor and those who minister among them. We are committed to creating materials, networks, and educational programs that will make that task easier and more effective.

Because we are a part of an interdenominational missions agency (see Appendix 1) with a specific focus on the urban poor, we are in a unique position to focus on the issues of theological education through the lens of a missionary vision.

We believe that The Urban Ministry Institute is best viewed not as the way to do theological education among the urban poor, but rather as a way of doing theological education that may serve as a resource and a springboard for continuing innovation by others who share our common task.

Conclusion

Extension seminaries, focused on the urban poor and adapted to the needs of Christian leaders in their ministry situations, are a key part of preparing the Church to fulfill its mission in the immediate future. The development, refinement, and proliferation of such centers for theological education deserves to be a high priority in the Church's vision, strategizing and allocating resources for ministry.

Reference List

Carpenter, Joel A. 1990. "Propagating the Faith Once Delivered," in *Earthen Vessels: American Evangelicals and Foreign Missions, 1880-1980*, eds. Joel A. Carpenter and Wilbert R. Shenk. Grand Rapids, MI: Wm. B. Eerdmans Publishing Co.

Cook, J. W. 1930. *The Bible Institute Movement.* Unpublished master's thesis: Northwestern Evangelical Seminary. Quoted in Jonathan N. Thigpen, "A Brief History of the Bible Institute Movement in America," in *Developing a Dynamic Bible Institute.* 1997. Wheaton, IL: Evangelical Training Association.

Daniel, Eleanor, John W. Wade, and Charles Gresham. 1980. *Introduction to Christian Education.* Cincinnati: Standard Publishing. Quoted in Jonathan N. Thigpen, "A Brief History of the Bible Institute Movement in America" in *Developing a Dynamic Bible Institute.* 1997. Wheaton, IL: Evangelical Training Association.

Freeman, Robert E. [Cited July 14, 1999]. Why Does Fuller Do Extended and Distance Education? In *Fuller Theological Seminary Internet Website.* URL: *www.fuller.edu/swm/faculty/ ML525/ supplemental/ linkwhyext.html.*

Kolb, David A. 1984. *Experiential Learning: Experience as the Source of Learning and Development.* Englewood Cliffs: Prentice-Hall.

Snook, Stewart G. 1992. *Developing Leaders through Theological Education by Extension.* A BGC Monograph. Wheaton, IL: Billy Graham Center-Wheaton College.

Ward, Ted and Samuel F. Rowen. "The Significance of the Extension Seminary," in *Evangelical Missions Quarterly* 9, no. 1 (Fall 1972).

Winter, Ralph D. 1969. "Theological Education in Historical Perspective," in *Theological Education by Extension*, edited by Ralph D. Winter. South Pasadena, CA: William Carey Library.

What Is a Satellite of The Urban Ministry Institute?

Identifying and recruiting partners in ministry is the only option for us if we truly intend to plant churches among the unreached urban poor, and to equip godly men and women to serve the Church in the city. Partnership is a time-tested principle which leads to dramatic results. Its power has been seen in every endeavor where God's people have sought to expand the Kingdom of God. The Lord God has made us partners with him as we serve as his very own ambassadors (2 Cor. 5.20). Rather than competing with each other, or even worse, ignoring the efforts of one another altogether, God desires that we join forces together in unity in order to mobilize his Church for evangelism, discipleship, and the growth of healthy congregations among the unreached urban poor (Phil. 1.27ff.). What an exciting, transforming vision!

A "satellite" of the Institute is a sister ministry, whether located in a church, Christian organization, prison, or mission that meets our requirements to equip leaders for the urban church, especially among the poor, in order to advance the Kingdom of God in the city. A satellite is a partner, a group of Christians who have committed themselves to train leaders for the urban church, maintaining their own identity and independence, while taking advantage of our staff, curricula, and experience as we strive together to raise up faithful laborers for the harvest (Matt. 9.35-38). Our desire is to provide each satellite with the most affordable and excellent theological resources that we can, enabling you to create your own unique training program that best suits your students and ministry situation.

We deeply believe in the Holy Spirit's ability to raise up faithful men and women who can teach deserving urban students the Word of God, and prepare them for the ministry. Our desire is to find new ways to cooperate with you as you fulfill your burden and calling to equip urban Christian leaders to minister effectively in their congregations and communities. We do not wish to hinder or squelch your vision for leadership development. On the contrary, we stand ready and eager to do whatever we can to assist you as you provide ministry training for the leaders in your church and community. As an evangelical ministry dedicated to teaching the Word of God, we want to find other churches and Christian organizations who share our belief in its power to transform, and partner with them to equip others to minister the Word effectively wherever God leads them.

In light of this, we encourage you to seriously consider becoming a satellite training center of the Institute. We pledge our most dedicated, prayerful, and focused effort to make you a relevant and dynamic training center for urban leaders. Our parent ministry, World Impact, Inc., is committed to planting as many urban churches among the urban poor in America as fast as possible. The role of The Urban Ministry Institute in this mandate is to assist everyone who desires to mobilize leaders in the urban church for more effective body life, outreach, and pioneer missions.

Partner with us in equipping leaders among the urban poor for the urban church!

The Strategic Role of the Local Church in Your Institute

The whole of biblical revelation and salvation history is organized around a profound drama, the romance of God with his creation, and in particular, his own precious people.

The Church is the very community of God, the body of Christ, and the agent of the Kingdom of God on earth today.

The story of God has the Church at its center, and the local congregation is the concrete expression of God's universal Church worldwide. As a training Institute, you must be careful to respect the role of the local congregation in the training of your students. To equip urban Christian leaders for the ministry is to prepare them to be effective disciplers in the context of existing urban churches, as well as to equip them to evangelize and do justice that leads to the formation of healthy, spiritually vital churches in urban areas where Christ is not yet known. We are convinced that the relative impact of your training will be directly connected to your commitment to strengthen and multiply healthy reproducing urban churches in your community, especially those committed to minister to the urban poor.

Below are several principles related to the central role that the local congregation should play in your Institute.

1. *The local congregation is a concrete expression of the Church Militant, the spiritual outpost authorized to make disciples and demonstrate the life of the Kingdom.* The Church nurtures and equips Christians for warfare, enabling them to represent Christ with honor as they "take ground" for God. No other institution can wield the sword of the Spirit against those spiritual forces undermining our urban neighborhoods. As a training Institute, one of your first priorities is to partner with the local congregations in your area to enrich and stimulate cooperation between them and other ministries in your community. You must seek to strengthen the worship, witness, and works of every local church in your area, for this is the place where believers reach full maturity in Christ (Eph. 4.7-16; Rom. 12.4-8; 1 Pet. 4.10-12). Please ensure that all of your students are members in good standing within their local congregations, are submitted to their pastoral leadership, and are open to fulfilling their ministry as their leaders and congregations confirm.

2. *The local congregation is both the ground and the end of all viable ministries which seek to fulfill the Great Commandment and the Great Commission.* As disciples of Jesus, we are not only called out of the world to love God and our neighbors (Matt. 22.30-31), we are also called to go into all the world and make disciples of all nations (Matt. 28.18-20). Individual Christians are called by God and gifted by the Holy Spirit to be ambassadors of Christ in the world, beginning in their own neighborhoods and wherever else the Spirit leads (2 Cor. 5.20).

The local congregation is the place God has ordained for believers to be equipped to do the work of the ministry, in order that the body of Christ might grow spiritually and numerically (Eph. 4.12-16). Your Institute's most important calling is to equip leadership for the urban church. Regardless of those urban leaders you train – whether they are pastors, Christian workers, missionaries, youth ministers, Sunday school teachers, or whomever else – you are enhancing God's Kingdom advance in your locale. Your Institute should strive to make Christians effective in their local churches so that every church they represent may be strengthened in Christ, becoming fruitful in doing good works and evangelizing the lost as God leads.

3. *The local congregation can be strategically mobilized to promote a biblical understanding of freedom, wholeness, and justice in the city, as well as to target unreached urban communities for evangelism and church planting.* As we equip leaders for spiritually vital ministry in the urban church, the Holy Spirit will provide opportunities for your students to minister to the pressing needs in your community or beyond. The Scriptures are God-breathed, sufficient to teach, correct, rebuke and instruct your students in righteousness in order that they might be completely furnished for every good work he calls them to do (2 Tim. 3.16-17). As you train your students to minister, and teach and model the Scriptures in your Institute, God will bear abundant spiritual fruit through your students, guiding them to disciple growing Christians, engage in good works, and reach out to touch the lost in your community. Training leaders to be effective in the context of their own local congregations will multiply ministry throughout your community, city, and around the world.

Three Levels of Ministry Investment

Rev. Dr. Don L. Davis

Evangelism – *winning souls for Christ*
Follow-up – *establishing new believers in Christ and the Church*
Discipleship – *equipping Christians to grow toward maturity*

(These activities are marked by missionary-led Bible study, discipling, teaching, and preaching)

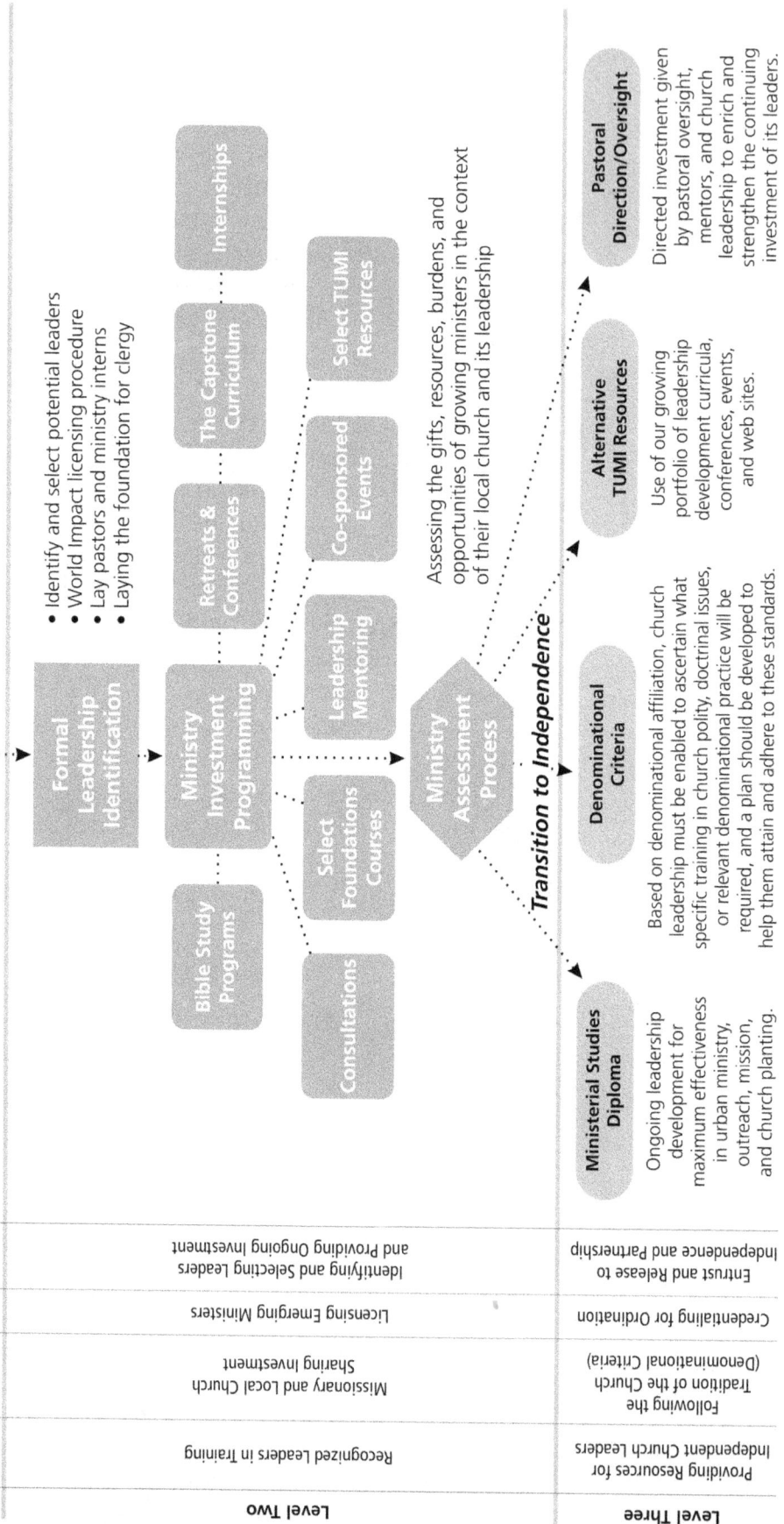

- Identify and select potential leaders
- World Impact licensing procedure
- Lay pastors and ministry interns
- Laying the foundation for clergy

Formal Leadership Identification

Ministry Investment Programming

Bible Study Programs · Retreats & Conferences · The Capstone Curriculum · Internships · Consultations · Select Foundations Courses · Leadership Mentoring · Co-sponsored Events · Select TUMI Resources

Ministry Assessment Process

Assessing the gifts, resources, burdens, and opportunities of growing ministers in the context of their local church and its leadership

Transition to Independence

Ministerial Studies Diploma
Ongoing leadership development for maximum effectiveness in urban ministry, outreach, mission, and church planting.

Denominational Criteria
Based on denominational affiliation, church leadership must be enabled to ascertain what specific training in church polity, doctrinal issues, or relevant denominational practice will be required, and a plan should be developed to help them attain and adhere to these standards.

Alternative TUMI Resources
Use of our growing portfolio of leadership development curricula, conferences, events, and web sites.

Pastoral Direction/Oversight
Directed investment given by pastoral oversight, mentors, and church leadership to enrich and strengthen the continuing investment of its leaders.

Level One	**Level Two**	**Level Three**
Win & Establish New Believers in Christ	Identifying and Selecting Leaders and Providing Ongoing Investment	Entrust and Release to Independence and Partnership
Grounding Converts	Licensing Emerging Ministers	Credentialing for Ordination
Missionary Investment	Sharing Investment	Following the Tradition of the Church (Denominational Criteria)
New & Growing Christians	Recognized Leaders in Training	Providing Resources for Independent Church Leaders

Evangel Process Overview
Planning Process for Evangel School Deans

I. The Evangel Team Members

The Evangel Schools of Urban Church Planting are designed to maximize workers for the harvest fields.

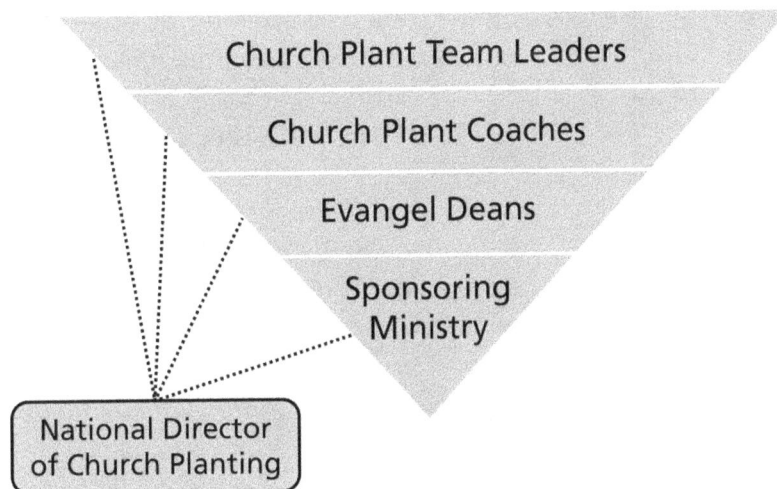

TUMI's National Director of Church Planting serves as a resource to every level of the Church Planting process.

II. Parallels between TUMI Satellite Structure and Evangel CPS Structure

A. **Local Leader.** Both training models are premised on a gifted local leader who trains leaders for his or her own context.

  1. TUMI Satellite: TUMI Site Coordinator

  2. Evangel CPS: Evangel Dean

B. **Contextualized Mentors.** Both training models are premised on the local leader recruiting others to form a training team to provide contextualized mentoring of developing leaders.

  1. TUMI Satellite System: TUMI Mentors and TUMI Professors

  2. Evangel Church Plant Schools: Assessor Coaches

C. **Core Content.** Both training models have a core curriculum which can be contextualized locally.

  1. TUMI: The Capstone Curriculum

  2. Evangel: *Ripe for Harvest Curriculum*

D. **Local Church.** Both training models are rooted in the local church.

  1. TUMI: Requires Pastor's reference to become student

  2. Evangel: Requires Pastor's reference to become Dean, Coach, or Team Leader

III. Process Overview

A. Dark boxes = interaction with TUMI National

B. Light boxes = local project

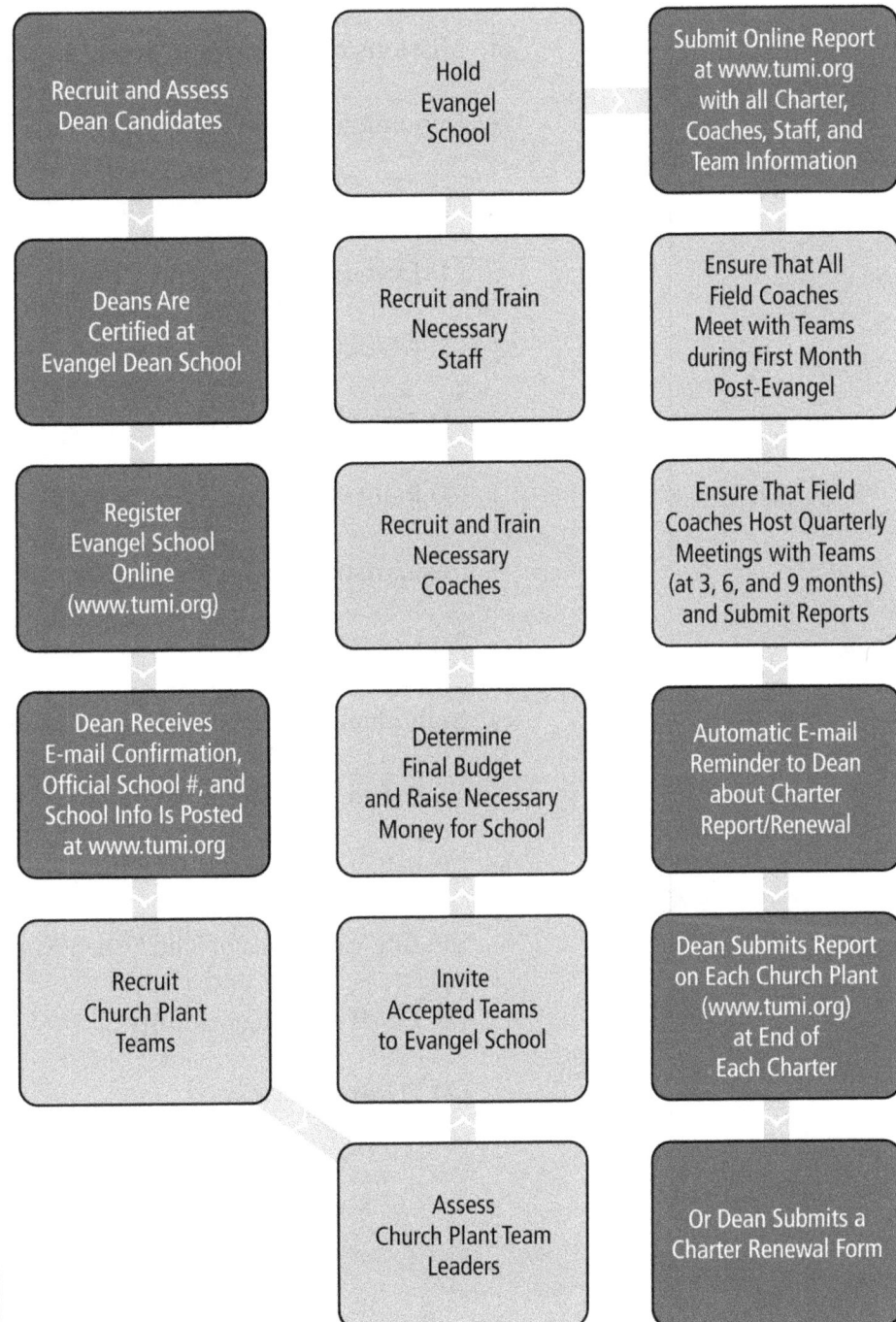

Recruit and Assess Dean Candidates

Hold Evangel School

Submit Online Report at www.tumi.org with all Charter, Coaches, Staff, and Team Information

Deans Are Certified at Evangel Dean School

Recruit and Train Necessary Staff

Ensure That All Field Coaches Meet with Teams during First Month Post-Evangel

Register Evangel School Online (www.tumi.org)

Recruit and Train Necessary Coaches

Ensure That Field Coaches Host Quarterly Meetings with Teams (at 3, 6, and 9 months) and Submit Reports

Dean Receives E-mail Confirmation, Official School #, and School Info Is Posted at www.tumi.org

Determine Final Budget and Raise Necessary Money for School

Automatic E-mail Reminder to Dean about Charter Report/Renewal

Recruit Church Plant Teams

Invite Accepted Teams to Evangel School

Dean Submits Report on Each Church Plant (www.tumi.org) at End of Each Charter

Assess Church Plant Team Leaders

Or Dean Submits a Charter Renewal Form

IV. Understanding Evangel School structure

A. Sponsoring ministry

1. Ensures proper spiritual authority for each Church Plant Team

2. Examples include

a. Missions organizations (World Impact)

b. Denominations

(1) Vineyard

(2) Evangelical Covenant Church

(3) Church of God in Christ

(4) Assembly of God

(5) Reformed Church of America

(6) Christian Reformed Church

(7) Free Methodist

c. Individual churches or church associations

(1) Urban Church Association of Los Angeles

(2) Valley Church in Cupertino

d. Satellite campuses of The Urban Ministry Institute

(1) TUMI – Orange County

(2) TUMI – Havana

B. TUMI International

1. TUMI provides resources for all Evangel Schools.

a. Annual Dean Training

b. Evangel School Resource Pack*

c. *Ripe for Harvest* (and Church Planters Toolkit)

d. Additional church planting courses for Team Leaders and Coaches

e. Online support and tracking of all Evangel Schools

f. Church Planting Certificate through TUMI satellite network

2. National Director of Church Planting (NDCP) is point of contact for all Evangel Schools.

a. Rev. Bob Engel serves as the NDCP and is a resource to all Evangel Deans. He provides coaching and consultation services as requested.

b. Oversees ongoing Dean certification process, Evangel Dean Training Schools, and Evangel Church Plant Tracks at International TUMI summit

* This package contains everything you need to host your own Evangel School, including video teachings and devotionals, PowerPoint presentations, event templates, Evangel graphics, music files and lead sheets, and all project supporting documents. An amazing array of practical helps and resources, this package is designed to provide Deans with all they need to host successful, informative, and fruitful sessions with coaches and church plant teams in your events.

Evangel Dean Training and Hosting Evangel Schools

What TUMI *Provides* to Deans in Order to Host Evangel Schools	What TUMI *Requires* from Deans in Order to Host Evangel Schools
What We Provide to Each Dean TEAM:	Each Evangel Dean TEAM Must:
Authority to host Evangel Schools with two Certified Deans	Purchase *Evangel Resources Package* before hosting any schools
Evangel Resources Package (purchased by team) that contains videos, graphics, PowerPoints, music/lead sheets, templates, etc.	Purchase *Ripe for Harvest* and *Planting Churches among the City's Poor: Vols. 1 and 2* for every Field Coach and Team Leader
Church Planter Tool Kit	Purchase a copy of *Ripe for Harvest* and *Front Matters: Prerequisite Readings for the Evangel School of Urban Church Planting* for every delegate of each school
Listing on site of upcoming school and link to registration	Two Certified Deans (one of which must be local) to host an Evangel School
Share social media posts on upcoming and hosted schools	Register upcoming school 60 days prior to hosting at *www.tumi.org/evangel*
	Complete *Evangel School Report Form* (and upload charters and pictures) after each school hosted at *www.tumi.org/evangel*
	Ensure that Field Coaches are oriented in PWR
	Pay annual license fee*
What We Provide to Each Individual DEAN:	Each Evangel DEAN Must:
Planting Churches among the City's Poor: Vols. 1 and 2, Ripe for Harvest, Evangel Dean Handbook	Renew Dean status every three years
Dean shirt	Renew status by attending Dean Training or alternate approved option by the Head Dean
Front Matters: Prerequisite Readings for the Evangel School of Urban Church Planting	If Dean status expires, attend Dean Training to renew
Training to host an Evangel School	
Certification to host an Evangel School for three years (with certificate and pocket card)	

* The First annual license fee is included with the registration of a Dean Team of two or more potential Deans.

In order to provide ongoing service and consultation to our Evangel School partners, we ask for a modest annual license fee due January 15, which keeps you certified as a team to host Evangel Schools.

Annual fees must be kept up to date in order to maintain approved Evangel School status with The Urban Ministry Institute.

Dean and Dean Team Requirements and Certification

Evangel Schools must operate under the supervision of TWO certified Evangel Deans.

I. Dean Certification

A. DEAN TRAINING: In order to be certified as a Dean of the Evangel School you must attend the Evangel School of Urban Church Planting, Dean Training.

B. CERTIFIED FOR 3 YEARS: Your Dean Certification authorizes you to host Evangel Schools for three years from the date of the completion of your training.

II. Dean Certification Renewal

A. RENEWAL: Dean Certification can be renewed for a 3-year period by:

1. Attending the Evangel School of Urban Church Planting, Dean Training

2. Attending alternate training (requires approval from NDCP) and your Pastor's or Spiritual Authority's approval (Reference Required)

B. EXPIRATION: If your Dean Certification expires, your certification can be renewed by attending the Evangel School of Urban Church Planting, Dean Training.

III. Dean TEAM Commissioning

A. COMMISSIONED AS DEAN TEAM:

1. After successfully completing the Evangel Dean Training, you will be commissioned as an Evangel Dean Team and certified to host Evangel Schools of Urban Church Planting.

2. You must include the Evangel School logo on any materials that you use for your school.

B. ANNUAL EVANGEL LICENSE FEE: In order to provide ongoing service and consultation to our Evangel Dean Team partners, we ask for a modest annual license fee due January 15.

1. The first annual license fee is included with the registration of a Dean Team of two or more potential Deans.

2. Annual fees must be kept up to date in order to maintain approved Evangel School status with The Urban Ministry Institute.

Three Sample Evangel School Budgets

Regional School at Newark Ministry Example
Budget for a three-night, two-and-a-half-day Church Plant School. School would begin on a Thursday night and finish Sunday at lunch.

Budget is for twenty-five church planters and church plant team members. School provides lunch and dinner in this budget (breakfast at hotel or on own).

Team Leader Expenses		
	Meeting in Newark Ministry Center	
Ripe for Harvest	$35.00	
Anthology, 1 and 2	$70.00	
Meals	$90.00	Meal cost includes snacks and drinks. $15.00 per meal x6 meals
Evangel Polo Shirt	$25.00	
Registration and Staff Fee	$25.00	
Total Fee	**$245.00**	

Church Plant Team Member Price		
	Lodging on Own	
Ripe for Harvest	$35.00	
Anthology, 1 and 2		
Meals	$90.00	Meal cost includes snacks and drinks. $15.00 per meal x6 meals
Evangel Polo Shirt	$25.00	
Registration and Staff Fee	$25.00	
Total Fee	**$175.00**	

Church Plant Coach Expenses		
	Lodging on Own	
Ripe for Harvest	$35.00	
Anthology, 1 and 2	$70.00	
Meals	$90.00	Meal cost includes snacks and drinks. $15.00 per meal x6 meals
Evangel Polo Shirt	$25.00	
Registration and Staff Fee		
Total Fee	**$220.00**	

Regional School at THE OAKS Example

Budget for a three-night, two-and-a-half-day Church Plant School. School would begin on a Thursday night and finish Sunday at lunch.

Budget is for twenty-five church planters and church plant team members. School provides lunch and dinner in this budget (breakfast at hotel or on own).

Team Leader Expenses	Lodging in Cabins	Lodging with Roommates	Lodge Room Alone	
Ripe for Harvest		$35.00		
Anthology, 1 and 2		$70.00		
Meals and Lodge rooms		$135.00		Includes 8 meals
Evangel Polo Shirt		$25.00		
Registration and Staff Fee		$100.00		Covers lodging and travel expenses for school staff as well as miscellaneous expenses
Total Fee		**$365.00**		

Church Plant Team Member Price	Lodging on Own	Lodging with Roommates	Room Alone	
Ripe for Harvest		$35.00		
Anthology, 1 and 2				
Meals and Lodge rooms		$135.00		Includes 8 meals
Evangel Polo Shirt		$25.00		
Registration and Staff Fee		$100.00		Covers lodging and travel expenses for school staff as well as miscellaneous expenses
Total Fee		**$295.00**		

Church Plant Coach Expenses	Lodging on Own	Lodging with Roommates	Room Alone	
Ripe for Harvest		$35.00		
Anthology, 1 and 2		$70.00		
Meals and Lodge rooms		$135.00		Includes 8 meals
Evangel Polo Shirt		$25.00		Covers lodging and travel expenses for school staff as well as miscellaneous expenses
Registration and Staff Fee				
Total Fee		**$265.00**		

Regional School in Wichita Example

Budget for a three-night, two-and-a-half-day Church Plant School. School would begin on a Thursday night and finish Sunday at lunch.

Budget is for twenty-five church planters and church plant team members. School provides lunch and dinner in this budget (breakfast at hotel or on own).

Team Leader Expenses	Lodging on Own	Room with Roommate	Room Alone	
Ripe for Harvest	$35.00	$35.00	$35.00	
Anthology, 1 and 2	$70.00	$70.00	$70.00	
Meals	$90.00	$90.00	$90.00	Meal cost includes snacks and drinks. $15.00 per meal x6 meals
Hotel		$110.00	$219.00	$73.00 per night at Wesley Inn
Evangel Polo Shirt	$25.00	$25.00	$25.00	
Registration and Staff Fee	$100.00	$100.00	$100.00	Covers lodging and travel expenses for school staff as well as miscellaneous expenses
Total Fee	**$320.00**	**$430.00**	**$539.00**	

Church Plant Team Member Price	Lodging on Own	Room with Roommate	Room Alone	
Ripe for Harvest	$35.00	$35.00	$35.00	
Anthology, 1 and 2				
Meals	$90.00	$90.00	$90.00	Meal cost includes snacks and drinks. $15.00 per meal x6 meals
Hotel		$110.00	$219.00	$73.00 per night at Wesley Inn
Evangel Polo Shirt	$25.00	$25.00	$25.00	
Registration and Staff Fee	$100.00	$100.00	$100.00	Covers lodging and travel expenses for school staff as well as miscellaneous expenses
Total Fee	**$250.00**	**$360.00**	**$469.00**	

Church Plant Coach Expenses				
	Lodging on Own	Room with Roommate	Room Alone	
Ripe for Harvest	$35.00	$35.00	$35.00	
Anthology, 1 and 2	$70.00	$70.00	$70.00	
Meals	$90.00	$90.00	$90.00	Meal cost includes snacks and drinks. $15.00 per meal x6 meals
Hotel		$110.00	$219.00	$73.00 per night at Wesley Inn
Evangel Polo Shirt	$25.00	$25.00	$25.00	Covers lodging and travel expenses for school staff as well as miscellaneous expenses
Registration and Staff Fee				
Total Fee	**$220.00**	**$330.00**	**$439.00**	

Evangel Church Planter Assessment
Pre-Evangel Team Leader Process Overview

I. **Enlistment: Steps to accepting a potential church plant team at your Evangel School**

A. **Host interview with potential Church Planter.** Evangel Deans are responsible to interview and do an initial evaluation of every church planter prior to attending Evangel. The Evangel Church Plant School should be the final tool of assessment, and as such the goal should be for all teams that attend the school to complete the school as commissioned teams with a charter.

B. **Complete Evangel Church Planter Assessment.** This one-page assessment is best used as a 360 review tool. One copy is given to the church plant team leader, one copy to the spouse, and one copy to the church planter's pastor. The assessments are scored by the Evangel Dean. This resource is especially targeted to help church planters working among the poor identify areas of strength and potential areas of growth.

C. **Submit and receive Pastor's Reference form to/from the applicant's pastor.** Every Church Planter is required to have at least one pastoral reference in order to bring a team to Evangel Church Plant School.

D. **Interview the Pastor on the applicant.** There are several objectives for this interview:

1. Introduce yourself, the name of your Evangel School, and affirm the pastor's recommendation.

2. Share the objectives of the Evangel School of Urban Church Planting (from Dean Handbook).

3. Ask if there is anything else he/she would like to share about the applicant.

4. Share the excitement we have to equip (person's name) to establish a new church for the glory of God.

5. Ask the pastor to close the time in prayer.

E. **Send link to "The Call to an Ancient-Evangelical Future" to Team Leader, and ask them to sign if in agreement.** The application will ask the potential planter if they have read, agree with, and have signed the document.

F. **Send link to Team Leader and ask that they purchase and read *Sacred Roots: A Primer on Retrieving the Great Tradition*.** The application will ask them to confirm that they have read this.

G. **Forward Evangel Application to Team Leader.** The Evangel application covers the basic information about a church plant team leader and the team that will be brought to Evangel, as well as is where the applicant will notify you that they read and agree with the "Ancient Future Call", and that they have purchased and read *Sacred Roots*.

II. Evangel School Basic Training

Purchase *Front Matters: Prerequisite Readings for the Evangel School of Urban Church Planting*. After all above is completed and church planter is approved and registered for the school, purchase Front Matters: Prerequisite Readings for the Evangel School of Urban Church Planting:

III. Resource Links

A. "The Call to an Ancient-Evangelical Future": *www.ancientfuturefaithnetwork.org/the-call/*

B. *Sacred Roots: A Primer on Retrieving the Great Tradition*

1. Softcover: *www.amazon.com/Sacred-Roots-Primer-Retrieving-Tradition/dp/1451520484/ref=tmm_pap_swatch_0?_encoding=UTF8&qid=&sr=*

2. Kindle: *www.amazon.com/gp/product/B0077E8MQQ/ref=as_li_tf_tl?ie=UTF8&camp=1789&creative=9325&creativeASIN=B0077E8MQQ&linkCode=as2&tag=theurbaninstitut*

C. See *www.tumi.org/evangel* for more resources on church planter assessments.

Understanding the Evangel Assessment Process

The following process is how an Evangel Dean will assess a church plant team leader.

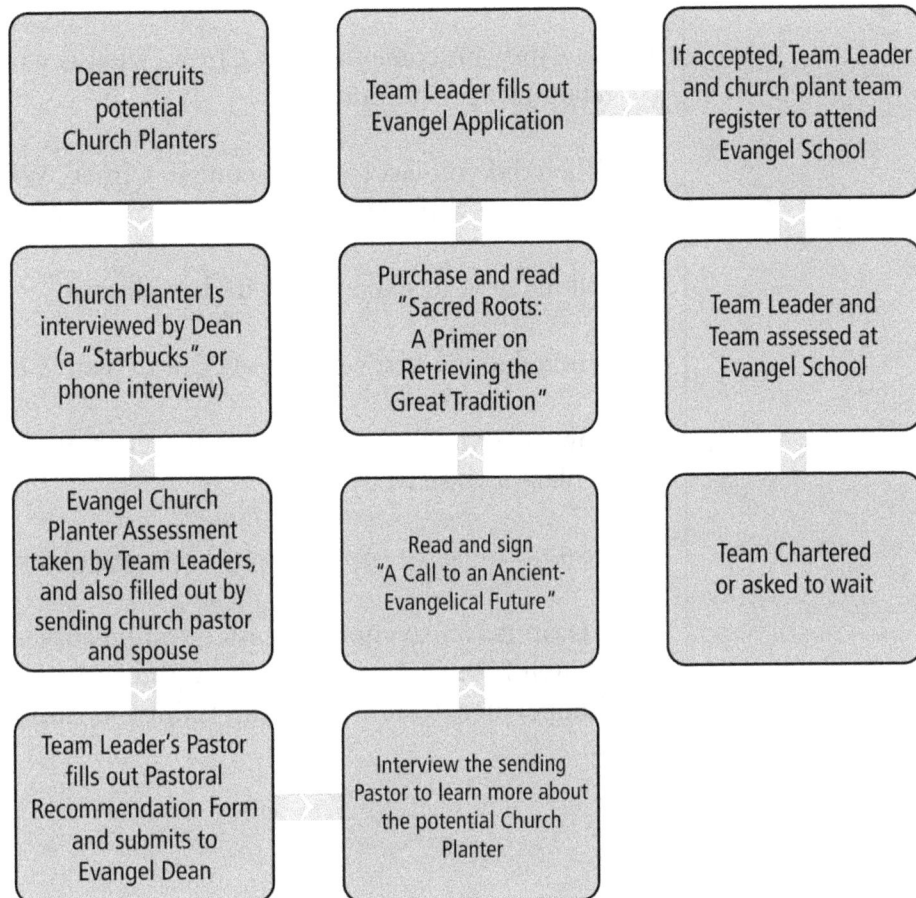

Dean recruits potential Church Planters	Team Leader fills out Evangel Application	If accepted, Team Leader and church plant team register to attend Evangel School
Church Planter Is interviewed by Dean (a "Starbucks" or phone interview)	Purchase and read "Sacred Roots: A Primer on Retrieving the Great Tradition"	Team Leader and Team assessed at Evangel School
Evangel Church Planter Assessment taken by Team Leaders, and also filled out by sending church pastor and spouse	Read and sign "A Call to an Ancient-Evangelical Future"	Team Chartered or asked to wait
Team Leader's Pastor fills out Pastoral Recommendation Form and submits to Evangel Dean	Interview the sending Pastor to learn more about the potential Church Planter	

Planter Interview Questions

Evangel Deans are expected to interview all church plant team leaders prior to their acceptance as candidates at an Evangel School of Urban Church Planting. Acceptance of candidates is at the Dean's discretion. However, the following questions may be helpful to consider.

1. How did you come to know Christ, what is your current relationship with him like?

2. When did you last lead someone to Christ? What has your experience with evangelism been like?

3. Tell me of your experiences in discipleship.

4. When did you first sense God's call to plant a church?

5. How does your spouse and family feel about God's call on your life to plant a church?

6. Does your pastor support your calling to plant a new church?

7. A Dean may also choose to ask questions based on the Evangel Church Planter Assessment Form categories of Character, Competence, Community, and Calling as outlined below.

Church Planter Self-Evaluation			To score, place a number between 1 and 10 on each line, where 1 is lowest and 10 is highest. Total the scores at bottom and right.

Church Planter Name:

Evaluator Name:

Calling	Character	Competence	Community
The Authority of God: God's leader acts on God's recognized call and authority, acknowledged by God's people.	**The Humility of Christ:** God's leader demonstrates the mind and lifestyle of Christ in his or her actions and relationships.	**The Power of the Holy Spirit:** God's leader operates in the gifting and anointing of the Holy Spirit.	**The Growth of the Church:** God's leader equips and empowers the body of Christ for mission and ministry.
___ Articulates a clear call from God and believes it (faith)	___ Passion for Christlikeness	___ Spiritual gift of evangelism	___ Disciples faithful individuals
___ Authentic testimony before God and others	___ Radical lifestyle for the Kingdom	___ Spiritual gift of teaching	___ Facilitates growth in small groups
___ Deep sense of personal conviction based on Scripture	___ Serious pursuit of holiness	___ Spiritual gift of pastoring	___ Pastors and equips believers in the congregation
___ Personal burden for a particular task or people	___ Discipline in personal life (ability to manage time without supervision)	___ Discipled by able mentor and has demonstrated joyful submission	___ Nurtures associations and networks among Christians and churches
___ Confirmation by leaders and the body	___ Planter and spouse share commitment to task and prioritize each other	___ Shows the biblical and theological competence necessary to pastor God's people	___ Advances new movements among God's people locally
___ Desire to plant a church is primarily from a desire to see lost come to Christ not because of problems in existing church or issues with pastor	___ Provides model in conduct, speech, and lifestyle (Fruit of the Spirit) and is worthy of imitation	___ Able to Evangelize, Follow Up, and Disciple	___ Committed to global mission
___ Possesses a rich theological understanding of the church and an even deeper love for Christ's body as motive for call	___ Knows self, both strengths and weaknesses	___ Strategic in the use of people and resources to accomplish the task	___ Participant and leader in congregational times of intercessory prayer
___ Prepared to suffer and engage in spiritual warfare	___ Displays perseverance and does not easily give up	___ Comfortable with chaos and starting from scratch	___ Participant and leader in tithing and generous giving
	___ Tend to be described by others as "independent, entrepreneurial, driving, hard-worker, decisive, confident, self-starter, optimistic, relational."	___ Ability to identify most important tasks and focus on them	___ Communicates kingdom vision for local congregation
	___ Understands and applied spiritual rhythms (Sabbath, Christian Year, Spiritual Retreats)	___ Have a track record of recruiting people to a team	___ Has participated in and led church discipline
		___ Have a history of starting new things	
		___ Demonstrates cross-cultural competence	
Score: ___ /80	Score: ___ /100	Score: ___ /120	Score: ___ /100

Total Score: _____ /400

Total Percent: _____ %

To score, place a number between 1 and 10 on each line, where 1 is lowest and 10 is highest. Total the scores at bottom and right.

Evaluator Name:

Church Planter Evaluation by Pastor			
Church Planter Name:			
Calling	**Character**	**Competence**	**Community**
The Authority of God: God's leader acts on God's recognized call and authority, acknowledged by God's people.	*The Humility of Christ:* God's leader demonstrates the mind and lifestyle of Christ in his or her actions and relationships.	*The Power of the Holy Spirit:* God's leader operates in the gifting and anointing of the Holy Spirit.	*The Growth of the Church:* God's leader equips and empowers the body of Christ for mission and ministry.
___ Articulates a clear call from God and believes it (faith)	___ Passion for Christlikeness	___ Spiritual gift of evangelism	___ Disciples faithful individuals
___ Authentic testimony before God and others	___ Radical lifestyle for the Kingdom	___ Spiritual gift of teaching	___ Facilitates growth in small groups
___ Deep sense of personal conviction based on Scripture	___ Serious pursuit of holiness	___ Spiritual gift of pastoring	___ Pastors and equips believers in the congregation
___ Personal burden for a particular task or people	___ Discipline in personal life (ability to manage time without supervision)	___ Discipled by able mentor and has demonstrated joyful submission	___ Nurtures associations and networks among Christians and churches
___ Confirmation by leaders and the body	___ Planter and spouse share commitment to task and prioritize each other	___ Shows the biblical and theological competence necessary to pastor God's people	___ Advances new movements among God's people locally
___ Desire to plant a church is primarily from a desire to see lost come to Christ not because of problems in existing church or issues with pastor	___ Provides model in conduct, speech, and lifestyle (Fruit of the Spirit) and is worthy of imitation	___ Able to Evangelize, Follow Up, and Disciple	___ Committed to global mission
___ Possesses a rich theological understanding of the church and an even deeper love for Christ's body as motive for call	___ Knows self, both strengths and weaknesses	___ Strategic in the use of people and resources to accomplish the task	___ Participant and leader in congregational times of intercessory prayer
___ Prepared to suffer and engage in spiritual warfare	___ Displays perseverance and does not easily give up	___ Comfortable with chaos and starting from scratch	___ Participant and leader in tithing and generous giving
	___ Tend to be described by others as "independent, entrepreneurial, driving, hard-worker, decisive, confident, self-starter, optimistic, relational."	___ Ability to identify most important tasks and focus on them	___ Communicates kingdom vision for local congregation
	___ Understands and applied spiritual rhythms (Sabbath, Christian Year, Spiritual Retreats)	___ Have a track record of recruiting people to a team	___ Has participated in and led church discipline
		___ Have a history of starting new things	
		___ Demonstrates cross-cultural competence	
Score: ___ /80	Score: ___ /100	Score: ___ /120	Score: ___ /100

Total Score: ___ /400

Total Percent: ___ %

To score, place a number between 1 and 10 on each line, where 1 is lowest and 10 is highest. Total the scores at bottom and right.

Church Planter Evaluation by Spouse

Church Planter Name:

Evaluator Name:

Calling	Character	Competence	Community
The Authority of God: God's leader acts on God's recognized call and authority, acknowledged by God's people.	**The Humility of Christ:** God's leader demonstrates the mind and lifestyle of Christ in his or her actions and relationships.	**The Power of the Holy Spirit:** God's leader operates in the gifting and anointing of the Holy Spirit.	**The Growth of the Church:** God's leader equips and empowers the body of Christ for mission and ministry.
___ Articulates a clear call from God and believes it (faith)	___ Passion for Christlikeness	___ Spiritual gift of evangelism	___ Disciples faithful individuals
___ Authentic testimony before God and others	___ Radical lifestyle for the Kingdom	___ Spiritual gift of teaching	___ Facilitates growth in small groups
___ Deep sense of personal conviction based on Scripture	___ Serious pursuit of holiness	___ Spiritual gift of pastoring	___ Pastors and equips believers in the congregation
___ Personal burden for a particular task or people	___ Discipline in personal life (ability to manage time without supervision)	___ Discipled by able mentor and has demonstrated joyful submission	___ Nurtures associations and networks among Christians and churches
___ Confirmation by leaders and the body	___ Planter and spouse share commitment to task and prioritize each other	___ Shows the biblical and theological competence necessary to pastor God's people	___ Advances new movements among God's people locally
___ Desire to plant a church is primarily from a desire to see lost come to Christ not because of problems in existing church or issues with pastor	___ Provides model in conduct, speech, and lifestyle (Fruit of the Spirit) and is worthy of imitation	___ Able to Evangelize, Follow Up, and Disciple	___ Committed to global mission
___ Possesses a rich theological understanding of the church and an even deeper love for Christ's body as motive for call	___ Knows self, both strengths and weaknesses	___ Strategic in the use of people and resources to accomplish the task	___ Participant and leader in congregational times of intercessory prayer
___ Prepared to suffer and engage in spiritual warfare	___ Displays perseverance and does not easily give up	___ Comfortable with chaos and starting from scratch	___ Participant and leader in tithing and generous giving
	___ Tend to be described by others as "independent, entrepreneurial, driving, hard-worker, decisive, confident, self-starter, optimistic, relational."	___ Ability to identify most important tasks and focus on them	___ Communicates kingdom vision for local congregation
	___ Understands and applied spiritual rhythms (Sabbath, Christian Year, Spiritual Retreats)	___ Have a track record of recruiting people to a team	___ Has participated in and led church discipline
		___ Have a history of starting new things	
		___ Demonstrates cross-cultural competence	
Score: ___ /80	Score: ___ /100	Score: ___ /120	Score: ___ /100

Total Score: ___ /400

Total Percent: ___ %

Resources Used to Develop the Evangel Church Planter Assessment
Unless otherwise noted, all resources below can be found in Volume 1 or 2 of *Planting Churches among the City's Poor: An Anthology of Urban Church Planting* (Wichita, KS: TUMI Press, 2015). The most important resources are listed in bold.

Davis, Don. **"Assessing Urban Christian Leaders."** In *The Evangel Dean Basic Training Manual: A Guide for Church Plant Movement Leaders to Equip Urban Church Planters*, 248-263. Wichita, KS: TUMI Press, 2015.

————. "Creedal Theology as a Blueprint for Discipleship and Leadership: A Time-Tested Criterion for Equipping New Believers and Developing Indigenous Leaders." 1:241–52.

————. "Designating Those Who Provide Leadership to Our Church Plant Teams." 2:134.

————. "Developing Urban Christian Leaders: A Profile." 2:165.

————. "Different Traditions of African-American Response: Interpreting a Legacy, Shaping an Identity, and Pursuing a Destiny as a Minority Culture Person." 1:257–59.

————. **"Discipling the Faithful: Establishing Leaders for the Urban Church."** 1:375.

————. "Fit to Represent: Multiplying Disciples of the Kingdom of God." 2:197.

————. "Forming the Church Plant Team and Understanding the Roles." 1:371–74.

————. "Identifying, Training, and Releasing Team Leaders and Coaches in World Impact." 2:73–77.

————. "Nurturing Authentic Christian Leadership." 2:163.

————. "Paul's Team Members: Companions, Laborers, and Fellow Workers." 1:260–62.

————. "Practical Steps in Church Planting: Knowing Your Call and Your Community." 1:349–55.

————. "Responsibilities of a Church Plant Team Leader." 1:336.

————. "Team Facilitation: Providing Ongoing Input to the Team as Team Leader." 2:177.

————. "Team Leader Identification Grid." 2:148–49.

————. "The Heartbeat of a Church Planter: Discerning an Apostolic/Pastoral Identity." 1:337–48.

————. "The Theology of the Church for Team Leaders." 1:200–10.

————. "Understanding Leadership as Representation: The Six Stages of Formal Proxy." 2:66.

Voss, Hank. "Assessment and Church Planters For/From the Urban Poor." In *The Evangel Dean Basic Training Manual: A Guide for Church Plant Movement Leaders to Equip Urban Church Planters*, 65–74. Wichita, KS: TUMI Press, 2015.

————. "Jesus' Practice of Silence and Solitude." 1:263.

————. "Seven Essential Practices of the Priesthood of All Believers." 1:264.

The forty items of the Church Planter Evaluation are discussed at multiple points in the resources above.

Evangel Church Plant Charter Form

Church Plant Name: _____

Church Planter: _____

Church Planter E-mail: _____ **Cell:** _____

Field Coach: _____

Field Coach E-mail: _____ **Cell:** _____

Church Expression (Check one):

_____ Small (House) Church [approximately 20-50]

_____ Community Church [approximately 60-150]

_____ Hub (Mother) Church [200+]

Sending Authority: _____

Primary Team Members and length of commitment:

Target Area: _____

Ethnicity and/or Unreached People Group(s): _____
[A people group is considered unreached (UPG) when there isn't an indigenous church in that people group (a church that looks like the people and is led by the people of the culture.]

Unengaged and Unreached People Group (if applicable): _____
[Unreached people groups are unengaged (UUPG) when there is no one strategizing to reach that group, i.e., there is no tangible intent of targeting that people group with the Gospel.]

Requested Length of Charter: _____

Times to Meet with Field Coach: _____

Times of Formal Evaluation (PWR, at least three times per year): _____

Values:

Vision Statement:

Key Goals:

Dean Approval:_____ **Date:** _____

Dean Approval:_____ **Date:** _____

Evangel Assessor Coach Approval:_____ **Date:** _____

Evangel Assessor Coach Approval:_____ **Date:** _____

* Charter must be reviewed and approved by Sponsoring Spiritual Authority of Church Plant Team.

Key Principles and Other Tools for Evangel Field Coaches and Assessor Coaches

Key Principles for Coaching

1. Make sure you have a clear understanding of expectations in the coaching relationship.

2. This is not a job put a co-laboring in the Gospel. Take time to know the church planter, his/her family, children, and team members. Family and personal character are critical for the task-oriented planter. Make sure there is good healthy family dynamics and a growing in the grace and knowledge of the Lord Jesus as a redeemed child of God.

3. Expect excellence from the planter. This includes prayer, any preparation work that has been assigned, and goals established prior to the Coaches meeting. Keep the church planter accountable to goals and assignments he/she has agreed to accomplish.

4. Though relationship is important, this is a meeting with the defined objective to guide the planter in their commissioned task to plant a church. Keep this allotted time as a professional time. Find a space in which both you and the planter can speak, listen, and focus.

5. Move the planter forward as you provide guidance. Not only review past action steps put be aggressive, in the Spirit, to set new actions steps. This is where you ask lots of questions and "pull out" of the planter what the Spirit is placing on his/her heart.

6. There is never not enough opportunity to encourage the planter. Celebrate a victory forward no matter how small. It is a guarantee that the spiritual enemy will do his part to bring discouragement. Always come prepared to share scripture words of endurance, promise, encouragement, identity in Christ.

7. Schedule your next meeting. Make sure you and the planter place a high priority on these meetings. If you have to reschedule, make sure you do it immediately.

Simple Checklist for the Field Coach
(Based on the 1-Year Evangel Charter)

I. **First Year**

    A. In-person visit to Team Leader in first month.

    B. Schedule time to pray regularly for Team and Team Leader by name.

    C. Schedule monthly Team Leader meeting either by phone call or by visit.

    D. Monthly report to sending authority (if applicable).

    E. Schedule four PWRs with the last one a review and planning time for the next year. Submit Evangel Quarterly Field Report to Dean (if applicable).

    F. Help Team Leader identify and recruit a potential team leader for a new church plant.

    G. Ensure that church plant is plugged into an Association (e.g. Urban Church Association) or Network.

    H. Plan for 1-year Antioch celebration.

Sample Questions for the Monthly Meeting

I. **Questions on the Team's Spiritual Growth and Community Life (Are they living as a called community?)**

   A. Are you and your team walking with the Lord, seeking God intently, and growing spiritually together?

   B. Are you and your team relating to each other in love, forgiveness, and unity? Do any conflicts exist which need to be resolved?

   C. Are you and your team remaining called and committed to its vision, united together around it? Is the team working well together toward its purpose?

   D. Are you and your team functioning as a gifted and serving body together, especially in your relationships with one another?

II. **Questions on Their Vision Together (Are they clear in their vision, values, and goals?)**

   A. Do you and your team understand its vision and can the members articulate it to each other, and those outside the team?

   B. Are you and your team able to articulate the values on which the Vision Statement was built and are you still committed to them?

   C. Because of your team's experience in ministry, does any part of the Vision Statement or Values need to be reconsidered or rewritten?

III. **Questions on the Team's Ministry Process and Results (Are they functioning wisely and effectively in ministry?)**

   A. What gains have you made as a ministry team in your church planting community during this past month?

   B. What are the greatest struggles you have had in implementing your vision?

C. What do your present schedules (i.e., personal and team schedules) look like and how does each ministry activity contribute to your ministry vision? What adjustments need to be made?

D. What is the quality of your ministry relationships currently? What individuals and families ought to be given further and deeper investment? How will you accomplish this?

IV. Questions for the Team's Ministry Planning and Strategy for the Next Ministry Period (Are they clear on the next steps the Spirit has for them to take?)

A. How do you and the team intend on changing/affirming its original strategic plan for ministry during the upcoming month? In other words, what goals do you need to pursue in order to ensure maximum progress toward your vision?

B. Do you and the team have assignments and dates to all your critical tasks in the plan, or at least set a date to establish these specific steps?

Sample Pre-Evangel Assessor Coach Information Letter
(Deans can put this on their website as well)

Greetings Evangel Assessor Coach,

Here is some information as you prepare to serve the church plant team you will be coaching/assessing at Evangel.

1) Attached is a schedule of the Evangel School of Urban Church Planting. Look over the schedule. It is important that you understand the overall schedule for the times we are together. If you have any questions on the overall schedule, please direct them to: [Name and contact information].

2) As Deans of [name of your Evangel School], we would like you to read over the two outlines on coaching from the Evangel Dean Handbook (attached). Please read over the outline entitled "The Coach and the Church Plant Team at Evangel." The outline is only ten pages, pay attention especially to page 153 ("Team Evaluation Form"). You will receive copies of this page for each of the teams you assess at Evangel and it will be used to help you determine if the team is ready to be chartered.

3) Attached are also two documents about charters. The first is the one-page charter you will help each team work on during Evangel. This is the one-page summary of their vision, values, and first-year strategy. Please review the document entitled "Evangel Church Plant Charter-2015." This is the single most important page (out of the many pages you will see when you get to boot camp). If you only read one page, read this page. Also review the three-page explanation of charters from the Evangel Dean Training entitled "Seminar: Charters, Coaches, and the Ongoing PWR Process" (attached).

Grace,

[Signature]

Sample Letter for Coaches Meetings at Evangel

Greetings Evangel Assessor and Field Coach,

Praise the Lord for your willingness to serve as an Evangel Coach! We settled on a schedule for special meetings, and I wanted all of you to be aware of them.

Special Coaches Meetings:

1) Coaches Orientation. Thursday night at Dinner (If you miss this meeting, please check in with [name of Dean] when you arrive at [name of Evangel School]).

2) First night at Evangel School: Each Coach will have opportunity to present how their team is doing and discuss any questions or concerns they have about the team they are responsible for evaluating ("staff" their team).

3) Second day: Coaches meeting to discuss any red flags about your team; opportunity to staff particular problems or opportunities you see with team.

4) Final Coaches meeting to confirm team's readiness to enter into the urban harvest field; sign certificates.

5) Celebration/Commissioning Service: note you will be taking pictures with your team.

Grace,

[Signature]

Sample Coaching Covenant

As your coach I promise to do the following:

- Enter into each coaching session prayerfully with an openness to the Holy Spirit.

- Work to gain your full trust by listening intently, asking clarifying questions, and keeping strict confidentiality (unless legally bound to share information due to its nature).

- Help you explore God's call for you...for today and for the future.

- Offer observations that may be helpful to you, always in a loving way.

- Offer knowledge and information that might be helpful.

- Never offer "answers" unless they have been specifically requested, and even then, they will be shared only after your own answers have been fully explored.

- Commit to meeting with you (either in person or by phone) one hour per month, and as special needs arise.

- I will monitor your commitment level as measured by tasks completed on time.

As a person being coached, I promise to do the following:

- Enter into each meeting prayerfully with an openness to the Holy Spirit.

- Openly share my thoughts and insights about my nature, my practices, and my passions (exploring who I am).

- Be open to your questions and your insights.

- Commit to meeting with you (either in person or by phone) one hour per month for one year.

- Carefully choose my commitments – then follow through on each of them.

Signed _____ Date _____

Urban Church Planting
A Topical Bibliography
By Rev. Dr. Don Davis and Dr. Hank Voss

> You should read twenty-five percent of your books from the first 1,500 years of church history, twenty-five percent from the last 500 years, twenty-five percent from the last 100 years, and twenty-five percent from recent years.
>
> ~ Rick Warren, 2010
>
> It has always therefore been one of my main endeavors as a teacher to persuade the young that firsthand knowledge is not only more worth acquiring than second-hand knowledge, but is usually much easier and more delightful to acquire. . . . It is a good rule, after reading a new book, never to allow yourself another new one till you have read an old one in between. If that is too much for you, you should at least read one old one to every three new ones.
>
> ~ C. S. Lewis, 1944

I. Endear: A Church Planter Loves God with All of His Heart

This manual is dedicated to Rev. Bob Engel, a faithful and fervent church planter. Rev Engel has served as an example to many of one who is "endeared" to Christ. Early in his work as a church planter, Rev. Engel came across a list of "Spiritual Classics" from a pastor named A. W. Tozer. Tozer grew up extremely poor and was only able to formally complete a fifth grade education. He eventually became an influential pastor in Chicago, but more importantly, he was known as a man passionately in *Pursuit of God*. When asked how he remained so passionate for God, Tozer pointed to his "teachers." These teachers were the authors of some 25 spiritual classics that had helped to shape his *Knowledge of the Holy*.

Rev. Engel recommended this list to me (Hank) more than a decade ago as one place to start for those interested in deepening their exposure to some of the giants of the faith. Most of the books on this list are over a hundred years old, some more than a thousand. They have proved valuable across generations, and much of their content is rooted in the Great Tradition. Church Planters will need to read with discernment, but for those willing to invest the time, there is much spiritual profit to be mined from these sacred roots. Many of these books are available for free as downloads at *www.ccel.org*. Since most of these books have been reprinted by dozens of publishers, only the authors and titles are listed below.

1. *The Dark Night of the Soul*, by John of the Cross

2. *Practice of the Presence of God*, by Brother Lawrence

3. *A Testament of Devotion*, by Thomas Kelly

4. *Introduction to the Devout Life*, by Francis of Sales

5. *The Imitation of Christ*, by Thomas a Kempis

6. *Confessions*, by Augustine

7. *Private Devotions*, by Lancelot Andrewes

8. *Adornment of the Spiritual Marriage*, by Jan van Ruysbroeck

9. *Amendment of Life*, by Richard Rolle

10. *The Ascent of Mt. Carmel*, by John of the Cross

11. *The Ascent of Mt. Zion*, by Berdardeno de Laredo

12. *Book of Eternal Wisdom*, by Henry Suso

13. *Centuries of Meditations*, by Thomas Traherne

14. *Christian Perfection*, by Fenelon

15. *The Cloud of Unknowing*, Anonymous

16. *The Goad of Love*, by Walter Hilton

17. *A Guide to True Peace*, by Molinos and others

18. *Hymns*, by Gerhard Tersteegen

19. *Letters of Direction*, by de Tourville

20. *On the Incarnation*, by Athanasius

21. *On the Love of God*, by Bernard of Clairvaux

22. *Poems*, by Frederick Faber

23. *Poems*, by Isaac Watts

24. *Proslogium*, by Anselm

25. *The Quiet Way*, by Gerhard Tersteegen

26. *Revelations of Divine Love*, by Julian of Norwich

27. *The Scale of Perfection*, by Walter Hilton

28. *Sermons*, by John Tauler

29. *Song of Songs*, by Bernard of Clairvaux

30. *The Spiritual Combat*, by Lorenzo Scupoli

31. *The Spiritual Guide*, by Michael Molinos

32. *Talks of Instruction*, by Meister Eckhart

33. *Theologia Germanica* (Winkworth translation), Anonymous

34. *The Vision of God*, by Nicholas of Cusa

35. *The Way of Christ*, by Jacob Boehme

There are many other lists of spiritual classics available for those interested in exploring the deep mines of the spiritual writings of the Great Tradition. Other lists of spiritual classics and introductions to their contents can be found in the volumes below.

Bernhard M Christensen. *The Inward Pilgrimage: An Introduction to Christian Spiritual Classics*, Rev. ed. Minneapolis: Augsburg, 1996.

Edward Donnelly, ed. *You Must Read: Books That Have Shaped Our Lives*. Carlisle, PA: Banner of Truth Trust, 2015.

Arthur Holder, ed. *Christian Spirituality: The Classics*. New York: Routledge, 2010.

Eugene Peterson. *Take and Read: Spiritual Reading: An Annotated List.* Grand Rapids: Eerdmans, 1995.

II. TUMI Resources

In general, there are few resources designed explicitly for church planters working among the urban poor. The Urban Ministry Institute provides one exception to this general rule. Between 1995 and 2015 more than fifty books, training courses, and booklets have been published to resource those working among the poor. The resources listed below are relevant to both church planting and to the continued growth and health of urban churches serving the poor. Those specifically focused on the topic of church planting are marked with an asterisk.

A. Select Books

Don Davis. *Black and Human: Rediscovering King as a Resource for Black Theology and Ethics.* [Orig. 2000]. Wichita, KS: TUMI Press, 2015.

————. *Let God Arise! A Sober Call to Prevailing Prayer for a Dynamic Spiritual Awakening and the Aggressive Advancement of the Kingdom in America's Inner Cities.* Wichita, KS: The Urban Ministry Institute Press, 2000.*

————. *Leading and Feeding Urban Church Plant Teams,* 2nd ed. Wichita, KS: The Urban Ministry Institute Press, 2007.*

————. *For the Next Generation: The Urban Ministry Institute Mentor Manual,* 2nd ed. Wichita, KS: The Urban Ministry Institute Press, 2008.

————. *Sacred Roots: A Primer on Retrieving the Great Tradition.* Wichita, KS: The Urban Ministry Institute Press, 2010.*

————. *Multiplying Laborers for the Urban Harvest: Shifting the Paradigm for Servant Leadership Education,* 15th ed. Wichita, KS: The Urban Ministry Institute Press, 2013.

————. *The SIAFU Network Guidebook: Standing Together for Christ in the City.* Wichita, KS: The Urban Ministry Institute Press, 2013.

Dr. Don L. Davis, ed. *Planting Churches among the City's Poor: An Anthology of Urban Church Planting Resources*. Wichita, KS: The Urban Ministry Institute Press, 2015. 2 Volumes.*

Rev. Don Allsman and Dr. Don L. Davis. *Fight the Good Fight of Faith: Playing Your Part in God's Unfolding Drama*. Wichita, KS: The Urban Ministry Institute Press, 2015.

Don Allsman, Don L. Davis, and Hank Voss, eds. *Ripe for Harvest: A Guidebook for Planting Healthy Churches in the City*. Wichita, KS: TUMI Press, 2015.*

B. Select Published Courses and Curriculum Resources

Much of TUMI's emphasis has focused on producing resources easily accessible to urban leaders with a low level of literacy. Nearly all of the resources in this section of the bibliography include audio or video instructional content representing hundreds of hours of lectures designed to equip urban church leaders for ministry in their own context.

Don L. Davis. *Nurturing an Apostolic Heart* (Foundations for Ministry Series). Wichita, KS: The Urban Ministry Institute Press, 2000.*

————. *The Gospel of John* (Foundations for Ministry Series). Wichita, KS: The Urban Ministry Institute Press, 2002.

————. *The Kingdom of God*, vol. 2, 16 vols. (The Capstone Curriculum). Wichita, KS: The Urban Ministry Institute Press, 2004.

————. *Bible Interpretation*, vol. 5, 16 vols. (The Capstone Curriculum). Wichita, KS: The Urban Ministry Institute Press, 2005.

————. *Conversion and Calling,* vol. 1, 16 vols. (The Capstone Curriculum). Wichita, KS: The Urban Ministry Institute Press, 2005.

————. *Doing Justice and Loving Mercy*, vol. 16, 16 vols. (The Capstone Curriculum). Wichita, KS: The Urban Ministry Institute Press, 2005.

————. *Evangelism and Spiritual Warfare*, vol. 8, 16 vols. (The Capstone Curriculum). Wichita, KS: The Urban Ministry Institute Press, 2005.*

————. *Focus on Reproduction*, vol. 12, 16 vols. (The Capstone Curriculum). Wichita, KS: The Urban Ministry Institute Press, 2005.*

————. *Foundations for Christian Mission*, vol. 4, 16 vols. (The Capstone Curriculum). Wichita, KS: The Urban Ministry Institute Press, 2005.*

————. *Foundations of Christian Leadership*, vol. 7, 16 vols. (The Capstone Curriculum). Wichita, KS: The Urban Ministry Institute Press, 2005.

————. *God the Father*, vol. 6, 16 vols. (The Capstone Curriculum). Wichita, KS: The Urban Ministry Institute Press, 2005.

————. *God the Son*, vol. 10, 16 vols. (The Capstone Curriculum). Wichita, KS: The Urban Ministry Institute Press, 2005.

————. *New Testament Witness to Christ and His Kingdom*, vol. 13, 16 vols. (The Capstone Curriculum). Wichita, KS: The Urban Ministry Institute Press, 2005.

————. *Old Testament Witness to Christ and His Kingdom*, vol. 9, 16 vols. (The Capstone Curriculum). Wichita, KS: The Urban Ministry Institute Press, 2005.

————. *Practicing Christian Leadership*, vol. 11, 16 vols. (The Capstone Curriculum). Wichita, KS: The Urban Ministry Institute Press, 2005.

————. *The Equipping Ministry,* vol. 15, 16 vols. (The Capstone Curriculum). Wichita, KS: The Urban Ministry Institute Press, 2005.

————. *A Compelling Testimony: Maintaining a Disciplined Walk, Christlike Character, and Godly Relationships as God's Servant* (Foundations for Ministry Series). Wichita, KS: The Urban Ministry Institute Press, 2006.

————. *A Biblical Vision, Part I: Mastering the Old Testament Witness to Christ and His Kingdom* (Foundations for Ministry Series). Wichita, KS: The Urban Ministry Institute Press, 2006.

————. *A Biblical Vision, Part II: Mastering the New Testament Witness to Christ and His Kingdom* (Foundations for Ministry Series). Wichita, KS: The Urban Ministry Institute Press, 2006.

————. *Winning the World: Facilitating Urban Church Planting Movements* (Foundations for Ministry Series). Wichita, KS: The Urban Ministry Institute Press, 2007.*

————. *Church Matters: Retrieving the Great Tradition* (Foundations for Ministry Series). Wichita, KS: The Urban Ministry Institute, 2007.*

————. *An Authentic Calling: Representing Christ and His Kingdom through the Church* (Foundations for Ministry Series). Wichita, KS: The Urban Ministry Institute Press, 2008.

————. *Master the Bible: How to Get and Keep the Big Picture of the Bible's Story* (Foundations for Ministry Series). Wichita, KS: The Urban Ministry Institute Press, 2008.

————. *Marking Time: Forming Spirituality through the Church Year* (Foundations for Ministry Series). Wichita, KS: The Urban Ministry Institute Press, 2009.

————. *Sacred Roots Workshop: Retrieving the Great Tradition in the Contemporary Church* (Foundations for Ministry Series). Wichita, KS: The Urban Ministry Institute Press, 2010.

————. *Ministry in a Multicultural and Unchurched Society* (Foundations for Ministry Series). Wichita, KS: The Urban Ministry Institute Press, 2012.

Don L. Davis and Terry G. Cornett. *Theology of the Church*, vol. 3, 16 vols. (The Capstone Curriculum). Wichita, KS: The Urban Ministry Institute Press, 2005.

Don L. Davis and Lorna Rasmussen, *Managing Projects for Ministry* (Foundations for Ministry Series). Wichita, KS: The Urban Ministry Institute Press, 2012.

Don L. Davis. *Church Resource CD*. Wichita, KS: The Urban Ministry Institute Press, 1999.

Don Davis and Don Allsman, eds. *The John Mark Curriculum*. Los Angeles: World Impact, 2000.*

C. Select Chapters, Articles, Shorter Works

Don L. Davis, "An Interview with Cornel West." *Iowa Journal of Cultural Studies* 12 (1993): 8–17.

————. "Overview and Framework for Church Planting Activity". Wichita, KS: The Urban Ministry Institute Press, 2000.*

————. *Making Joyful Noises: Mastering the Fundamentals of Music*. Wichita, KS: The Urban Ministry Institute Press, 2000.

————. "Creedal Theology: A Blueprint for Urban Leadership Momentum," in *Gaining Momentum: The Urban Ministry Institute Satellite Summit Workbook*. Wichita, KS: The Urban Ministry Institute Press, 2006, 77–94.

————. "Fleshing out the Universal Priesthood: Recommended Order for Morning and Evening Sacrifices to God," in *The Wondrous Cross: TUMI Annual 2009-2010*. Wichita, KS: The Urban Ministry Institute Press, 2009, 425–36.

————. *The Most Amazing Story Ever Told*. Wichita, KS: The Urban Ministry Institute Press, 2011.

————. *The SIAFU Network Chapter Meeting Guide: How to Inspire Souls and Transform Hearts through Your SIAFU Gathering*. Wichita, KS: The Urban Ministry Institute Press, 2013.

Terry Cornett and Don Davis. *Empowering People for Freedom, Wholeness, and Justice: Theological and Ethical Foundations for World Impact's Development Ministries*. Wichita, KS: The Urban Ministry Institute Press, 1996.

Carl Ellis, ed. with Don Davis and Pastor R. C. Smith. *Saving Our Sons: Confronting the Lure of Islam With Truth, Faith & Courage* (Chicago, IMANI Books, 2007).

Hank Voss. "Twenty Five Years of Church Planting Among the Poor: A Report," in *Planting Churches among the City's Poor: An Anthology of Urban Church Planting Resources, Vol. 1.* Ed. Don L. Davis. Wichita, KS: TUMI Press, 2015. pp. 471–510.

III. "Urban Ministry" and Church Planting among the Poor

World Impact has identified three expressions of the church for strategic purposes. These three expressions require different types of planters, resources, and strategic plans. All three expressions can be healthy representations of Christ's kingdom in urban neighborhoods. The first expression is the Small ("House") Church. These churches are gatherings of 20-50 people for smaller expressions of the body of Christ in a local neighborhood. The second expression is the Community ("Storefront") Church. These churches range between 50 and 200 people and are among the most common expression of the church found in North America today. The third expression of the church is the Hub ("Mother") Church. These churches are larger than 200 people and tend to serve as rally points for other churches in a particular neighborhood.

A. Church Plant Expressions

1. Planting Small "House" Churches

Bunch, David, Jarvey Kneisel and Barbara Oden. *Multihousing Congregations: How to Start and Grow Christian Congregations in Multihousing Communities.* Atlanta, GA: Smith Publishing, 1991.

This is an older resource, but it is one of the only resources that provides specific ideas for those planting a church in an apartment complexes, trailer parks, or other multi-housing units.

Joel Comiskey. "Cell Church Reading List and Bibliography," accessed June 2, 2015, *http://www.joelcomiskeygroup.com/ articles/churchLeaders/cellreadinglistbibliography.htm.*

198 • The Evangel Dean Basic Training Manual

Comiskey has written more than twenty-five books on cell churches (two noted below). His dissertation (available for free online) was on cell churches in Latin America and a number of his books are available in both Spanish and English. He currently teaches church planting at Tozer Seminary and consults with church plant groups interested in the cell church model. This bibliography lists 81 books he recommends on cell churches. He ranks them in the order he recommends that a cell church planter to read them.

Joel Comiskey. *2000 Years of Small Groups: A History of Cell Ministry in the Church.* Moreno, CA: CCS Publishing, 2014.

Joel Comiskey. *Biblical Foundations for the Cell-Based Church: New Testament Insights for the 21st Century Church.* Moreno, CA: CCS Publishing, 2012.

Randy Frazee and Max Lucado. *The Connecting Church 2.0: Beyond Small Groups to Authentic Community.* Grand Rapids: Zondervan, 2013.

This book is not designed exclusively for small churches, but it describes the impact a small group of committed believers can have when they focus on single geographical area. This is an important book for those wrestling with the incarnational aspect of church planting.

David Garrison. *Church Planting Movements: How God Is Redeeming a Lost World.* Midlothian, VA: WIGTake, 2004.

An important book for those seeking to understand church plant movements. This is the core textbook for TUMI's course on church plant movements.

Michael Green. *Church without Walls: A Global Examination of the Cell Church.* Waynesboro, GA: Paternoster, 2002.

Joel Comiskey ranks this as the most important book on the "Small Church." Michael Green has been writing on evangelism for more than fifty years, his early book *Evangelism in the Early Church* is a seminal book.

Larry Kreider and Floyd McClung. *Starting a House Church*. Chosen Books, 2007.

Larry Kreider is one of the leaders of the House to House Network. This association of house churches has dozens of resources for those working with Small Church models. Several of these resources are listed below and many more can be found at *www.h2hp.com*.

Larry Kreider et al. *The Biblical Role of Elders for Today's Church: New Testament Leadership Principles for Equipping Elders*. Ephrata, PA: House To House Publication, 2015.

Larry Kreider. *House Church Networks: A Church for a New Generation*. Ephrata, PA: House to House, 2001.

Brian Sauder and Larry Kreider. *Helping You Build Cell Churches: A Comprehensive Training Manual for Pastors, Cell Leaders and Church Planters*, Updated edition. Ephrata, PA: House to House, 2000.

Scoggins, Dick. *Handbook for House Churches*. [on-line], accessed 1 December 1999, *http://genesis.acu.edu/cplant/archive/contr036*; Internet.

This resource was designed for a network of house churches on the East Coast. The group is known as the Fellowship of Church Planters, and it is available for free at the website above.

2. Planting Community Churches

Don Allsman, Don L. Davis, and Hank Voss, eds. *Ripe for Harvest: A Guidebook for Planting Healthy Churches in the City*. Wichita, KS: TUMI Press, 2015.*

This book is TUMI's primary textbook for the Evangel School of Church Planting. It is relevant for all expressions of the church, but is included here so as not to be missed.

Carter, Ryan, ed. *Christ the Victor Church: The Guidebook: Ancient Faith for an Urban Movement*. N.P.: CreateSpace, 2014.

The Christ the Victor (CTV) movement began in Wichita, KS and is heavily influenced by TUMI's Sacred Roots theme. This guidebook is designed for planters who are interested in planting a CTV church plant.

Davis, Don. *Focus on Reproduction*, vol. 12, 16 vols. (The Capstone Curriculum). Wichita, KS: The Urban Ministry Institute Press, 2005.*

TUMI's primary church plant course is relevant to all three church plant expressions, but is included here so as not to be missed.

Nebel, Tom. *Big Dreams in Small Places: Church Planting in Smaller Communities*. St Charles, IL: ChurchSmart Resources, 2002.

This book is focused on church planting in rural areas. It is relevant to urban church planting in that many rural areas are very poor and there are thus principles which can be gleaned by those working among the urban poor.

3. Planting Mother (Hub) Churches

Keller, Tim and J. Allen Thompson. *Church Planting Manual*. Redeemer Church Planting Center, New York, 2002.

Tim Keller and Allen Thompson have planted many urban churches over several decades. Their church plants are usually not focused on starting with the urban poor, but they are attentive to the importance of serving the poor through ministries of mercy.

Moore, Ralph. *Starting a New Church: The Church Planter's Guide to Success*. Ventura, CA: Regal Books, 2002.

Pastor Moore founded the Hope Chapel movement which has planted a number of churches among the urban poor. His book includes chapters on the importance of preaching for church planting.

Searcy, Nelson and Kerick Thomas. *Launch: Starting a New Church from Scratch.* Regal Books, 2007.

> This book focuses on planting with a large nucleus from the very first service. It places much emphasis on starting large and has helpful ideas for those committed to planting a "Hub Church."

Smith, Efrem. *The Post-Black & Post-White Church: Becoming the Beloved Community in a Multi-Ethnic World.* San Francisco: Jossey-Bass Publishers, 2012.

> Rev. Smith's book is specifically focused on the importance of planting a multi-ethnic church. The book describes lessons learned from church planting and will be especially helpful for those hoping to plant a large Hub Church in an urban area.

B. Associations, Denominations and Partnerships

Carter, Ryan, ed., *Christ the Victor Church: The Guidebook: Ancient Faith for an Urban Movement.* N.P.: CreateSpace, 2014.

> The Christ the Victor (CTV) movement began in Wichita, KS and is heavily influenced by TUMI's Sacred Roots theme. This guidebook is designed for planters who are interested in planting a CTV church plant and provides a helpful example for other movements interested in training church planters within their movement.

Mannoia, Kevin. *Church Planting: The Next Generation.* Indianapolis, IN: Light and Life Communication, 1994.

> This book is now over twenty years old, but it is still helpful for movements and denominations that are thinking through the "systems" they hope to use as their group plants churches. His emphasis on systems helps a family of churches think through how they can work together to recruit, assess, train, encourage, and empower church planters.

Romo, Oscar I. *American Mosaic Church Planting in Ethnic America.* Nashville: Broadman Press, 1993.

This book describes the church planting system in use in the early nineties in the Southern Baptist denomination.

C. Urban Church Planting

Bunch, David, Jarvey Kneisel and Barbara Oden. *Multihousing Congregations: How to Start and Grow Christian Congregations in Multihousing Communities.* Atlanta, GA: Smith Publishing, 1991.

This is an older resource, but it provides specific ideas for those planting a church in apartment complexes, trailer parks, or other multi-housing units.

Carter, Ryan, ed. *Christ the Victor Church: The Guidebook: Ancient Faith for an Urban Movement.* N.P.: CreateSpace, 2014.

As noted above, this resource is especially designed for church planters working among the urban poor.

Carter, Matt and Darrin Patrick. *For the City: Proclaiming and Living Out the Gospel.* Grand Rapids, MI: Zondervan, 2011.

This book focuses especially on church planting in urban contexts, but is not especially targeted on church planters working among the poor.

Conn, Harvie, M. ed. *Planting and Growing Urban Churches: From Dream to Reality.* Grand Rapids, MI: Baker Book House, 1996.

This is a "big picture" book on why church planting in the cities is especially important. Harvie Conn was a cross-cultural missionary for many years and has written a number of books calling the evangelical church to prioritize urban missions.

Francis, Hozell C. *Church Planting in the African American Context.* Grand Rapids, MI: Zondervan Publishing House, 2000.

This is one of several books published in the last two decades that focuses on the specific issues facing church planters targeting African-American communities.

Greenway, Roger S. and Timothy M. Monsma. *Cities: Missions' New Frontier*, 2nd Ed. Grand Rapids, MI: Baker Books, 2000.

Greenway has written a number of books on urban mission and his books offer a big picture perspective on why urban church planting needs to be a priority.

Grigg, Viv. *Cry of the Urban Poor.* MARC, a division of World Vision, 1992.

Grigg is now a professor at Azusa Pacific University teaching on urban transformational development. He has written a number of books on the urban poor. This book focuses especially on the need for church planting work among the international urban poor communities, but many of its ideas are relevant to those working with U.S. poor as well.

Hiebert, Paul G. and Eloise Hiebert Meneses. *Incarnational Ministry: Planting Churches in Band, Tribal, Peasant, and Urban Societies.* Grand Rapids, MI: Baker Publishing House, 1995.

This book is a classic and provides important sociological insight for those planting churches in urban communities, both in the United States and internationally.

Kyle, John E. ed. *Urban Mission: God's Concern for the City.* Downers Grove, IL: InterVarsity Press, 1988.

Overstreet, Don. *Sent Out: The Calling, the Character, and the Challenge of the Apostle/Missionary.* Bloomington, IN: Crossbooks, 2009.

Rev. Overstreet has helped to plant or coach more than 500 churches among the poor during the past fifty years. He currently serves as a church plant strategy coordinator in Los Angeles.

Overstreet, Don and Mark Hammond. *God's Call to the City.* Bloomington, IN: Crossbooks, 2011.

Rev. Overstreet is a strategy coordinator for the Southern Baptists and Mark Hammond has planted many African American churches in the greater Los Angeles Area. This book reflects on the implications of the book of Jonah for church planting among the poor.

Phillips, Keith. *Out of Ashes*. Los Angeles, CA: World Impact Press, 1996.

This book describes some of the philosophical and theological foundations behind World Impact's church planting strategy.

Ratliff, Joe S. and Michael J. Cox. *Church Planting in the African-American Community*. Nashville, TN: Broadman Press, 1993.

One of the first books that specifically focused on church planting in African-American contexts.

Sanders, Alvin. *Bridging the Diversity Gap: Leading Toward God's Multi-Ethnic Kingdom*. Indianapolis: Wesleyan Publishing House, 2013.

Steffen, Tom. *Passing the Baton: Church Planting That Empowers*. La Habra, CA: Center for Organizational & Ministry Development, 1997.

Steffon teaches at Biola University. This book describes church planting among the poor in an international setting, but its emphasis on empowerment of the poor from the beginning of the church planting process makes it especially relevant for those planting among the poor in the U.S.

IV. General on Church Planting

The following books and articles have proven helpful to many church planters.

Allen, Roland. *Missionary Methods, St. Paul's or Ours?* Grand Rapids, MI: William B. Eerdmans Publishing Company, 1962.

Chaney, Charles L. *Church Planting at the End of the Twentieth Century*. Wheaton, Il: Tyndale House Publishers, Inc., 1993.

Logan, Robert E. *Beyond Church Growth*. Old Tappan, New Jersey: Fleming H. Revell Co., 1989.

Malphurs, Aubrey. *Planting Growing Churches for the 21 Century: A Comprehensive Guide for New Churches and Those Desiring Renewal*, 2nd ed. Grand Rapids, MI: Baker Book House, 1998.

Mull, Marlin. *A Biblical Church Planting Manual from the Book of Acts*. Eugene, OR: Wipf and Stock Publishers, 2003.

Shenk, David W. and Ervin R. Stutzman. *Creating Communities of the Kingdom: New Testament Models of Church Planting*. Scottdale, PA: Herald Press, 1988.

Stetzer, Edward J. *Planting Missional Churches*. Nashville, TN: B&H Publishers, 2006.

Ed Stetzer and Warren Bird. "The State of Church Planting in the United States: Research Overview and Qualitative Study of Primary Church Planting Entities." (*The Leadership Network*, 2007), *www.christianitytoday.com/assets /10228.pdf*.

V. Free Church Planting Resources

Cheyney, Tom, J. David Putman and Van Sanders, eds. *Seven Steps for Planting Churches*. Alpharetta, GA: North American Mission Board, SBC, 2003.

A free resource that describes a seven-step process for church planting. It is available at *www.churchplantingvillage.net*.

Davis, Don. *www.tumi.org*.

There are hundreds of free sermons, lectures, papers, diagrams, and other resources relevant to urban church planters developed by Dr. Don Davis at *www.tumi.org*.

———. *Winning the World: Facilitating Urban Church Planting Movements* (Foundations for Ministry Series). Wichita, KS: The Urban Ministry Institute Press, 2007.

This entire course on church planting movements is available for free at *www.biblicaltraining.org*. The website *www.biblicaltraining. org* has dozens of other free seminary courses on it as well.

Chris, Richard H., compiler. *Reaching a Nation through Church Planting*. Alpharetta, GA: North American Mission Board, SBC, 2002.

This book provides a collection of essays and resources on church planting. It is available for free at *www.churchplantingvillage.net*.

Scoggins, Dick. *Handbook for House Churches*. [on-line], accessed 1 December 1999, *http://genesis.acu.edu/cplant/archive/contr036*; Internet.

A free resource on planting house churches.

Ed Stetzer and Warren Bird, "The State of Church Planting in the United States: Research Overview and Qualitative Study of Primary Church Planting Entities" (*The Leadership Network*, 2007), *www.christianitytoday.com/assets /10228.pdf*.

This forty-page research report provides one of the most important big picture surveys of church planting in the United States currently available.

Gary Teja and John Wagenveld, eds. *Planting Healthy Churches*. Sauk Village, IL: Multiplication Network Ministries, 2015.

Free downloadable resource for students interested in church planting; PowerPoint and other teaching resources are also available.

VI. Women Church Planting

It can be difficult to find resources designed to support women involved in church planting. The following resources are either by or about women involved with church planting.

Allen, Tricia. "Single Church Planter: Singles Must Step Up to Lead." *Wesleyan Life* 6 (Summer 2011): 6-7.

Chilcote, Paul Wesley. "Lessons from the 'Society Planting': Paradigm of Early Methodist Women: 2012 AETE Presidential Address." *Witness: Journal of the Academy for Evangelism in Theological Education* 27 (2013):5–30.

Emmanuel Gospel Center. "The Unsolved Leadership Challenge: A Report on Greater Boston Church Planters and What They Believe about Women in Leadership," October 2014, *http://egc. org/sites/egc.org/files/The%20Unsolved%20Leadership%20 Challenge_Church%20Planters%20and%20Women%20in%20 Leadership_0.pdf*.

Dale, Felicity. *Getting Started: A Practical Guide to House Church Planting*. Karis Publishing, Inc., 2003.

Hamp, Angie. *Confessions of a Church Planter's Wife: Coming Clean about the Dirty Side of Church Planting*. N.P.: Create Space, 2011.

Hoover, Christine. *The Church Planting Wife: Help and Hope for Her Heart*. Chicago: Moody Publishers, 2013.

————. *Partners in Planting: Help and Encouragement for Church Planting Wives*. An ebook available at "Grace Covers Me." *www. gracecoversme.com*. 2014.

Thomas, Shari. *The Primary Sources of Stress and Satisfaction among PCA Church Planting Spouses*. Atlanta: Mission to North America, 2005.

Wilson, Linda. "Issues for Women in Church Planting." *Evangelical Missions Quarterly* 39, no.3 (July 2003): 362–366.

Reddin, Opal. *Planting Churches That Grow*. Springfield, MO: Central Bible College Press, 1990.

VII. Specialized Bibliographies

Dr. Don L. Davis, ed. *Planting Churches among the City's Poor: An Anthology of Urban Church Planting Resources*. Wichita, KS: The Urban Ministry Institute Press, 2015. 2 Volumes.*

Both volumes of the anthology include a five-page bibliography of resources especially relevant for urban church planters.

Joel Comiskey, "Cell Church Reading List and Bibliography," accessed June 2, 2015, *http://www.joelcomiskeygroup.com/articles/ churchLeaders/cellreadinglistbibliography.htm*.

Comiskey has written more than twenty-five books on cell churches. His doctoral research was on cell churches in Latin America and a number of his books are available in both Spanish and English. He currently teaches church planting at Tozer Seminary and consults with church plant groups interested in the cell church model. This bibliography lists eighty-one books he recommends on cell churches. They are ranked by him in the order that he would recommend a cell church planter to read them.

Ed Stetzer, "Church Planting Bibliography," *The Exchange*, April 20, 2009, *http://www.christianitytoday.com/edstetzer*.

This free online bibliography is an annotated list of seventy books related to church planting in North America. The content of each book is briefly summarized and Stetzer usually provides a one or two sentence evaluation of the books merits for church planters. Seven of the seventy books (10%) have some relevancy to urban church planting, although none are specifically concerned with the challenge of planting churches among the urban poor in North America. Two of the seventy books are written by women.

Hank Voss, "A Select Bibliography of Works by Rev. Dr. Don L. Davis," in *Black and Human: Rediscovering King as a Resource for Black Theology and Ethics*, ed. Don L. Davis. Wichita, KS: TUMI Press, 2015, pp. 295–310.

This bibliography covers more than 100 resources developed by Dr. Don Davis relevant to those involved with urban church planting and cross cultural missions.

Top Ten Principles for Elders

1. **Elders serve because we are willing, not because we must (1 Pet. 5.1-4).**

   So I exhort the elders among you, as a fellow elder and a witness of the sufferings of Christ, as well as a partaker in the glory that is going to be revealed: [2] shepherd the flock of God that is among you, exercising oversight, not under compulsion, but willingly, as God would have you; not for shameful gain, but eagerly; [3] not domineering over those in your charge, but being examples to the flock. [4] And when the chief Shepherd appears, you will receive the unfading crown of glory.

2. **Elders are leaders in pursuit of the character of Christ. Twenty-two of the twenty-four characteristics or qualifications of elders have to do with character (1 Tim. 3.1-7; Titus 1.5-9). We love God and people (Mark 12.29-31).**

   This is why I left you in Crete, so that you might put what remained into order, and appoint elders in every town as I directed you – [6] if anyone is above reproach, the husband of one wife, and his children are believers and not open to the charge of debauchery or insubordination. [7] For an overseer, as God's steward, must be above reproach. He must not be arrogant or quick-tempered or a drunkard or violent or greedy for gain, [8] but hospitable, a lover of good, self-controlled, upright, holy, and disciplined. [9] He must hold firm to the trustworthy word as taught, so that he may be able to give instruction in sound doctrine and also to rebuke those who contradict it (Titus 1.5-9).

   The saying is trustworthy: If anyone aspires to the office of overseer, he desires a noble task. [2] Therefore an overseer must be above reproach, the husband of one wife, sober-minded, self-controlled, respectable, hospitable, able to teach, [3] not a drunkard, not violent but gentle, not quarrelsome, not a lover of money. [4] He must manage his own household well, with all dignity keeping his children submissive, [5] for if someone does not know how to manage his own household, how will he care for God's church? [6] He must not be a recent convert, or he may become puffed up with conceit and fall into the condemnation of the devil. [7] Moreover, he must be well thought of by outsiders, so that he may not fall into disgrace, into a snare of the devil (1 Tim 3.1-7).

3. **Elders are servants (Matt. 20.26-27; 23.11-12); we are eager to serve even though it is often hard (1 Pet. 5.2). Our model in service is Christ and we seek to follow his example (John 13.3-17).**

It shall not be so among you. But whoever would be great among you must be your servant, [27] and whoever would be first among you must be your slave . . . [11] The greatest among you shall be your servant. [12] Whoever exalts himself will be humbled, and whoever humbles himself will be exalted (Matt. 20.26-27; 23.11-12).

Jesus, knowing that the Father had given all things into his hands, and that he had come from God and was going back to God, [4] rose from supper. He laid aside his outer garments, and taking a towel, tied it around his waist. [5] Then he poured water into a basin and began to wash the disciples' feet and to wipe them with the towel that was wrapped around him. [6] He came to Simon Peter, who said to him, "Lord, do you wash my feet?" [7] Jesus answered him, "What I am doing you do not understand now, but afterward you will understand." [8] Peter said to him, "You shall never wash my feet." Jesus answered him, "If I do not wash you, you have no share with me." [9] Simon Peter said to him, "Lord, not my feet only but also my hands and my head!" [10] Jesus said to him, "The one who has bathed does not need to wash, except for his feet, but is completely clean. And you are clean, but not every one of you." [11] For he knew who was to betray him; that was why he said, "Not all of you are clean." [12] When he had washed their feet and put on his outer garments and resumed his place, he said to them, "Do you understand what I have done to you? [13] You call me Teacher and Lord, and you are right, for so I am. [14] If I then, your Lord and Teacher, have washed your feet, you also ought to wash one another's feet. [15] For I have given you an example, that you also should do just as I have done to you. [16] Truly, truly, I say to you, a servant is not greater than his master, nor is a messenger greater than the one who sent him. [17] If you know these things, blessed are you if you do them (John 3.3-17).

4. **Elders live as examples for the church they lead (1 Pet. 5.3). We examine ourselves (Acts 20.28-31a) and obey the Lord's voice (Cf. Ezek. 34).**

Pay careful attention to yourselves and to all the flock, in which the Holy Spirit has made you overseers, to care for the church of God, which he obtained with his own blood. [29] I know that after my departure fierce wolves will come in among you, not sparing the flock; [30] and from among your own selves will arise men speaking twisted things, to draw away the disciples after them. [31] Therefore be alert. . . (Acts 20.28-31a).

5. **The elders' most important responsibility is to make space for hearing the Word and listening to the Lord in prayer (Acts 6.4; 1 Tim. 3.2; Titus 1.9; James 5.13–20). We are devoted to the Word of God.**

But we will devote ourselves to prayer and to the ministry of the word (Acts 6.4).

Let the elders who rule well be considered worthy of double honor, especially those who labor in preaching and teaching (1 Tim. 5.17).

Is anyone among you suffering? Let him pray. Is anyone cheerful? Let him sing praise. [14] Is anyone among you sick? Let him call for the elders of the church, and let them pray over him, anointing him with oil in the name of the Lord. [15] And the prayer of faith will save the one who is sick, and the Lord will raise him up. And if he has committed sins, he will be forgiven. [16] Therefore, confess your sins to one another and pray for one another, that you may be healed. The prayer of a righteous person has great power as it is working. [17] Elijah was a man with a nature like ours, and he prayed fervently that it might not rain, and for three years and six months it did not rain on the earth. [18] Then he prayed again, and heaven gave rain, and the earth bore its fruit. [19] My brothers, if anyone among you wanders from the truth and someone brings him back, [20] let him know that whoever brings back a sinner from his wandering will save his soul from death and will cover a multitude of sins (James 5.13-20).

6. **Elders prioritize a clear conscience before God (Acts 20.28). We know we will ultimately give account to God for how we have shepherded God's people (Heb. 13.7). We value the fear of the Lord (Prov. 9.10).**

Pay careful attention to yourselves. . . . (Acts 20.28a).

Obey your leaders and submit to them, for they are keeping watch over your souls, as those who will have to give an account. Let them do this with joy and not with groaning, for that would be of no advantage to you (Heb. 13.7).

The fear of the Lord is the beginning of wisdom, and the knowledge of the Holy One is insight (Prov. 9.10).

7. **Elders are courageous about speaking the Word of the God (Acts 20.20, 26-27, 31). We are not afraid to speak the truth in love (Eph. 4.15-16; Ezek. 33.1-9).**

". . . how I did not shrink from declaring to you anything that was profitable, and teaching you in public and from house to house . . . Therefore I testify to you this day that I am innocent of the blood of all, [27] for I did not shrink from declaring to you the whole counsel of God. . . . Therefore be alert, remembering that for three years I did not cease night or day to admonish every one with tears" (Acts 20.20, 26-27, 31).

The word of the Lord came to me: [2] "Son of man, speak to your people and say to them, If I bring the sword upon a land, and the people of the land take a man from among them, and make him their watchman, [3] and if he sees the sword coming upon the land and blows the trumpet and warns the people, [4] then if anyone who hears the sound of the trumpet does not take warning, and the sword comes and takes him away, his blood shall be upon his own head. [5] He heard the sound of the trumpet and did not take warning; his blood shall be upon himself. But if he had taken warning, he would have saved his life. [6] But if the watchman sees the sword coming and does not blow the trumpet, so that the people are not warned, and the sword comes and takes any one of them, that person is taken away in his iniquity, but his blood I will require at the watchman's hand. [7] "So you, son of man, I have made a watchman for the house of Israel. Whenever you hear a word from my mouth, you shall give them warning from me. [8] If I say to the wicked, O wicked one, you shall surely die, and you do not speak to warn the wicked to turn from his way, that wicked person shall die in his iniquity, but his blood I will require at your hand. [9] But if you warn the wicked to turn from his way, and he does not turn from his way, that person shall die in his iniquity, but you will have delivered your soul. (Ezek. 33.1-9).

Rather, speaking the truth in love, we are to grow up in every way into him who is the head, into Christ, [16] from whom the whole body, joined and held together by every joint with which it is equipped, when each part is working properly, makes the body grow so that it builds itself up in love (Eph. 4.15-16).

8. **Elders work with servant leaders (*diaconos*) to equip the church for ministry and mission (Eph. 4.11-12). We value other leaders in the church.**

   And he gave the apostles, the prophets, the evangelists, the shepherds and teachers, [12] to equip the saints for the work of ministry, for building up the body of Christ (Eph. 4.11-12).

9. **Elders exercise oversight like shepherds (1 Pet. 5.2; Gal. 5.22-6.2; cf. Ezek. 34).**

   Shepherd the flock of God that is among you, exercising oversight, not under compulsion, but willingly (1 Pet. 5.2).

10. **Elders are honored at our church. We treat elders with great honor and respect (1 Tim. 5.17; 1 Thess. 5.12–13; Heb. 13.7).**

    Let the elders who rule well be considered worthy of double honor, especially those who labor in preaching and teaching (1 Tim. 5.17).

    We ask you, brothers, to respect those who labor among you and are over you in the Lord and admonish you, [13] and to esteem them very highly in love because of their work. Be at peace among yourselves (1 Thess. 5.12-13).

    Remember your leaders, those who spoke to you the word of God. Consider the outcome of their way of life, and imitate their faith (Heb. 13.7).

Preaching and Teaching

Dr. Hank Voss

"Preach the Gospel through the Scriptures, in the power of the Holy Spirit."

Step	Strategy	Scripture
1. Pray and Plan	First, our daily walk must continually be in the Word (listen, read, study, memorize, meditate, apply). Secondly, prayer must begin and continue throughout the whole process. Without the anointing of the Holy Spirit, no eternal fruit will be found. Third, if preaching every week, a plan is essential. The Revised Common Lectionary (RCL) offers a Christ Centered plan that can be adapted whenever needed. It preaches through the whole Bible over a three year period, but always keeps the focus on Christ.	Pss. 1; 119; Josh. 1.8; Eph. 6.18-20
2. Study Scripture	At TUMI, we encourage pastors to study the Scriptures using a three step method; Step One: Understanding the Original Situation; Step Two: Find General Principles; Step Three: Apply General Principles Today. Don't be afraid to preach what you have heard in Scripture. The preacher's greatest virtue is courage, and his greatest vice is cowardliness.	1 Tim. 4.13; 2 Tim. 2.15; Josh. 1.9
3. Study Audience	The better we know our audience, the better we will be able to speak God's Word to them in their particular context. The first step to knowing one's audience is to pray for them. Secondly, even while preaching, keep listening.	2 Tim. 1.3
4. Outline or Write Sermon	All Scripture is valuable, and every Scripture contains deep mysteries. But since we who preach are finite, we must listen carefully to what the Holy Spirit would have us speak from each particular text to each particular audience. The Holy Spirit may surprise us last minute, but it is wise to outline or write out one's message ahead of time – especially in the first ten years of preaching.	2 Tim. 3.16-17; Matt. 28.19-20
5. Preach Message	Dr. Don Davis suggests there are three essential steps to preaching effective sermons. 1) Establish **Contact** with the hearers through spotlighting issues, concerns, ideas or experiences that resonate with the audience; 2) Deliver **Content** of Scripture. Paint a picture of the Scripture's message to show not merely tell the Bibles theme. 3) Make **Connections** between the Bible's content and particular responses of God's people.	2 Tim. 4.1-2

Step	Strategy	Scripture
6. Evaluate and Give God Glory	For at least your first ten years as a preacher, always ask a friend to be ready to give you a *torta* (sandwich) after you preach. First the bread (something encouraging), then the meat (something to work on), finally another piece of bread (another encouraging thing). Whenever you preach, always give the Father glory for what the Holy Spirit does in drawing people to his Son through the preaching of his Word.	1 Tim. 4.16

More Resources for Preaching

Planning your preaching. Dr. Don Davis uses the Revised Common Lectionary to plan his preaching. His sermons and outlines can be found at *www.tumimedia.org*. TUMI also produces a calendar and devotional book every year that can be used to plan the next year's preaching. These resources are available at *http://www.tumistore.org/church-resources*.

Three-Step Bible Study Method. More information on these three steps can be downloaded at *www.tumi-la.org* under the "resources" tab and by clicking "exegetical papers."

Books and Audio

Cothen, Joe. *Equipped for Good Work: A Guide for Pastors.* Gretna, LA: Pelican, 2002. This book is used in two TUMI classes. It has two chapters on preaching and some helpful planning worksheets for sermons and sermon plans.

"Invitation to Biblical Preaching." Notes (in English or Spanish) and four MP3 Lectures can be downloaded at *www.TUMI-LA.org*. Dr. Don Sunukijian's book, *Invitation to Biblical Preaching: Proclaiming Truth with Clarity and Relevance* can be purchased at Amazon in English or Spanish.

Four TUMI classes especially helpful for improving your preaching are:

1. Don Davis. *Bible Interpretation*, vol. 5, 16 vols. Capstone Curriculum. Wichita, KS: The Urban Ministry Institute, 2005.

2. Don Davis. *New Testament Witness to Christ and His Kingdom*, vol. 13, 16 vols. Capstone Curriculum. Wichita, KS: The Urban Ministry Institute, 2005.

3. Don Davis. *Old Testament Witness to Christ and His Kingdom*, vol. 9, 16 vols. Capstone Curriculum. Wichita, KS: The Urban Ministry Institute, 2005.

4. Don Davis. *The Equipping Ministry*, vol. 15, 16 vols. Capstone Curriculum. Wichita, KS: The Urban Ministry Institute, 2005.

Suffering for the Gospel
The Cost of Discipleship and Servant-Leadership
Rev. Dr. Don L. Davis

To embrace the Gospel and not to be shamed of it (Rom. 1.16) is to bear the stigma and reproach of the One who called you into service (2 Tim. 3.12). Practically, this may mean the loss of comfort, convenience, and even life itself (John 12.24-25). As ambassadors of Christ, appealing to men and women to come to him, we must not even count our lives as dear to ourselves, but be ever willing to lay our very lives down for the Good News (Acts 20.24). All of Christ's apostles endured insults, rebukes, lashes, and rejections by the enemies of their Master (cf. 2 Cor. 6, 11). Each of them sealed their calling to Christ and to his doctrines with their blood in exile, torture, and martyrdom. Listed below are the fates of the apostles according to traditional accounts.

Matthew suffered martyrdom by being slain with a sword at a distant city of Ethiopia.

Mark expired at Alexandria, after being cruelly dragged through the streets of that city.

Luke was hanged upon an olive tree in the land of Greece.

John was put in a caldron of boiling oil, but escaped death in a miraculous manner, and was afterward exiled to and branded at Patmos.

Peter was crucified at Rome in an inverted position, with his head downward.

James, the Greater, was beheaded at Jerusalem.

James, the Less, was thrown from a lofty pinnacle of the temple, and then beaten to death with a fuller's club.

Bartholomew was flayed alive.

Andrew was bound to a cross, where he preached to his persecutors until he died.

Thomas was run through the body with a lance at Coromandel in the East Indies.

Jude was shot to death with arrows.

Matthias was first stoned and then beheaded.

Barnabas of the Gentiles was stoned to death at Salonica.

Paul, after various tortures and persecutions, was at length beheaded at Rome by the Emperor Nero.

And what more shall I say? For time will fail me if I tell of Gideon, Barak, Samson, Jephthah, of David and Samuel and the prophets, who by faith conquered kingdoms, performed acts of righteousness, obtained promises, shut the mouths of lions, quenched the power of fire, escaped the edge of the sword, from weakness were made strong, became mighty in war, put foreign armies to flight. Women received back their dead by resurrection; and others were tortured, not accepting their release, in order that they might obtain a better resurrection; and others experienced mockings and scourgings, yes, also chains and imprisonment. They were stoned, they were sawn in two, they were tempted, they were put to death with the sword; they went about in sheepskins, in goatskins, being destitute, afflicted, ill-treated (men of who the world was not worthy), wandering in deserts and mountains and caves and holes in the ground. And all these, having gained approval through their faith, did not receive what was promised, because God had provided something better for us, so that apart from us they should not be made perfect.

~ Hebrews 11.32-40

"Framework" for an Urban Church Association

Rev. Bob Engel

I. Core Commitments

A. Mission

B. Vision

C. Objectives

D. Theological

II. A Shared Spirituality/Way of Wisdom

A. A shared history and identity

B. A shared liturgy and celebration

C. A shared membership

D. A shared catechism and doctrine

E. A shared government and authority

F. A shared leadership development structure

G. A shared financial policy and procedure

H. A shared care and support ministry

I. A shared evangelism and outreach

III. Key Elements

A. Share in fellowship

B. Share resources

C. Share in mission and ministry

IV. Strategy

    A. Levels of Commitment

        1. Members

        2. Affiliates

        3. Observers

    B. Communication

    C. Participation

        1. Monthly - Local

        2. Quarterly – District

        3. Annually - Regional

A Quick Guide to an Urban Church Association

A QUICK GUIDE
TO AN
URBAN CHURCH
ASSOCIATION

urban church association

Table of Contents

FRAMEWORK

PURPOSE STATEMENT: WHO WE ARE

MISSION: OUR CALLING

OBJECTIVES: HOW WE ACCOMPLISH OUR MISSION

THEOLOGICAL COMMITMENTS: WHAT WE STAND ON

CORE COMMITMENTS: HOW WE FELLOWSHIP TOGETHER

PARTICIPATION: HOW WE CHOOSE TO OPERATE AS AN ASSOCIATION

LEVELS OF COMMITMENT: WAYS TO BE INVOLVED

2

CORE COMPONENTS

PURPOSE STATEMENT: The UCA's purpose is to expand and advance God's Kingdom among the urban poor by evangelizing, the making of disciples, planting reproducing churches, and establishing regional associations that will lead to the facilitating of church plant movements for the glory of God.

MISSION: The UCA is a mission focused network of churches and leaders dedicated to one another's growth and welfare as we identify, equip, and release called and gifted Christian leaders to plant new church plants and pastor existing churches that will multiply and grow.

OBJECTIVES:

1. Fellowship – to encourage, inspire and strengthen one another in vital Christian discipleship through regular gatherings and consistent communication.
2. Resource – to pool our gifts, knowledge, and strengths for kingdom minded work.
3. Mission – to work together as a unified Church towards our mission and vision of transforming our city and region for the glory of God.

THEOLOGICAL COMMITMENT: As members of The Urban Church Association we commit to defend the "Great Tradition" (the faith "that has been believed, in all places, by all people, at all times") as expressed in the Nicene Creed.

CORE COMMITMENTS:

Endearment
> We are devoted to God and each other because God loved us first and sent His son for our salvation. Apart from Him we can do nothing for His glory in the work of ministry (I John 4:19-21; John 3:16; John 15:1-8).

Evangelism
> We sow the seed of the gospel broadly and abundantly (I Corinthians 9:16-23; Acts 1:8; Acts 8:4).

3

Equipping

We make disciples, teaching them to obey all that Jesus commanded (Matthew 28:18-20).

Empowering

We release disciples to lead the church (Acts 14:23).

Embrace

We gather as an Association for fellowship, to share resources, and to participate in missions ministry (I Corinthians 1:2; Philippians 1:5).

PARTICIPATION

- **Monthly – Through monthly UCA attendance**
- **Quarterly – Pastoral fellowship times**
- **Annually – Unity Service and Leadership Retreat**

EVERY ASSOCIATION MEMBER ALSO PARTICIPATES IN THE FOLLOWING:

A shared membership: The UCA is comprised of churches that value community and are passionate about working alongside likeminded churches for mutual health, leadership training, and church planting. UCA churches work together to accomplish the difficult task of building the Kingdom in the urban context.

A shared fellowship: Members will gather monthly to build the unity and strength of the body through, fellowship, worship, prayer, teaching, and encouragement. The UCA members take annual leadership retreats together, hold each other accountable and uphold those who are struggling in our midst. The UCA also intentionally cares not only for pastoral leaders, but for their spouse and families when a need arises. The UCA strives to be a holistic organization that cares not only for church health, but for pastoral, and family health as well.

A shared structure of operation: The UCA follows a predetermined framework that will work to ensure healthy communication, unity of the body, and growth of its members. Each decision that the UCA makes will be agreed upon by the whole body, to preserve unity of vision, and purpose within the body.

A shared support system for pastors and their churches: The UCA will uphold each other and their families through prayer and community as they minister together. Pastors and their spouses will have the ability to meet on a regular basis with fellow ministers and find support and encouragement in the midst of ministry. The UCA will also strive to come alongside and minister to and with any church within the association. If a particular church in the association is struggling with leadership change, financial difficulties, or is in need of prayer ministry the UCA will gather and find appropriate ways to support that church within the UCA body.

A shared leadership development structure: In order to ensure the reproduction of quality leadership in sending leaders and starting new churches, it is vital for each church to fully utilize the training of The Urban Ministry Institute (tumi.org) or implement a clear leadership training process specific to each church.

A shared mission, vision, and outreach: UCA members will plan, set goals, and implement strategic initiatives towards evangelism, making disciples and church planting. UCA churches reproduce their church through church planting. Churches will utilize The Urban Ministry Institute to equip emerging leaders for the urban church and empower church planting movements to reach and transform the inner cities of America and around the world.

A shared care and support ministry: Members will pray for one another and share resources with other association members. The association can provide pastors to guest speak if a pastor is not present or is in need of rest. The association will strive to care for each other and share resources that are beneficial to each church body. Such resources would include counseling, prayer ministry, and justice and compassion resources.

LEVELS OF COMMITMENT

All Urban Church Associations will have two possible levels of involvement: members and affiliates.

- **Members – Fully invested and committed Churches**
- **Affiliates – Churches supporting UCA goals and initiatives**

Members:
- Members must agree with our purpose, objectives and common commitments.
- Members must agree to participate fully in the strategy to which the association has committed itself.
- Only members will have voting rights in the association.
- Members participate in whatever communication tool is adopted by the association as one way to demonstrate obedience to our Lord's command to "love one another."
- Members participate with the UCA monthly, quarterly and annually:
  - Monthly – Every association church sends at least one leader to the association meeting.
  - Quarterly – The UCA will hold pastoral fellowship gatherings.

6

- Annually – All churches and their leaders in the association will gather for worship, celebration, encouragement, the Word and prayer in a unity service.
  - UCA leadership will also have an annual retreat time for fellowship, strategy development and refreshment.

Affiliates:
- Affiliate churches must be in agreement with our purpose and commitments.
- Affiliate churches must be willing to come alongside and support our mission, vision, and objectives through prayer, partnerships, and resourcing.
- Affiliate churches must attend at least one monthly gathering per year to remain a part of the association.
- Affiliate churches will remain in regular communication with the association and annually request affiliate status.

Visitor Policy:
- Various pastors and leaders are welcome to observe and participate in a UCA gathering. However observers should be hosted by a full member of the association. Visitors should be brought in intentionally and should only be invited if they are looking to join the UCA as members, affiliates, or as possible ministry partners.
- If a pastor would like to bring a visitor to the UCA please inform the UCA facilitator ahead of the fellowship time.

UCA STRUCTURE AND GOVERNMENTAL PROCEDURES

- Electing a Facilitator of the UCA
  - Facilitation of the UCA will transition from one pastor to another every two years. This period can be as short as one year if the association or facilitator deems it necessary.
  - The pastor can only be elected if he/she volunteers for the position.
  - The UCA facilitator will be elected through unanimous vote only.
- Responsibility of Facilitator
  - The facilitator will faithfully uphold the commitments of the UCA and will strive to grow and maintain the health of the UCA.
  - The facilitator will faithfully attend each gathering. (If an emergency should occur he/she will be responsible for temporarily passing on facilitation of the group.)
- UCA's commitment to the Facilitator
  - The UCA will faithfully support and follow the lead of the facilitator.
  - Major decisions regarding the UCA and its initiatives cannot be made by the facilitator alone but must be put to a vote by the members for approval. Any changes that are made must be unanimous to uphold the unity of the UCA.
  - If a facilitator is failing in faithfulness (to commitments, leadership, or is abusing authority) the members of the UCA can call a vote to remove that pastor from his/her role of authority.
  - If any areas of theology of vision threatens to break unity of the UCA, the UCA will gather together to discuss as to set forward a decision regarding the disagreement. This should be avoided if possible as the heart of the UCA should be unity before personal preference.

8

MEMBERSHIP REQUIREMENTS

CHURCH NAME _____

COMMITS TO THE FOLLOWING:

- ☐ Supporting the UCA's purpose, mission, objectives, and theological commitments.

- ☐ Participate fully in the strategies agreed upon by the UCA.

- ☐ Communicating and interacting with one another in a way that demonstrates obedience to our Lord's command to "love one another" and to build healthy, cooperative relationships with other members of the association.

- ☐ Sending at least one leader to monthly fellowships.

- ☐ Pastors, Spouses, and Elders who are in pastoral training will gather for fellowship and encouragement quarterly.

- ☐ Utilize membership in the association to promote unity and growth of the association.

_____

Church Name

_____   _____

Pastor's Signature   Date

9

Suggested Outline for Monthly Fellowship

Prayer

Joining together as a body to pray on behalf of our families, churches, and community to prepare for God's transforming work.

Worship

Spending intentional time together, lifting up the name of the Lord, and glorifying Him through our voices, words, and actions. We worship together in order to give God glory, and align our hearts with His.

Support and Encouragement

This is a time to acknowledge our weaknesses, our hardships, our victories in Christ, and celebrating God's redemptive work together.

Training

Teaching each other effective tools for, evangelism, discipleship, leadership training, personal and family care, and church growth.

Planning

Engaging pastors to work together to target areas of ministry as a UCA. Planning events, and developing strategies for church and UCA growth.

Exhortation

Encouraging and challenging each other to fulfill God's calling on their lives and in their churches to the fullest extent. This is a time designed to exhort each other pursue God's Kingdom work with passion and strength, and should leave each Pastor prepared for the work that God has called them to in ministry.

10

WE BELIEVE
WE NEED EACH OTHER
And though a man might prevail against one who is alone, two will withstand him—a threefold cord is not quickly broken. Ecclesiastes 3:12
3701 E 13th St N Wichita, KS 67208 | worldimpactmidwest.org/uca

Evangel Session Summary

Dr. Hank Voss

I. Summary of Evangel's Sessions and Activities

Sessions	Devotionals and Seminars	Exercises
Session 1 (5 hrs, 45 mins)	**Devotional 1: The Power of Praise**	
	1. What Is a Church?	
	2. Church Planting Overview	
	3. Using Wisdom in Ministry: The PWR Process	
		1. Establishing Context
		2. Defining Vision and Values
		Presentation 1
Session 2 (4 hrs, 45 mins)	**Devotional 2: Freedom in Christ**	
	4. The Difference That Difference Makes: Cross-Cultural Church Planting and the Issue of Culture	
	5. Theology of the Poor for Church Planters	
	6. Building the Team for Success: Principles of Effective Team Play	
		3. Prepare: Be the Church
		Presentation 2

Sessions	Devotionals and Seminars	Exercises
Session 3 (5 hrs, 45 mins)	Devotional 3: Prayer Is the Walkie-Talkie of Faith	
	7. Evangelism and Follow-up as Mission: Incorporation into the Body of Christ	
	8. Christus Victor: An Ancient Biblical Motif for Connecting the Dots in Urban Spiritual Formation and Cross-Cultural Missions	
	9. Conducting Events and Projects	
		4. Launch: Expand the Church
		5. Assemble: Establish the Church
		Presentation 3

Sessions	Devotionals and Seminars	Exercises
Session 4 (6 hrs, 15 mins)	Devotional 4: God Is a Warrior	
	10. Effective Discipling in the Church	
	11. Discipling Urban Christian Leaders	
	12. Preaching and Teaching: The Fine Art of Communicating the Truth	
	13. Selecting a Credible Criteria for Independence: Navigating toward a Healthy Transition	
		6. Nurture: Mature the Church
		7. Transition: Release the Church
		Presentation 4
Session 5 (3 hrs, 15 mins)	Devotional 5: Adapt to Win	
	14. The Importance of Review	
		8. Bringing It All Together: The Team Charter
		Presentation 5
(1 hr)	Commissioning Service	

II. Core Content Summary

Devotional/Seminar	Author	Core Content Summary
Session 1		
Devotional 1 The Power of Praise	Davis (33-40)	Experiencing the Power of Praise Seven Reasons to Praise Five Principles for Powerful Praise
Seminar 1 What Is a Church?	Davis (47-50)	Definition of Church Church Planting, the Story of God and Sacred Roots Three Expressions of Church
Seminar 2 Church Planting Overview	Davis (54-64)	PLANT Evangelism, Equipping, and Empowering Pauline Perspective on Church Planting Ten Principles of Church Planting
Seminar 3 Using Wisdom in Ministry: The PWR Process	Allsman (65-76)	Using Wisdom in Ministry Prepare, Work, Review (PWR) Introducing the Church Plant Charter
Session 2		
Devotional 2 Freedom in Christ	Davis (121-132)	Freedom From Freedom to Be and to Do
Seminar 4 The Difference That Difference Makes: Cross- Cultural Church Planting and the Issue of Culture	Davis (139-154)	The Gospel vs. Culture in an Age of Global Urbanization The Concept of Difference as Culture Implications of Culture for Evangelism A Biblical Theology of Culture
Seminar 5 Theology of the Poor for Church Planters	Cornett (155-168)	The Urban Poor as Mission Field Participating in Jesus' Mission to the Poor Grace and Mission with the Poor Mission to the Poor Characterized by Respect and Expectation
Seminar 6 Building the Team for Success: Principles of Effective Team Play	Davis (169-184)	Ten Universal Principles for Church Plant Teams Diagnostic Team Effectiveness Rating Chart Using Ten Principles

Devotional/Seminar	Author	Core Content Summary
Session 3		
Devotional 3 Prayer Is the Walkie-Talkie of Faith	Davis (223-229)	Prayer Is a War Time Walkie-Talkie, Not a Domestic Intercom Let God Arise: A Dedicated Prayer Movement for the Cities of the World Seven A's of Let God Arise
Seminar 7 Evangelism and Follow-up as Mission: Incorporation into the Body of Christ	Davis (237-248)	Evangelism as Sharing the Good News Follow-Up: Incorporating and Nurturing New Members in God's Family
Seminar 8 Christus Victor: An Ancient Biblical Motif for Connecting the Dots in Urban Spiritual Formation and Cross-Cultural Missions	Davis (249-274)	"To Christ the Victory" as a Rally Cry "To Christ the Victory" as Measure for Ministry and Witness "To Christ the Victory" in Our Time: Using the Church Year Benefits of Fleshing Out Christ as Victor in Our Worship and Mission
Seminar 9 Conducting Events and Projects	Allsman (275-283)	Projects in the Bible and in Church Planting Prepare, Work, Review Case Studies
Session 4		
Devotional 4 God Is a Warrior	Davis (341-352)	The Lord Is a Warrior Who Liberates (e.g. Exodus) The Lord Fights with His People (Conquest of Canaan) The Lord Will Win (Promised Land) Implications of Spiritual Warfare for Urban Church Planting

Devotional/Seminar	Author	Core Content Summary
Seminar 10 Effective Discipling in the Church	Davis (359-376)	Great Commission, Kingdom of God, and the Church Why Disciple? What Does It Look Like? The Role of the Discipler The Role of the Local Church in Discipleship Internal Conviction and Internal Persuasion The Word of God and the Disciple Discipleship "How To's" and Fruit
Seminar 11 Discipling Urban Christian Leaders	Davis (377-382)	Four Markers for Leadership Development in the Church Commission, Character, Competence, Community
Seminar 12 Preaching and Teaching: The Fine Art of Communicating the Truth	Davis (383-393)	Goals and Importance of Preaching the Teaching Gifts in the Church Images of the Biblical Teacher and Preacher Contemporary Educational Models for Teaching (Richards, Groome) TUMI's Model for Contextual Teaching and Preaching Contact, Content, Connection
Seminar 13 Selecting a Credible Criteria for Independence: Navigating toward a Healthy Transition	Davis (394-398)	Principles for Cross-Cultural Church Planters Eight Categories for Evaluation
Session 5		
Devotional 5 Adapt to Win	Davis (443-449)	Understand Church Planting's Axioms of Adaptation Trouble Will Come; Change Will Come; Team Is Necessary
Seminar 14 The Importance of Review	Allsman (457-460)	Freedom and Adaptation at Half Time Review and Prepare Again

III. Prerequisite Reading Assignments

These readings are to be completed before attendance at Evangel School. The page numbers listed refer to *Front Matters: Prerequisite Readings for the Evangel School of Urban Church Planting*.

Session	Team Exercise	Reading Assignments
Session 1	Seeing the Big Picture: Establishing the Context	"Preface: How to Use This Guidebook" (pp. 11–22) "Introduction: Sacred Roots, Church Planting, and the Great Tradition" (pp. 23–28)
Session 1	Seeing the Big Picture: Establishing Values and Vision	"A Call to An Ancient Evangelical Future" (pp. 29-32) "On World Impact's 'Empowering the Urban Poor'" (pp. 36-41)
Session 2 Session 3 Session 4	Prepare: Be the Church Launch: Expand the Church Assemble: Establish the Church Nurture: Mature the Church Transition: Release the Church	"Church Planting Overview" (pp. 42-55) "Church Planting Models" (pp. 33-35)
Session 5	Bringing It All Together: The Team Charter	"Summary of Key Cross-Cultural Church Planting Principles" (pp. 56-61)

IV. Team Exercises

All page numbers in the table below refer to *Ripe for Harvest*.

Session	Team Exercise	Exercise Purpose	Reading Assignments, Team Discussions, and Team Worksheets
Session 1 Exercise 1	Seeing the Big Picture: Establishing the Context (pp. 79-92)	• Comprehend the role of the Church in God's Kingdom-building effort. • Drafting a brief narrative of the history and origin of your church plant team and its call. • Mapping out what the target area, demographics, and resources available for this work. • Do a SWOT analysis on the internal strengths and weaknesses and external opportunities and threats you will face in this effort.	RA: *Preface: How to Use This Guidebook* (pp. 11-22) RA: *Introduction: Sacred Roots, Church Planting, and the Great Tradition* (pp. 23-28) RA: *A Call to an Ancient Evangelical Future* (pp. 83-86) RA: *Church Planting Models* (pp. 87-89) RA: *What Is a Church?* (pp. 90-92) TD: *Seeing the Big Picture: Establishing Context* (11 questions, pp. 81-82)
Session 1 Exercise 2	Seeing the Big Picture: Establishing Values and Vision (pp. 95-102)	• Dialogue about possible pictures of what we believe God has put on our hearts to achieve. • Discuss the various alternative values openly and carefully together. • Reaching consensus together on our shared values, bringing them together clearly and concisely. • Craft a vision statement that describes what we hope to see God do in our effort.	RA: *Seeing the Big Picture: Defining Values/Vision* (p. 95-99) TW: *Values Ranking Worksheet (Individual)* (p. 100) TW: *Values Ranking Worksheet (Team)* (p. 101) TD: *Seeing the Big Picture: Defining Values/Vision* (5 questions, p. 102) TP: Team Prayer

Session	Team Exercise	Exercise Purpose	Reading Assignments, Team Discussions, and Team Worksheets
Session 2 Exercise 3	Prepare: Be the Church (pp. 188-205)	• Seek God regarding the target population and community. • Seek God regarding the formation of your church plant team, the initial church which community believers can join. • Select reproducible models to contextualize standard church practices. • Initiate discussions about associations, denominations, or other affiliations.	RA: *On World Impact's "Empowering the Urban Poor"* (pp. 195-200) RA: *Responding to God's Call to the Poor* (pp. 201-202) RA: *As You Form Your Plan, Keep Your Overall Purpose in Mind* (pp. 203-204) RA: *Key Roles of a Church Planting Team* (p. 205) TD: *Prepare: Be the Church* (40 questions, pp. 191-194) TP: Team Prayer
Session 3 Exercise 4	Launch: Expand the Church (pp. 288-291)	Brainstorm and discuss how you might: • Invite mature believers to join the church. • Recruit and organize volunteers to conduct ongoing evangelistic events and holistic outreach to win associates and neighbors to Christ. • Engage the community as God leads and follow-up new believers. • Adjust if there is no response in your initial target area.	TD: *Launch: Expand the Church* (15 questions, pp. 290-291) TP: Team Prayer

Session	Team Exercise	Exercise Purpose	Reading Assignments, Team Discussions, and Team Worksheets
Session 3 Exercise 5	Assemble: Establish the Church (pp. 296-321)	Brainstorm and discuss how you might: • Train others through cell groups or Bible studies to follow up and disciple new believers. • Continue evangelism with *oikos* groups • Identify and train emerging leaders, focusing on preparing leaders for Transition at a satellite campus of The Urban Ministry Institute (TUMI). • Assemble the groups where the Word is rightly preached, the sacraments are rightly administered and discipline is rightly ordered. • Announce to the neighborhood the beginning of public worship.	RA: *Welcome to the Family: Membership Responsibilities and Leadership* (p. 301-321) TD: *Assemble: Establish the Church* (23 questions, pp. 298-300) TP: Team Prayer
Session 4 Exercise 6	Nurture: Mature the Church (pp. 402-411)	Brainstorm and discuss how you might: • Establish relationships and structures to disciple individuals, groups, and church leaders. • Help growing, faithful members identify and fulfill key roles in the new church based on their burden and gifting. • Create infrastructure and processes which give clear governance to the body.	RA: *The Dynamic Dozen: Foundational Principles of the Nurture Phase* (pp. 406-409) RA: *Drafting a Constitution: Key Tool for Nurturing Community* (p. 410) RA: *Nurture and Transition Dimensions* (p. 411) TD: *Nurture: Mature the Church* (14 questions, pp. 404-405) TP: Team Prayer

Session	Team Exercise	Exercise Purpose	Reading Assignments, Team Discussions, and Team Worksheets
Session 4 Exercise 7	Transition: Release the Church (pp. 416-425)	Brainstorm and discuss how you might: • Commission the church to its mission in the world. • Appoint elders and leaders, and enable the church to select and install the pastor. • Finalize all infrastructure to ensure church independence and autonomy. • Build and foster church affiliations and associations.	RA: *The Self-Governing Seven: Central Principles for the Transition Phase* (pp. 421-423) RA: *Transition* (pp. 424-425) TD: *Transition: Release the Church* (12 questions, pp. 419-420) TP: Team Prayer
Session 5 Exercise 8	Bringing It All Together: The Team Charter (pp. 464-467)	Fill out a charter that details your overall church planting strategy, including major items such things as overall goal deadline, who will serve as field coach, under whose authority, with what team members, for what expression of the church.	TD: *Bringing It All Together* (pp. 464-466) TD: *Evangel School of Urban Church Planting Charter Form* (p. 467) TP: Team Prayer

Additional Readings,
Seminars, and Team Exercises

TUMI

READING

What Is a Church?

Rev. Dr. Don Davis

The Church is the community of God's people who acknowledge Jesus as Lord, who carry out his purposes on earth, comprised of everyone past, present and future, from every place on the earth and throughout history. The Church is God's agent of the Kingdom of God, the body and bride of Christ, who as custodian of God's revelation has responded to his work in theology, worship, discipleship and witness (see *The Story of God: Our Sacred Roots*). Each local church is an embassy, serving as an outpost of his Kingdom.

There is a single story revealed in the Bible (see *Once Upon a Time*). The God of the universe, existing in three Persons (Father, Son, and Holy Spirit), is the Creator of all things, visible and invisible, who made human beings in His own image. Despite the rebellion of Satan and the first human pair, God sent a Savior who would overcome evil and win everything back for the glory of God.

In this unfolding drama, there is an objective foundation (the sovereign work of God in creation, Israel, and Christ) and a subjective response (the Church's participation in God's Kingdom). On the objective side, the Father is the Author and Director of the Story, the Son is the Champion and Lead Actor of the Story, and the Spirit is the Narrator and Interpreter of the Story. The Bible is the Script and Testimony of the Story.

On the subjective side, the People of the Story respond in orthodox theology as confessors of the faith, worship together as royal priests, are formed as disciples of Christ as sojourners in this world, and witness to God's love as his holy ambassadors. This understanding creates the foundation for every expression in a local church (see *Christus Victor: An Integrated Vision for the Christian Life and Witness*) including doctrine, use of gifts, spirituality, justice and compassion, evangelism and mission, and worship.

The Church is called to faithfully embody and defend God's revelation through the apostle's testimony, fulfilling its identity as one, holy, universal, and apostolic community (see *There Is a River*). The Church is to faithfully pass down what the Spirit gave to Christ's people in terms of what they believe, how they are to worship, and what their Scriptures would be. These foundational beliefs undergird the faith for all believers, everywhere, and is called the "Great Tradition" (see *The Nicene Creed*) which is embraced by all orthodox believers. This represents the teaching and practice of the apostles, written in the Bible, summarized in the creeds and councils of the Church, and defended by believers throughout history.

Church planting is simply an extension of the subjective expression of this Grand Cosmic Drama. A church plant is a new leaf on the Tree of God's design, going back to its Sacred Roots. Our identity is based on the guardianship and cross-cultural transference of the Great Tradition, which guards against heresy, sectarianism, syncretism, schism and pragmatism.

Once we see the broad landscape of the Church (big "C") we can then think more responsibly and clearly about the church (little "c"). In World Impact's conceptual dictionary, we acknowledge that the Church has historically and practically today expressed its community in three ways. These expressions will prove to be essential in our outworking of church planting among city folk, and encompasses all facets of our church planting strategy (including assessment for church planters, training and chartering church plant teams, and providing resources and directions through our coaches and funding).

(The purposes of these expressions is not to determine the absolute line between, say, 50 and 51 members in a church. Obviously, these numbers are not given for hard-and-fast distinctions between expressions. Rather, the numbers are meant to help provide us with a sense of the congregations regular, ongoing, size and makeup. Churches breathe in their member-ship, but do tend to settle at a particular attendance within margins. Do not see the numbers as absolute boundaries but rather as suggestive guidelines in terms of how a particular church tends to grow and function.)

Our three expressions are as follows:

The Small Church (or "house church," 20-50 or so people).
The small (or house) church can be understood as a *small store in a shopping mall*. It needs the connections to other small churches to both survive and thrive. Small churches are able to meet virtually anywhere and can operate with a tiny footprint with little to no financial burdens. They can focus on a specific block, housing development, or network of families. This expression allows for a strong discipleship focus of indigenous leadership development which can take place in this smaller connected group.

Community Church (60-150 or so people)

The community church is the most common expression of church, numerically speaking, in the world today. This expression can be understood as a *grocery or convenience store in a neighborhood or community*. This expression focuses on a particular geographic identity and proximity, highlighting the affinity, connection, and unique context of the congregation and the surrounding community. It is developed around a deep calling and connection to a particular neighborhood, and typically requires a semi-stable place to meet (e.g., a park, community center, or school). This expression especially depends on and is enriched by explicit partnerships formed with other community churches, which effectively strengthens and feeds their growth and mission as individual assemblies.

Mother Church (200+ people)

The mother church (or "hub church") represents a larger assembly of believers, and can be understood as *a Walmart Superstore or Super Target, a store which houses a number of select entities that supply its patrons with many choices and opportunities*. This kind of church, which has both the economic and spiritual resources for multiplication, can leverage its resources and capabilities to become both a sending/empowering church which reproduces itself many times over. Ideally, a mother or hub church is a congregation that is lead by clear missional intents that allow it to leverage its capabilities and gifts to become a center of compassion, mercy, and justice ministries. It can also come to serve as the nurturing headquarters for church planters and ministry starters, and can easily operate as an incubator of other effective ministries among the unreached urban poor. Such an expression usually is more rooted in a particular built-to-suit facility that allows it to leverage these kinds of capabilities.

Seminar

Assessing Urban Christian Leaders

Rev. Dr. Don L. Davis

Who Are Prepared to Represent God's Interests in the City: Those Who Know Their God!

"The Lord is a man of war, Jehovah is his name." Those who enlist under His banner shall have a Commander who will train them for the conflict, and give them both vigor and valor. The times of which Daniel wrote were of the very worst kind, and then it was promised that the people of God would come out in their best colors: they would be strong and stout to confront the powerful adversary.

Oh, that we may know our God; His power, His faithfulness, His immutable love, and so may be ready to risk everything in His behalf. He is One whose character excites our enthusiasm, and makes us willing to live and to die for Him. Oh, that we may know our God by familiar fellowship with Him; for then we shall become like Him, and shall be prepared to stand up for truth and righteousness. He who comes forth fresh from beholding the face of God will never fear the face of man. If we dwell with Him, we shall catch the heroic spirit, and to us a world of enemies will be but as the drop of a bucket. A countless array of men, or even of devils, will seem as little to us as the nations are to God, and He counts them only as grasshoppers. Oh, to be valiant for truth in this day of falsehood.

~ C.H. Spurgeon, *Faith's Checkbook.*

I. **The Central Question: How Do We Identify the Apostolic Church Planters Whom the Holy Spirit Has Chosen to Midwife a New Local Church Expression?**

II. Four Critical Categories for Assessing Urban Church Planters Working among the Poor

New Testament Senses of Apostleship

The term "apostles" designates three different groups of people. Initially, only the original disciples (meaning "students, learners") of Jesus were called apostles (meaning "those sent forth with a mission"). Later, the name was given to missionaries involved in church planting who were also eyewitnesses of Christ's resurrection, such as Paul himself (1 Cor. 9.1-1) and a group of Jesus' followers other than the Twelve (1 Cor. 15.5, 7). Finally, the designation was extended to people who had never seen Christ but who were involved with apostles in pioneer missionary efforts – Apollos (1 Cor. 4.6, 9); Epaphroditus (Phil. 2.25); Silvanus and Timothy (1 Thess. 1.1, cf. 2.6). The definition of "apostles" as one of the higher gifts to be desired bears evidence to the continued accessibility to this ministry for qualified individuals (1 Cor. 12.28, cf. 31). Corinthian Christians could aspire to become apostles, prophets, or teachers. The term apostle was still used in this broad sense in the post-apostolic writings of the Didache. In his writings Paul also refers to some of his associates as his "co-workers" or his "fellow workers." Under his pen, this terms seems to have become a technical label to designate people who identified closely with him in his church-planting efforts as frontline, pioneer missionaries. Interestingly, the same people whom Paul calls "apostles" are also referred to as his "co-workers" – Barnabas (1 Cor. 9.5-6, cf. Acts 14.14; Col. 4.10-11), Epaphroditus (Phil. 2.25), Timothy (Rom. 16.21). In 2 Corinthians 8.23, Titus is a co-worker and his lesser companions are apostles. We can therefore deduce that there exists some interchangeability between the terms apostles and co-workers.

~ Gilbert Bilezikian. *Beyond Sex Roles: What the Bible says about a Woman's Place in Church and Family.* Grand Rapids: Baker Book House, 1986. pp. 197-98.

A. *Calling:* responding to the call of the Lord to plant his church (Cf. "Missionary Calling: The Ground of Apostolic Mission," in *Planting Churches among the City's Poor: An Anthology of Urban Church Planting Resources*, Vol. 2, pp. 98–113)

   1. Definition: recognized the call of God and replies with prompt obedience to his lordship and leading

2. Key Scripture:

   a. 2 Tim. 1.6-14

   b. 1 Tim. 4.14

   c. Acts 1.8

   d. Matt. 28.18-20

3. Critical concept: on the authority of God – God's leader acts on God's recognized call and authority, acknowledged by the saints and God's leaders.

4. Central elements:

   a. A clear call from God

   b. Authentic testimony before God and others

   c. Deep sense of personal conviction based on Scripture

   d. Personal burden for a particular task or people

   e. Confirmation by leaders and the body

5. Satanic strategy to abort: operate on the basis of personality or position rather than on God's appointed call and ongoing authority

6. Key steps:

   a. Identify God's call.

   b. Discover your burden.

   c. Be confirmed by leadership.

7. Results: deep confidence towards God arising from God's call

B. *Character:* personal maturity and growth as a disciple of Christ, and leader in his church

   1. Definition: reflects the character of Christ in their personal convictions, conduct, and lifestyle.

   2. Key Scripture:

      a. John 15.4-5

      b. 2 Tim. 2.2

      c. 1 Cor. 4.2

      d. Gal. 5.16-23

   3. Critical concept: in the humility of Christ – God's leader demonstrates the mind and lifestyle of Christ in his or her actions and relationships.

   4. Central elements:

      a. Passion for Christlikeness

      b. Radical lifestyle for the Kingdom

      c. Serious pursuit of holiness

      d. Discipline in the personal life

      e. Fulfills role-relationships as bond-slave of Jesus Christ

      f. Provides an attractive model for other sin their conduct, speech, and lifestyle (the fruit of the Spirit)

   5. Satanic strategy to abort: substitute ministry activity and/or hard work and industry for godliness and Christlikeness

6. Key steps:

   a. Abide in Christ.

   b. Discipline for godliness.

   c. Pursue holiness in all.

7. Results: powerful Christlike example provided for others to follow

C. *Competence:* knowledgeable and practiced experience using the gifts and endowments of the Holy Spirit.

   1. Definition: respond in the power of the Spirit with excellence in carrying out their appointed tasks and ministry

   2. Key Scripture:

      a. 2 Tim. 2.15

      b. 2 Tim. 3.16-17

      c. Rom. 15.14

      d. 1 Cor. 12

   3. Critical concept: by the power of the Spirit – God's leader operates in the gifting and anointing of the Holy Spirit.

   4. Central elements:

      a. Endowments and gifts from the Spirit

      b. Sound discipling from an able mentor

      c. Skill in the spiritual disciplines

      d. Ability in the Word

      e. Capable to evangelize, follow up, and disciple new converts

      f. Strategic in the use of resources and people to accomplish God's task

5. Satanic strategy to abort: function on natural gifting and personal ingenuity rather than on the Spirit's leading and gifting

6. Key steps:

      a. Discover the Spirit's gifts.

      b. Receive excellent training.

      c. Hone your performance.

7. Results: dynamic working of the Holy Spirit

D. *Community:* participation in and submission to authority in the context of the local church. (*Only church men and women should vie to be church planters for Christ.*)

1. Definition: regards multiplying disciples in the body of Christ as the primary role of ministry.

2. Key Scripture:

      a) Eph. 4.9-15

      b) 1 Cor. 12.1-27

3. Critical concept: for the growth of the Church – God's leader uses all of his or her resources to equip and empower the body of Christ for her goal and task.

4. Central elements:

   a) Genuine love for and desire to serve God's people

   b) Disciples faithful individuals

   c) Facilitates growth in small groups

   d) Pastors and equips believers in the congregation

   e) Nurtures associations, networks among Christians and churches

   f) Advances new movements among God's people locally

5. Satanic strategy to abort: exalts tasks and activities above equipping the saint and developing Christian community

6. Key steps:

   a) Embrace the Church of God.

   b) Learn leadership's contexts.

   c) Equip concentrically.

7. Results: multiplying disciples in the Church

Assessing Urban Church Planters

	Calling	Character	Competence	Community
Definition	Recognizes *the call of God* and replies with prompt obedience to his lordship and leading	Reflects *the character of Christ* in his/her personal convictions, conduct, and lifestyle	Responds in *the power of the Spirit* with excellence in carrying out their appointed tasks and ministry	Regards multiplying disciples in *the body of Christ* as the primary role of ministry
Key Scripture	2 Tim. 1.6-14; 1 Tim. 4.14; Acts 1.8; Matt. 28.18-20	John 15.4-5; 2 Tim. 2.2; 1 Cor. 4.2; Gal. 5.16-23	2 Tim. 2.15; 3.16-17; Rom. 15.14; 1 Cor. 12	Eph. 4.9-15; 1 Cor. 12.1-27
Critical Concept	The Authority of **God**: God's leader acts on God's recognized call and authority, acknowledged by the saints and God's leaders	The Humility of **Christ**: God's leader demonstrates the mind and lifestyle of Christ in his or her actions and relationships	The Power of the **Spirit**: God's leader operates in the gifting and anointing of the Holy Spirit	The Growth of the **Church**: God's leader uses all of his or her resources to equip and empower the body of Christ for his/her goal and task
Central Elements	A clear call from God Authentic testimony before God and others Deep sense of personal conviction based on Scripture Personal burden for a particular task or people Confirmation by leaders and the body	Passion for Christlikeness Radical lifestyle for the Kingdom Serious pursuit of holiness Discipline in the personal life Fulfills role-relationships and bond-slave of Jesus Christ Provides an attractive model for others in their conduct, speech, and lifestyle (the fruit of the Spirit)	Endowments and gifts from the Spirit Sound discipling from an able mentor Skill in the spiritual disciplines Ability in the Word Able to evangelize, follow up, and disciple new converts Strategic in the use of resources and people to accomplish God's task	Genuine love for and desire to serve God's people Disciples faithful individuals Facilitates growth in small groups Pastors and equips believers in the congregation Nurtures associations and networks among Christians and churches Advances new movements among God's people locally
Satanic Strategy to Abort	Operates on the basis of personality or position rather than on God's appointed call and ongoing authority	Substitutes ministry activity and/or hard work and industry for godliness and Christlikeness	Functions on natural gifting and personal ingenuity rather than on the Spirit's leading and gifting	Exalts tasks and activities above equipping the saints and developing Christian community
Key Steps	Identify God's call Discover your burden Be confirmed by leaders	Abide in Christ Discipline for godliness Pursue holiness in all	Discover the Spirit's gifts Receive excellent training Hone your performance	Embrace God's Church Learn leadership's contexts Equip concentrically
Results	Deep confidence in God arising from God's call	Powerful Christlike example provided for others to follow	Dynamic working of the Holy Spirit	Multiplying disciples in the Church

III. Applying the Four Categories

A. Drafting a working profile of a Church Plant Team Pastor

1. S/he maintains *a mature walk with Jesus Christ* that is worthy to be imitated.

   Phil. 4.8-9 – Finally, brothers, whatever is true, whatever is honorable, whatever is just, whatever is pure, whatever is lovely, whatever is commendable, if there is any excellence, if there is anything worthy of praise, think about these things. What you have learned and received and heard and seen in me – practice these things, and the God if peace will be with you.

2. S/he represents the Lord through a compelling personal witness and solid reputation *among outsiders and among believers.*

   2 Cor. 6. 3-11 – We put no obstacle in any one's way, so that no fault may be found with our ministry, but as servants of God we commend ourselves in every way: by great endurance, in afflictions, hardships, calamities, beatings, imprisonments, riots, labors, sleepless nights, hunger; by purity, knowledge, patience, kindness, the Holy Spirit, genuine love; by truthful speech, and the power of God; with the weapons of righteousness for the right hand and for the left; through honor and dishonor, through slander and praise. We are treated as impostors, and yet are true; as unknown, and yet well known; as dying, and behold we live; as punished, and yet not killed; as sorrowful, yet always rejoicing; as poor, yet making many rich; as having nothing, yet possessing everything. We have spoken freely to you, Corinthians; our heart is wide open.

3. S/he affirms with confidence *the calling of God* to represent him in pioneer church planting.

   Gal. 1.1 – Paul, an apostle – not from men nor through man, but through Jesus Christ and God the Father, who raised him from the dead.

4. S/he *submits joyfully to their leaders* under the authority of Jesus Christ.

   1 Tim. 1.18-19 – This charge I entrust to you, Timothy, my child, in accordance with the prophecies previously made about you, that by them you may wage the good warfare, holding faith and a good conscience. By rejecting this, some have made shipwreck of their faith.

5. S/he *possesses a rich theological view of the Church*, with an even deeper love for the body of Christ.

   2 Cor. 11.2 – I feel a divine jealousy for you, for I betrothed you to one husband, to present you as a pure virgin to Christ.

   Col. 1.24-27 – Now I rejoice in my sufferings for your sake, and in my flesh I am filling up what is lacking in Christ's afflictions for the sake of his body, that is, the church, of which I became a minister according to the stewardship from God that was given to me for you, to make the word of God fully known, the mystery hidden for ages and generations but now revealed to his saints. To them God chose to make known how great among the Gentiles are the riches of the glory of this mystery, which is Christ in you, the hope of glory.

6. S/he *identifies and pastors with sensitivity* the members of his/her church plant team (apostolic band).

   Phil. 2.19-24 – I hope in the Lord Jesus to send Timothy to you soon, so that I too may be cheered by news of you. For I have no one like him, who will be genuinely concerned for your welfare. They all seek their own interests, not those of Jesus Christ. But you know Timothy's proven worth, how as a son with a father he has served with me in the gospel. I hope therefore to send him just as soon as I see how it will go with me, and I trust in the Lord that shortly I myself will come also.

7. S/he *coordinates the gifted men and women under their care*, enabling the diverse members to make the maximum contribution possible to the church planting endeavor.

   Col. 4.10-17 – Aristarchus my fellow prisoner greets you, and Mark the cousin of Barnabas (concerning whom you have received instructions – if he comes to you, welcome him), and Jesus who is called Justus. These are the only men of the circumcision among my fellow workers for the kingdom of God, and they have been a comfort to me. Epaphras, who is one of you, a servant of Christ Jesus, greets you, always struggling on your behalf in his prayers, that you may stand mature and fully assured in all the will of God. For I bear him witness that he has worked hard for you and for those in Laodicea and in Hierapolis. Luke the beloved physician greets you, as does Demas. Give my greetings to the brothers at Laodicea, and to Nympha and the church in her house. And when this letter has been read among you, have it also read in the church of the Laodiceans; and see that you also read the letter from Laodicea. And say to Archippus, "See that you fulfill the ministry that you have received in the Lord."

8. S/he has a *burden for the lost*, and constantly seeks creative ways to share the good news of the Gospel with those who haven't heard, with a passion to incorporate all those who respond in a local assembly of believers.

    Rom. 15.18-22 – For I will not venture to speak of anything except what Christ has accomplished through me to bring the Gentiles to obedience – by word and deed, by the power of signs and wonders, by the power of the Spirit of God – so that from Jerusalem and all the way around to Illyricum I have fulfilled the ministry of the gospel of Christ; and thus I make it my ambition to preach the gospel, not where Christ has already been named, lest I build on someone else's foundation, but as it is written, "Those who have never been told of him will see, and those who have never heard will understand." This is the reason why I have so often been hindered from coming to you.

9. S/he *equips the Christian community to function as a congregation of believers,* training the leaders and members to grow in the grace of Jesus Christ.

    Gal. 4.12-19 – Brothers, I entreat you, become as I am, for I also have become as you are. You did me no wrong. You know it was because of a bodily ailment that I preached the gospel to you at first, and though my condition was a trial to you, you did not scorn or despise me, but received me as an angel of God, as Christ Jesus. What then has become of the blessing you felt? For I testify to you that, if possible, you would have gouged out your eyes and given them to me. Have I then become your enemy by telling you the truth? They make much of you, but for no good purpose. They want to shut you out, that you may make much of them. It is always good to be made much of for a good purpose, and not only when I am present with you, my little children, for whom I am again in the anguish of childbirth until Christ is formed in you!

10. S/he allows the *emerging church* to develop its own identity and destiny under the leadership of the Holy Spirit.

Acts 20.25-32 – And now, behold, I know that none of you among whom I have gone about proclaiming the kingdom will see my face again. Therefore I testify to you this day that I am innocent of the blood of all of you, for I did not shrink from declaring to you the whole counsel of God. Pay careful attention to yourselves and to all the flock, in which the Holy Spirit has made you overseers, to care for the church of God, which he obtained with his own blood. I know that after my departure fierce wolves will come in among you, not sparing the flock; and from among your own selves will arise men speaking twisted things, to draw away the disciples after them. Therefore be alert, remembering that for three years I did not cease night or day to admonish everyone with tears. And now I commend you to God and to the word of his grace, which is able to build you up and to give you the inheritance among all those who are sanctified.

B. Church planter's practical responsibilities: a suggested job description

However you wish to describe the practical responsibilities of a church planter in a poor neighborhood, you cannot ignore the overarching categories of commission, character, competence, and community. While these general principles shape our understanding of the kind of individuals the Spirit will use in such an effort, they must be seen as "deep concepts," i.e., the kind of truths that make up the DNA of the planter, and will affect his/her operation in all their duties and relationships. Below is an example of a description of the planter's duties, informed by an ongoing, steady application of the categories discussed above.

1. To faithfully intercede for oneself, one's members and volunteers, the community, and the entire effort during the Charter period

2. To relate and communicate regularly with the church plant team members and his/her field coach and/or church authority on the status of the plant

3. To commence and superintend the training and resourcing provided for each member of the team for their growth and development

4. To attend the Evangel Church Plant School with core team members, and if possible, his field coach to develop a Team Charter

5. To oversee the formation and implementation of the team's church planting strategy

6. To insure that each team member has received adequate orientation and training for his/her role

7. To care for the spiritual and emotional welfare of the team, both as individuals, and as a whole

8. To lead team meetings, and its processes of planning, preparing, evaluating, and making adjustments to the Charter

9. To help team members resolve interpersonal conflict

10. To secure resources, personnel, and counseling for the team's ongoing challenges and opportunities

11. To set an example of service and spirituality for the team

C. The problem with taxonomies: not falling off the cliff(s) of extremism

1. God employs different criteria, different readings of data, and different analyses of prospective futures than us!

2. 1 Sam. 16.6-7 – When they came, he looked on Eliab and thought, "Surely the LORD's anointed is before him." [7] But the LORD said to Samuel, "Do not look on his appearance or

on the height of his stature, because I have rejected him. For the LORD sees not as man sees: man looks on the outward appearance, but the LORD looks on the heart."

> The eldest son, Eliab, impresses Samuel as a suitable candidate, but his appearance is deceptive, as Saul's had been. The Lord sees not as man sees becomes an important maxim (cf. 1 Chr. 28:9), which illuminated the prophetic vision of the servant of the Lord, "marred beyond human semblance", "despised and rejected by men" but declared to be supremely great (Isa. 52:14; 53:3). There is a corrective here to *merely superficial judgment* (italics mine).
>
> ~ *Tyndale Old Testament Commentaries.* 1 and 2 Samuel. 1 Sam. 16:6-10.

3. The Lord searches and knows the heart of all people, and relates to them on the basis of what he chooses and wills (1 Kings 8.39; 1 Chron. 28.9; Ps. 7.9; Jer. 11.20; 17.9-10; Acts 1.24).

4. Allow the Holy Spirit to use whomever he selects for whatever reason he may choose

   Moses – a murderer! (cf. Exod. 3.11-15)

   Paul – a religious persecutor! (cf. Phil. 3.6-7 with Acts 8.3)

IV. Testing the Categories: Concepts, Case Studies, and Controversial Candidates

1 Sam. 16.7 – But the LORD said to Samuel, "Do not look on his appearance or on the height of his stature, because I have rejected him. For the LORD sees not as man sees: man looks on the outward appearance, but the LORD looks on the heart."

A. How can people with a shady background and no formal training lead the church of God? Unlikely choices for church planting among the poor? *Discuss the viability and desirability of selecting any one of the following to lead a church plant effort in the city.*

1. Elementary school graduate called to church plant

2. PF TUMI grad call to plant

3. Registered sex offender

B. Transcending wooden/knee jerk application of assessment tools: a corrective

1. Am I using the data received from the assessment tool as *a prophetic lens* (self-fulfilling prophecy) or a data gathering instrument?

2. How am I evaluating the candidate through these tools in terms of *their future usefulness and deployability* in kingdom service?

3. How can I tell that I am evaluating the data objectively, as well as *in confidence and faith in the Lord's ability to transform and transcend the past?*

V. The Need for Discernment and Discretion: A Plea for Godly Wisdom

John 7.24 – Do not judge by appearances, but judge with right judgment.

A. The power of discernment: exercising wisdom (beyond data management)

1. It involves the ability to select the proper course of action (Prov. 15.21; Phil. 1.9-10; cf. Prov. 3.21-23; 8.8-9; 10.21; 11.12; 18.1; 24.30; Hos. 14.9).

2. Discernment is able to distinguish good from evil (2 Sam. 14.17; Gen. 3.22; Job 6.30; 34.3-4; Isa. 7.15).

3. It allows us to distinguish the holy from common (Lev. 10.10; 11.47; Ezek. 22.26; 44.23).

4. The discernment of the Spirit enables us to see beyond outward appearances or past occurrences (Prov. 28.11; 1 Sam. 16.7; Isa. 11.3).

5. Discernment detects and understands the significance and meaning of events (Deut. 32.29-30; 1 Chron.12.32; Esther 1.13; cf. Matt. 24.32-33; Mark 13.28-29; Luke 12.54-56).

B. Freedom of the Holy Spirit

1. The Spirit is free to choose whomever he wishes to do whatever he wills (1 Cor. 12.4-8, 11; 2 Cor. 3.17-18).

2. The Spirit never calls a man or woman to do or be anything without providing the requisite will and ability to do that thing (Eph. 3.20-21).

SEMINAR
The Evangel Strategy

Dr. Hank Voss

> How is it possible that the gospel should be credible, that people should come to believe that the power which has the last word in human affairs is represented by a man hanging on a cross? I am suggesting that the only answer, the only hermeneutic of the gospel, is a congregation of men and women who believe it and live by it.
>
> ~ Lesslie Newbigin. *The Gospel in a Pluralist Society.* p. 227

> For a day in your courts is better than a thousand elsewhere. I would rather be a doorkeeper in the house of my God than dwell in the tents of wickedness.
>
> ~ Psalm 84.10

I. The Beauty of the Church

A. The Church is the place where the Lord has chosen to display his beauty

1. Isaiah 61 and Crowns of Beauty

2. "Jerusalem" and the Zion songs (Pss. 46, 48, 76, 84, 87, 122)

3. The bride of Christ and the mystery of the Church (Eph. 5)

4. Like Israel in the Old Testament, the Church does not always display Christ's beauty.

B. A healthy Church that displays Christ's beauty is the best way to bring the Evangel (Gospel) to the cities of the world.

1. "The Congregation as hermeneutic of the Gospel" (Lesslie Newbigin)

2. The moon's beauty lies in its reflection of the sun's light.

II. Understanding Evangel's Chief Metaphor

A. Matt. 13.3–9, 18–23

[3] And he told them many things in parables, saying: "A sower went out to sow. [4] And as he sowed, some seeds fell along the path, and the birds came and devoured them. [5] Other seeds fell on rocky ground, where they did not have much soil, and immediately they sprang up, since they had no depth of soil, [6] but when the sun rose they were scorched. And since they had no root, they withered away. [7] Other seeds fell among thorns, and the thorns grew up and choked them. [8] Other seeds fell on good soil and produced grain, some a hundredfold, some sixty, some thirty. 9 He who has ears, let him hear."

". . . Hear then the parable of the sower: [19] When anyone hears the word of the kingdom and does not understand it, the evil one comes and snatches away what has been sown in his heart. This is what was sown along the path. [20] As for what was sown on rocky ground, this is the one who hears the word and immediately receives it with joy, [21] yet he has no root in himself, but endures for a while, and when tribulation or persecution arises on account of the word, immediately he falls away. [22] As for what was sown among thorns, this is the one who hears the word, but the cares of the world and the deceitfulness of riches choke the word, and it proves unfruitful. [23] As for what was sown on good soil, this is the one who hears the word and understands it. He indeed bears fruit and yields, in one case a hundredfold, in another sixty, and in another thirty."

B. The significance of Jesus' sower parable

1. Jesus' use of parables and metaphors

2. Our use of parables and metaphors

3. Other "plant" parables

C. Implications from Evangel's basic parable

Metaphor	Implications
Seed	
Sower	
Soil	
Roots	
Stages of Growth (Tree/Plant/Vine)	
Fruit	

III. Does an Agricultural Metaphor Work for Urban Leaders?

A. The modern city often lacks the beauty of God's larger creation.

   1. The city can choke out life.

      a. The absence of green places among urban poor communities

      b. The air quality in urban poor communities

   2. God's ultimate intent for the city is green.

      a. The new creation will be a garden city, an urban Eden.

      b. The tree of life will grow in the midst of the New Jerusalem (Rev 22.1–2).

   3. Just because we are urban church planters, doesn't mean God wants us to be ignorant of his great creation.

B. Why keep an agricultural metaphor in the city?[1]

    1. It works in a different way in the city than it does in the country, but it is worth keeping.

        a. The metaphor is deeply biblical.

            (1) Agricultural metaphors (roots, plants, trees, vines, etc.) appear more than 1,000 times in Scripture.

            (2) The Church finds its place in the Kingdom, and the Kingdom includes all of Creation.

        b. It is powerful.

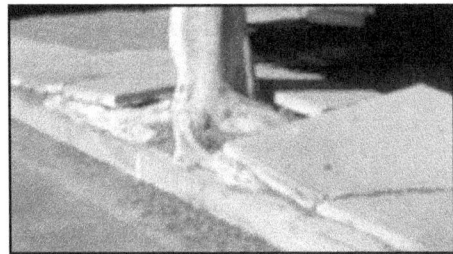

            (1) Urbanites in the inner city know the power of roots under a sidewalk.

            (2) Case Study: *Roots: The Saga of an American Family*

IV. Evangel as Part of a Larger Church Plant System

A. The contexts of an Evangel church planter

    1. *Specific soil.* Every church planter is called to a specific community.

    2. *Specific family heritage.* Every church planter brings a specific vision of the church relating to church background and experiences.

    3. *Specific sending church.* Every church planter operates under accountability and has been commissioned to the task of church planting by a specific church or group of churches.

---

1 Some suggest agricultural metaphors don't work for urban ethnic leaders (*http://www.stuffwhitechristianslike.com/2010/07/86-agricultural-imagery.html*)

4. *Specific strategy and resources.* Every church planter operates with a strategy and is equipped with resources even if they cannot articulate that strategy or list all the resources.

B. The ABCs of training church planters among the poor

1. The ABCs are simple and memorable.

   a. They help us keep the big picture.

   b. The actual process is more complicated.

2. Evangel's ABCs: Assessment, Boot Camp, Coaching

   a. *Assessment:* the process of recruiting and assessing church planters called to work among the poor

   b. *Boot Camp:* the process of training and commissioning church planters to plant churches among the poor

   c. *Coaching:* the process of encouraging and mentoring church planters to grow in wisdom as they plant churches among the poor

3. Assessment is a process which includes:

   a. The recruitment of church planters

   b. The assessment of potential church planters

4. Boot Camp is a process which includes

   a. Strategic planning of church planters before, during, and after the Evangel Urban Church Plant School

   b. A public commissioning of a church planter and a team to plant a church in a specific location during a specific amount of time as summarized by a one-page charter

5. Coaching is a process which includes:

   a. A Field Coach who helps the church planter and the Church Plant Team pursue wisdom by meeting regularly with them for Planning and Review of church plant efforts (the PWR process) as designated by the team charter.

b. Helping the new church connect with a locale expression of the Church for engaging in Kingdom mission (e.g. Urban Church Association) as well as embracing a specific church tradition (e.g. denomination, non-denominational, etc.)

V. A Brief Overview of The Evangel School of Urban Church Planting

A. Vision

1. Vision: to recruit, empower, and release urban leaders who will plant churches and launch indigenous church planting movements

2. Big Idea: Our church plant team will be spiritually, strategically, and tactically ready to plant a church

B. Objectives

Urban Church Planters and their Teams will:

1. Leave Evangel with a clear theological vision for church planting.

2. Embrace a culturally sensitive model and expression of the church.

3. Apply biblical wisdom as they evangelize, equip, and empower throughout the P.L.A.N.T. phases of planting.

4. Represent Christ's Kingdom with excellence in their locale.

5. Complete the process of prayer, reflection, teaching, and counsel in order to discover God's unique call for their church plant as reflected in a one-page authorized plan (Charter).

6. Leave Evangel with a Field Coach who has committed to at least three specific times for planning and review in the next year.

C. Components of Evangel School

1. People

    a. People at Evangel

       (1) Deans: Provide overall leadership for the school

       (2) Coaches

          (a) School Assessor Coaches: Assist with evaluating and coaching teams at the school

          (b) Team Field Coaches: Assist with evaluating and coaching teams both at the school and after the school is completed

       (3) Support Personnel: All those assisting in various ways with running the school including leading worship, teaching sessions, helping with technology, food, etc.

       (4) Church Planters: the identified leaders of potential church plant teams (including apostolic church planters, founding pastors, and planters of various expressions of the church.

       (5) Primary Team Members: Members of a church plant team who are committed to working under a church planter for a period of time designated by the team charter.

    b. People involved but not usually present at Evangel

       (1) Financial Donors. Those who give to help make a school possible.

       (2) Intercessors. Those recruited by all who attend the school to be praying for the school.

       (3) Sponsoring Churches, associations, and networks. Those sending church planters to the school.

2. Budget

    a. Options for paying for a school

       (1) Sponsoring churches, associations, and networks raise money for school

(2) Church planters and teams pay for school

(3) Donors pay for school

(4) Combination of above

    b. Sample budgets available in the appendix

3. Content

    a. Evangel's content is based around five sessions.

Session 1	See the Big Picture
Session 2	Prepare
Session 3	Launch and Assemble
Session 4	Nurture and Transition
Session 5	Bringing It All Together

    b. Throughout the five sessions there are a variety of activities.

(1) Worship and Devotionals

(2) Seminar Teachings

(3) Team Exercises

(4) Team Presentations

(5) Chartering and Commissioning Service

VI. Evangel and Certification

A. Evangel Schools must operate under the supervision of TWO certified Evangel Deans.

1. Being Commissioned at an Evangel Dean Training School certifies you and authorizes you to host Evangel Schools for three years from the date of the completion of your training.

2. Dean Certification can be renewed for a three-year period by attending an Evangel Church Plant Track at the International TUMI Summit or participating in another Evangel Dean School.

3. If your Dean Certification expires, renewal of your certification must be completed by attending another Evangel Dean School.

B. Advantages of Evangel School Certification

1. Charter opportunity: ensure supportive accountability and ongoing instruction in connection to one's supervising authority.

2. Discounts on all Evangel and TUMI products at the TUMI store

3. Permission to use Evangel name and promotional materials

4. Access to a large collection of resources for hosting Evangel Schools, including videos, PowerPoints, templates, graphics, music and project planning files

5. Connection to a growing network of coaches and church planters working with the urban poor through the quarterly *Urban Church Leader: News and Notes* (newsletter)

6. Lasting connection to a solid evangelical urban missions organization devoted to the Great Tradition of the Church

SEMINAR
Toward a Flexible Strategy for Ministry
Coordinating the Team for Success
Lorna Rasmussen and Don Davis

TUMI defines *Ministry Stewardship* as the process of authorizing our trusted and gifted people to freely deploy our goods in connection to our key operations and projects, consistent with their authority and duties, and our corporate fiscal year priorities and goals.

What Exactly Is a Project?

Projects may be large or small. . . . Projects may involve many people or just you. . . . Projects may be planned formally or informally. . . . Projects may be tracked formally or informally. . . . Projects may be performed for external or internal clients and customers. . . . Projects may be defined by a legal contract or an informal agreement. . . . Projects may be business related or personal. No matter what the characteristics of your project, you define it by the same three ingredients: outcomes, start and end dates, and resources. The information you need to plan and manage your project is the same, although the ease and the time required to develop it may differ. The more thoroughly you plan and manage your projects, the more likely you are to succeed.

~ Stanley E. Portny, *Project Management for Dummies*. Indianapolis, IN: Wiley Publishing, Inc., 2001, pp. 10-11.

- Identify Your Burden and Call: Based on your call, history, and vision, what are the dreams you have for your enterprise?

- Set Goals: What practically can you do, sponsor, produce, or executive this year to make your dreams a reality now? What possible goals do you have to make your dreams come true?

- Establish Priorities: Of all the possible things you could accomplish, which goals are the most important to pursue right now? What will you seek to do this year?

- Execute Projects: What projects will you initiate that will enable you to fulfill your goals for this year?

- Review Efforts: How did the accomplishment of this project help or hinder us in our strategic goals and purposes? What did we learn, what should we do again, what should we change, and what should we drop (if we do this again)?

Requires commitment, Priorities, Resources and Tools
The key to accomplishment is settling clearly on what you will give your time and attention to. "If you try to chase two rabbits, you will not catch either of them" (Chinese proverb).

I. **Clarify Your Dream: Set your context. What has the Lord called you to be and to do?**

    Nehemiah sets goals to build the wall and rebuild the house of God, Neh. 2.2-8.

    A. Definition

        1. Dreaming big involves using your imagination and faith to visualize what would happen if the Lord granted you fulfillment of your call and vision.

        2. What is your call, your history, and your dream?

    B. Elements

        1. Clarify your vision; set the context for your work, based on your history and experience.

        2. Understand your call; reaffirm why you exist, and "what your business is."

        3. Release the imagination of your faith; if God would grant you anything, what would you ask for? Why does your enterprise exist?

    C. Illustration: Evangel School of Urban Church Planting

        1. TUMI Project Portfolio

        2. How do we use our imagination to determine possible rabbits to chase?

        3. Hosting the *Evangel School of Urban Church Planting* clarifies our dream to identify, equip, and empower partners who are investing in emerging leaders around the world.

II. Set Goals: Brainstorm possibilities. What possible things can you do this year to make your dream a reality?

Nehemiah spies out the city in order to set specific goals for the work, Neh. 2.11-15.

A. Definition

1. Setting goals involves making a list of all the possible things you could do this calendar or fiscal year that would help you accomplish the dream God has given.

2. This step involves reading your situation, brainstorming a list of possible activities or initiatives that would "move the ball down the field" this year in fulfilling your call.

B. Elements

1. At the start, do not limit yourself; brainstorm freely and openly as you make your list.

2. Do a SWOT (Strengths, Weaknesses, Opportunities, Threats) analysis. Understand internally what your strengths and liabilities are, and externally what your opportunities and threats are right now.

3. Silence the judge and the critic; think of every possible goal you might want to seek. (Reserve the sorting and evaluating for the next step.)

C. Illustration: Evangel School of Urban Church Planting

1. TUMI Project Portfolio

2. How do we use our imagination to determine possible rabbits to chase?

3. Hosting the Evangel School of Urban Church Planting clarifies our dream to identify, equip, and empower partners who are investing in emerging leaders around the world.

III. Establish Priorities: Concentrate on things for first importance. Of all the things you pursue, which things will you commit to accomplish this year as your priorities?

Based on his situation and the opposition he faced, Nehemiah set priorities as to the construction and the security of the project, Neh. 4.15-20.

A. Definition

    1. Establishing priorities involves sorting your goals into things you might do versus things you must do, those SMART goals you intend to pursue

    2. Using the SMART acrostic can help you determine your priorities right now; goals are SMART when they are Specific, Measurable, Attainable, Realistic, and Time-based.

B. Elements

    1. Ask yourself which goals on your brainstorm list are absolutely important right now for you to pursue in light of where you are now as an enterprise?

    2. Those deemed important should be "cleaned up" to match the SMART format

    3. Those important, SMART-formatted goals should be sorted in order of urgency, importance, and confidence.

C. Illustration: Evangel School of Urban Church Planting

    1. TUMI Project Portfolio

    2. How do we use our imagination to determine possible rabbits to chase?

    3. Hosting the Evangel School of Urban Church Planting clarifies our dream to identify, equip, and empower partners who are investing in emerging leaders around the world.

IV. Execute Projects: Do your priorities with all your might. What specific projects will you execute to accomplish your priorities this year?

Nehemiah and his team engage the construction until the wall is done, Neh. 4.6-14 .

A. Definition

    1. Executing projects involves coordinating resources (e.g., people, technologies, facilities, funds) according to specific desired qualifications and outcomes toward a specific time frame or deadline.

    2. Resources + specifications + time frames = project management (the constraints of cost, quality, and time)

B. Elements

    1. Propose it!

        a. What you want to accomplish – be absolutely specific.

        b. Objectives: What are the key objectives you hope to achieve by hosting the event, creating the resource, or putting on the production?

        c. Due dates: When must it be done?

        d. Team members (project manager, team members, support team)

        e. Draft budget

        f. Lay out steps to complete project (back-of-the-napkin type of thing – not thorough, just main/key points).

        g. Receive approval: Get buy-in from your stakeholders (leaders) to ensure authorization (authority to act) and support (resources).

2. Execute it!

    a. Plan – create Work Breakdown Structure (prepare):

        (1) Make a list of everything that has to be done (and in what in order).

        (2) Assign tasks and due dates.

        (3) Put the plan on "paper" (Smartsheet, Evernote, Microsoft Project, Word).

    b. Engage the plan, but expect change (work).

        (1) Don't take change personally.

        (2) Keep the big picture in mind.

        (3) Keep the plates spinning: regular, brief, decisive.

            (a) Attend to a number of different important areas at the same time – making adjustments as quickly as possible.

            (b) Discipline yourself to the project: LOOK at your plan and COMMUNICATE with the team continuously!

        (4) Be flexible: Adjust the plan as you go, change as you need it.

3. Wrap it up (evaluate and celebrate!)

    a. Wrap up final details: close project with excellence (pay final bills, put everything away, clean up).

    b. Review: Evaluate project.

        (1) Host a project team meeting for the core members of your team.

(2) Open dialogue: No project is done without open dialogue, critical analysis, and honest evaluation of results both throughout the event and after. We evaluate everything in order to assess "How did the accomplishment of this project help or hinder us in our strategic goals and purposes?"

(3) Record evaluation: All insights should be archived (written down, recorded, and stored for future reference). If your efforts are not worthy to be evaluated, then they are not important enough to be initiated.

c. Celebrate the completion of this project as a team.

d. Get feedback from key team members, participants and stakeholders.

> **Note: Skilled project management was not the real reason for the completion of the work,** *Neh. 6.15-16 (ESV) – . . . So the wall was finished on the twenty-fifth day of the month Elul, in fifty-two days. [16] And when all our enemies heard of it, all the nations around us were afraid and fell greatly in their own esteem, for they perceived that this work had been accomplished with the help of our God.*

C. Illustration: Evangel School of Urban Church Planting

   1. Illustrating Project Proposal

      a. TUMI Project Process: *www.tumi.org/project*

      b. TUMI Project Proposal: back-of-the-napkin checklist

      c. Budget worksheet: Project Planning budget worksheet (Excel)

      d. Post-its (Mural.ly: Online project brainstorming platform)

2. Illustrating Project Execution

a. Word Processor: Notepad, Word, WordPerfect – anything to make a list with

b. Post-its (Mural.ly: online project brainstorming platform)

c. Evernote: online tool for project collaboration – *www.evernote.com*

d. Smartsheet: online project software (easy to use!) – *www.smartsheet.com* (Where the buck stops!)

e. Microsoft Teams: online tool for project collaboration

3. Illustration Project Wrap-up

a. Always celebrate every project victory with the team!

b. Project Review: Dialogue about the project's good, bad, and ugly (e.g. what happened, what we should do again, what never to do again).

Toward a Strategy for Ministry: Coordinate Your Team for Success

- Identify Your Burden and Call: Based on your call, history, and vision, what are the dreams you have for your enterprise?

- Set Goals: What practically can you do, sponsor, produce, or executive this year to make your dreams a reality now? What possible goals do you have to make your dreams come true?

- Establish Priorities: Of all the possible things you could accomplish, which goals are the most important to pursue right now? What will you seek to do this year?

- Execute Projects: What projects will you initiate that will enable you to fulfill your goals for this year?

- Review Efforts: How did the accomplishment of this project help or hinder us in our strategic goals and purposes? What did we learn, what should we do again, what should we change, and what should we drop (if we do this again)?

Toward a Flexible Strategy for Ministry

Lorna Rasmussen, Don Davis • Adapted from Don Allsman's PWR Concept

Execute Projects

Do your priorities with all your might. What specific projects will you execute to accomplish your priorities this year?

Establish Priorities

Concentrate on things of first importance. Of all the things you pursue, which things will you commit to accomplish this year as your priorities?

Review Efforts

What did we learn, what should we do again, what should we change, and what should we drop?

Work

Review

Toward a Flexible Strategy for Ministry

Prepare

Set Goals

Brainstorm possibilities. What possible things can you do this year to make your dream a reality?

Identify Your Call and Burden

Set your context. What has the Lord called you to be and to do?

The Need for Commitment, Priorities, Resources, and Tools

The key to accomplishment is settling clearly on what you will give your time and attention to.

"If you try to chase two rabbits you will not catch either of them."

~ Old Chinese Proverb ~

Seminar

Charters, Coaches, and the Ongoing PWR Process

Dr. Hank Voss

> Look carefully then how you walk, not as unwise but as wise, making the best use of the time, because the days are evil. Therefore do not be foolish, but understand what the will of the Lord is.
>
> ~ Ephesians 5.15–17
>
> The Charter is the culmination of the strategic planning process and equips the team to proceed with wisdom and authority.
>
> ~ Don Allsman[1]

I. A Brief History of "Charters"

A. Charters and cities

B. Charters at World Impact

II. Wisdom and Charters

A. The pursuit of wisdom

B. The importance of balancing strategy and tactics

C. The benefits of a charter

D. The limits of a charter

III. Fifteen Components of an Evangel Charter

A. Church plant name

---

1   Don Allsman, "Using Wisdom in Ministry: The PWR Process," in *Ripe for Harvest: A Guidebook for Planting Healthy Churches in the City*, ed. Don Allsman, Don L. Davis, and Hank Voss. Wichita, KS: TUMI Press, 2015. p. 65.

B. Church planter

C. Coach

D. Church expression

E. World Impact partnership model

F. Urban Church Association

G. Primary team members (length of commitment)

H. Target area and ethnicity

I. Requested length of charter

J. Times to meet with field coach

K. Times of formal evaluation (PWR, at least three times a year)

L. Values

M. Vision statement

N. Key goals

O. Signatures

    1. Deans

    2. Assessor Coach

    3. Commissioned by (sponsoring spiritual authority of church planter)

IV. Charters and the PWR Process Especially Important for the Urban Poor

A. The poor and planning: divine appointments or demonic assignment?

B. The Charter and freedom: the importance of adapting to win

V. The Charter and the Field Coach

A. The Charter as a map for PLANT process

1. Creating and commissioning

2. Evaluating and adapting

3. Completing and celebrating

4. Debriefing and disbanding

B. The Charter and the three-year coaching cycle

VI. Resources for the Field Coach

A. The Capstone Curriculum and other coaching resources

1. "Summary of the Capstone Curriculum"[2]

2. Other Resources

B. "Providing Formal Feedback for the Team as Field Coach"[3]

---

2   Don L. Davis, ed., *Planting Churches among the City's Poor: An Anthology of Urban Church Planting Resources,* Vol. 2. Wichita, KS: TUMI Press, 2015.

3   Ibid., p. 179.

SEMINAR

Families of Churches
Movements, Associations, and Denominations
Dr. Hank Voss

> Christians have expressed their faith in Jesus Christ in various ways through particular movements and traditions which embrace and express the Apostolic Tradition and the Great Tradition in unique ways.
>
> ~ Rev. Dr. Don Davis. *Sacred Roots: A Primer on the Great Tradition.* p. 46.

I. The Nicene Marks of the Church

A. The Church is located in the article on the Holy Spirit.

B. The four marks: One, Holy, Catholic, and Apostolic

II. Understanding the Church in Relation to Three Levels of Tradition[1]

A. The Authoritative ("Apostolic") Tradition

B. The Great Tradition

C. Specific church traditions: the founders of movements, denominations and orders

  1. The history of denominations in the United States

  2. Views of denominations

  3. The recent rise of associations and networks

---

1   Don Davis, *Sacred Roots: A Primer on Retrieving the Great Tradition.* Wichita, KS: The Urban Ministry Institute, 2010. pp. 41–47.

III. Church Plant Movements and Denominations

A. Definition of a Church Plant Movement (CPM)

B. Denomination and mission agency approaches to Church Planting Movements

C. The relationship between denominations and locale church associations

IV. What about Licensing and Ordination for the Urban Poor?

A. Tradition-based factors

1. Examples:

   a. Evangelical Free response

   b. Reformed Church in America response

   c. Southern Baptist response

   d. Non-Denominational response(s)

   e. Church of God in Christ

2. Implications:

   a. License to preach (and to plant)

   b. Ordination: the "acid test"

V. Forming Church Planting Partnerships

A. A brief biblical theology of partnership

B. Four models of partnership

1. Model 1

2. Model 2

3. Model 3

4. Model 4

C. Practical aids to partnership

1. MOUs

2. Sample Partnership Agreements (See *Planting Churches among the City's Poor: An Anthology of Urban Church Planting Resources*, Vol. 2, pp. 367-386.)

VI. Implications for Evangel Church Plant Schools

A. Know how your Evangel School fits into the family tree

B. Implications for partnerships with denominations

C. Implications for partnerships with urban church associations

D. Implications for preparing church planters for licensing and ordination

VII. Resources for Further Study

A. *Church Matters*, by Don Davis[2]

B. *The Missional Church and Denominations*, Craig Van Gelder, ed.[3]

C. *Handbook of Denominations in the United States*, Craig Atwood, Frank Mead and Samuel Hill[4]

---

2   Don L. Davis. *Church Matters: Retrieving the Great Tradition.* Wichita, KS: TUMI/ World Impact, 2007.

3   Craig Van Gelder, ed. *The Missional Church and Denominations.* Grand Rapids, MI: Eerdmans, 2008.

4   Craig D. Atwood, Frank S. Mead, and Samuel Hill. *Handbook of Denominations in the United States.* 13 ed. Abingdon, 2010.

SEMINAR

Church Plants and Urban Church Associations
The Need for a Local Embrace
Rev. Dr. Don L. Davis

> My last request is, that all the faithful ministers of Christ would, without any more delay, unite and associate for the furtherance of each other in the work of the Lord, and the maintaining of unity and concord in his churches.
>
> ~ Richard Baxter. *The Reformed Pastor,* 1656.

I. The Theology of the Locale Church

Once a church has been planted, the work for spiritual formation and multiplication has begun. Every healthy assembly must not only grow in its theology, worship, discipleship, and witness, but it must also extend a hand of fellowship, connection, and shared mission with other pastors, congregations, and movements in its distinctive locale. No urban church can possibly survive (let alone thrive) without the cultivation of ongoing love, support, and camaraderie with other congregations. This was true in the time of the apostles, and is equally relevant today.

A. The intimate relationship between Movements and Associations

Please refer to *The Threefold Cord of Urban Cross-Cultural Church Planting Movements* on page 299.

B. Leadership authority and responsibility has historically corresponded to the various dimensions of Christian community.

Please refer to *The Communal Context of Authentic Christian Leadership* on page 300.

C. Whatever the model, Association is mandatory!

Please refer to *Church Planting Models* on page 301.

II. The Practical Application of a Locale Theology: The Urban Church Association (UCA)

A. The mechanical inworkings of an effective UCA (cf. "A Model of an Urban Church Association").

1 Pet. 5.8 – Be sober-minded; be watchful. Your adversary the devil prowls round like a roaring lion, seeking someone to devour.

2 Cor. 2.10-11 – Anyone whom you forgive, I also forgive. Indeed, what I have forgiven, if I have forgiven anything, has been for your sake in the presence of Christ, [11] so that we would not be outwitted by Satan; for we are not ignorant of his designs.

1. The reality of the enemy and the great need for connection and association among urban churches

2. How predators hunt – by isolation:

   a. Stragglers: those who don't keep up with the pack

   b. The weak and infirm: those who are vulnerable due to ill-health

   c. The young and inexperienced: those not yet strong enough to be independent

   d. The reckless: those rebellious and recalcitrant

3. Why churches tend to grow in bunches, and fail alone

   a. Churches that are alone easily tend to forget their place in the grander story and schema of the Kingdom ("tempest in a tea cup" syndrome).

   b. Churches that are alone lose answerability to a larger context where their doctrine, practice, and behavior can be encouraged and challenged.

   c. Churches that are alone may easily isolate themselves from the larger body of Christ, spawning either heresy or schism (or both).

d. Churches that are alone often find it difficult if not impossible to fund and underwrite their mission and projects which flow from their vision.

e. Churches that are alone tend to exaggerate the importance of everything they experience in their body as being binding on the conscience and practice of all believers everywhere.

B. That We May Be One (John 17): Toward a Theology of Church Association

Please refer to "That We May Be One: Elements of an Integrated Church Planting Movement among the Urban Poor" in *Planting Churches among the City's Poor: An Anthology of Urban Church Planting Resources*, Vol. 2, p. 152.

> It is a most invaluable part of that blessed "liberty wherewith Christ hath made us free," that in his worship different forms and usages may without offence be allowed, provided the substance of the Faith be kept entire; and that, in every Church, what cannot be clearly determined to belong to Doctrine must be referred to Discipline; and therefore, by common consent and authority, may be altered, abridged, enlarged, amended, or otherwise disposed of, as may seem most convenient for the edification of the people, "according to the various exigency of times and occasions."
>
> ~ 1789 Preface to the *Book of Common Prayer*. 1928 Episcopal edition.

Nevertheless, as was affirmed by the emerging leaders of the then American Episcopal Church, the freedom that we have in Christ allows for different forms and usages of worship in the body of Christ without any offense whatsoever, as long as we are faithful to the historic orthodox beliefs of the Church as taught to us by the prophets and apostles of our Lord. Doctrine must remain anchored and complete; discipline, however, can be based on the contingencies and exigencies of the people who embrace them, as long as all that is shaped and conceived builds up the body of Christ, and glorifies God our Father through our Lord Jesus Christ.

1. *A shared history and identity* (i.e., a common name and heritage). CPMs among the urban poor will seek to link themselves to and identify themselves by a well defined and joyfully shared history and persona that all members and congregations share.

2. *A shared liturgy and celebration* (i.e., a common worship). CPMs among the urban poor should reflect a shared hymnody, practice of the sacraments, theological focus and imagery, aesthetic vision, vestments, liturgical order, symbology, and spiritual formation that enables us to worship and glorify God in a way that lifts up the Lord and attracts urbanites to vital worship.

3. *A shared membership, well-being, welfare, and support* (i.e., a common order and discipline). CPMs among the urban poor must be anchored in evangelical and historically orthodox presentations of the Gospel that result in conversions to Jesus Christ and incorporation into local churches.

4. *A shared catechism and doctrine* (i.e., a common faith). CPMs among the urban poor must embrace a common biblical theology and express it practically in a Christian education that reflects their commonly held faith.

5. *A shared church government and authority* (i.e., a common polity). CPMs among the urban poor must be organized around a common polity, ecclesial management, and submit to flexible governing policies that allow for effective and efficient management of their resources and congregations.

6. *A shared leadership development structure* (i.e., a common pastoral strategy). CPMs among the urban poor are committed to supplying each congregation with godly undershepherds, and seek to identify, equip, and support its pastors and missionaries in order that their members may grow to maturity in Christ.

7. *A shared financial philosophy and procedure* (i.e., a common stewardship). CPMs among the urban poor strive to handle all of their financial affairs and resources with wise, stream-lined, and reproducible policies that allow for the good management of their monies and goods, locally, regionally, and nationally.

8. *A shared care and support ministry* (i.e., a common service). CPMs among the urban poor seek to practically demonstrate the love and justice of the Kingdom among its members and towards others in the city in ways that allow individuals and congregations to love their neighbors as they love themselves.

9. *A shared evangelism and outreach* (i.e., a common mission). CPMs among the urban poor network and collaborate among their members in order to clearly present Jesus and his Kingdom to the lost in the city in order to multiply new congregations in unreached urban areas as quickly as possible.

10. *A shared vision for connection and association* (i.e., a common partnership). CPMs among the urban poor must seek to make fresh connections, links, and relationships with other movements for the sake of regular communication, fellowship, and mission.

C. Types and kinds of Church Associations

Please refer to "Associations and Urban Church Planting Movement: The Efficiency and Reproductive Power of Standardization" in *Planting Churches among the City's Poor: An Anthology of Urban Church Planting Resources*, Vol. 2, pp. 167-171.

1. Churches based on relationship and camaraderie (between pastors, members, leaders)

2. Churches linked because of denominational legacy (e.g., EFCA, Presbyterian, United Methodist, National Baptist Convention)

3. Churches under a particular pastoral authority or "bishop"

4. Churches connected to sacramental, liturgical, doctrinal, or governance practice (e.g., Charismatic Episcopal Church, Pentecostal churches)

5. Churches based on ethnic, national, or cultural heritage and background (e.g., Greek Orthodox, Korean Baptist)

6. Churches that emerged from a movement of church planting (e.g., Vineyard, Victory Outreach)

7. Churches in a distinctive city, locale, and region

D. The pieces of the puzzle: creating a template for Church Association

If we admit that every urban congregation fundamentally needs association to survive and grow, regardless of model, size, or governance structure, we must train church planters to plant churches that long for intimate connection with other congregations. Association is a solid biblical and historical concept that allows for freedom of expression, to be structured in any number of legitimate ways.

Please refer to "Looking Toward the Horizons: Facilitating an Association of Urban Congregations" (*Planting Churches among the City's Poor: An Anthology of Urban Church Planting Resources*, Vol. 2, pp. 172-176) to find a ready template of the various elements by which a group of like-minded churches can unite around.

III. Evangel Schools and UCAs – The Concept of a Locale Church

The concept of the Locale Church: "The presence and association of all Christ-honoring congregations in a particular geographical area, regardless of form, denomination, or structure (whether traditional, community, mega-churches, or cell or house churches) which together represent the body of Christ and kingdom witness in a region."

A. Elements of the locale church (i.e., regional church)

1. In the NT, the churches throughout Asia Minor and the Roman empire were connected and built upon the apostolic witness concerning the person and work of Jesus Christ; in every sense, the early Church was:

   a. *One*: Eph. 4.4-6 – There is one body and one Spirit – just as you were called to the one hope that belongs to your call – one Lord, one faith, one baptism, one God and Father of all, who is over all and through all and in all.

b. *Holy*: 1 Pet. 2.9 – But you are a chosen race, a royal priesthood, a holy nation, a people for his own possession, that you may proclaim the excellencies of him who called you out of darkness into his marvelous light.

c. *Catholic*: Titus 2.14 – who gave himself for us to redeem us from all lawlessness and to purify for himself a people for his own possession who are zealous for good works.

d. *Apostolic*: Eph. 2.19-20 – So then you are no longer strangers and aliens, but you are fellow citizens with the saints and members of the household of God, built on the foundation of the apostles and prophets, Christ Jesus himself being the cornerstone.

2. The kind of experience they were undergoing in their location and condition, 1 Thess. 2.14 – For you, brothers, became imitators of the churches of God in Christ Jesus that are in Judea. For you suffered the same things from your own countrymen as they did from the Jews.

3. Their cultural background, Rom. 16.3-4 – Greet Prisca and Aquila, my fellow workers in Christ Jesus, who risked their necks for my life, to whom not only I give thanks but all the churches of the Gentiles give thanks as well.

4. Their spiritual condition, Acts 15.41 – And he went through Syria and Cilicia, strengthening the churches.

5. Their particular geographical location and proximity

a. 2 Cor. 8.1 – We want you to know, brothers, about the grace of God that has been given among the churches of Macedonia.

b. Rev. 1.4 – John to the seven churches that are in Asia: Grace to you and peace from him who is and who was and who is to come, and from the seven spirits who are before his throne.

B. The problem with the Hodges Three-Selfs Paradigm of Church Identity

The Melvin Hodges paradigm emphasizes the need for indigenous independence in church starts and development. According to Hodge, churches must be self-governing (the indigenous church controls its own affairs and direction), self-supporting (the indigenous church supports its activities and leaders on the basis of its own funding and resources), and self-propagating (the indigenous church produces outreach and mission through its own efforts, evangelizing, discipling, and reproducing daughter churches). This paradigm is problematic if by "self" we mean completely separate and autonomous from the influence and support of any other congregations.

1. No church can be fully autonomous (i.e., a law to itself; we are all connected to apostolic witness, to the communion of saints, and to our common head and source, the Lord Jesus Christ), Eph. 4.4-6.

2. Likewise, no church can be expected to meet its own needs entirely; the apostles defined self-support in ways that ignored Hodge's element of complete indigenous support (e.g., the Jerusalem famine and the Macedonian offering, cf. Acts 15, 2 Cor. 8-9).

3. The early Church was a network of congregations and their leaders bound together by their common parentage by the Holy Spirit and their shared oversight by the apostles, along with their shared persecution and opposition from both Jewish and Roman sources, e.g., 1 Cor. 12.13; 2 Cor. 11.9.

4. Urban churches today desperately require the benefits of ongoing connection, oversight, partnership, and support from one another.

   a. Scattered, alienated, and disconnected flocks: the importance of the unity of the Church in our witness to Christ, John 17.21-23.

   b. Under-supported, financially strapped congregations: need for interconnected livelihood and growth of urban congregations, 2 Cor. 8.1-4; Acts 11.27-30.

    c. Poorly coordinated outreach and mission: the need for coordinated efforts at outreach, evangelism, social service, and mission, Acts 15.22.

5. Principles and practice of the locale church relationships

    a. Recognize the truth that all pastors need to be pastored.

    b. Further acknowledge that, in spite of the "self-" principles of church governance, all churches need relationships with other churches if they are to mature.

    c. Acknowledge the historical benefit of having congregational oversight (i.e., bishop or council) in the life of vulnerable, fledgling congregations and their leaders.

      (1) Regional relationships are key to connecting pastors and churches.

      (2) Regional relationships ensure the sharing of provision among churches which cannot meet their full need alone.

      (3) Regional relationships establish some level of self-chosen oversight for pastors who are accustomed to functioning as Lone Rangers.

      (4) Regional relationships open up the possibility of new outreach and mission by connecting believers of good will around issues and projects which require our attention as believers in our locale.

IV. Challenges to the Locale Church

Please refer to *Defining Our Convictions, Distinctives, and Applications* on the following page.

Defining Our Convictions, Distinctives, and Applications
Discerning the Elements of Community Identity

Rev. Dr. Don L. Davis

Our Core Convictions

This circle represents our most fundamental convictions and commitments, our Affirmation of Faith, the Gospel and those truths contained in the early Christian creeds (i.e., The Nicene Creed). These convictions are anchored in the Word of God, and represent our core belief and essential doctrines.

As members of the one, holy, apostolic, and universal body of Christ, *we should be ready and willing to die for our core convictions. They can never be compromised or altered.*

Our Ministry Applications
Our Community Distinctives
Our Core Convictions

Expressing Our Community Identity

Our Community Distinctives

This circle represents our unique distinctives as a missions organization and missionary community dedicated to living out our core convictions in the inner cities of America.

We are a religious missionary order community, living out the Gospel in the inner cities of America. We seek to honor and glorify God and delight in him in the city, knowing him and making him known through our evangelism, discipleship, and church planting. We seek to empower churches and their leaders through works of righteousness that impact them where they live, targeted to the whole person and the whole family. Our desire is to seek the transformation of the inner city as thousands of churches are planted in urban poor neighborhoods in every unreached community in America.

As members of an urban religious missionary order, we articulate and embody our fundamental distinctives in the inner cities of America. *We should be ready and willing to defend our unique distinctives as a community whose very existence seeks to flesh these out in the city.*

Our Ministry Applications

This circle represents the ways in which we have expressed our convictions and distinctives in our strategies, policies, and decisions. Our applications represent our unique methods of fleshing out our convictions and distinctives as the World Impact community, and as such also represent our accumulated legacy and wisdom in *how best* to accomplish our purposes in the city.

As urban cross-cultural church planters, we must be *ready and willing to dialogue about our applications and methods in order to discover the best possible means to accomplish our objectives to know God and make him known in the cities where we live.*

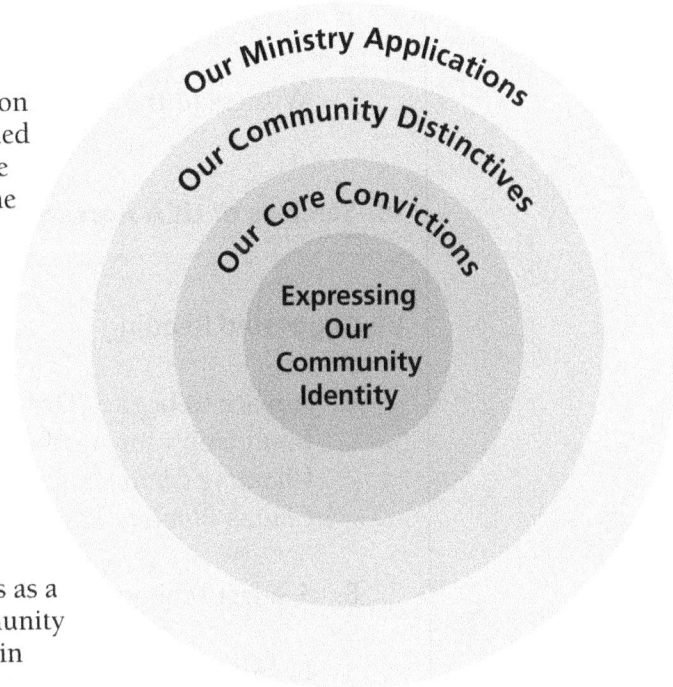

V. Benefits of Kingdom Partnership at the Locale Level

A. Church planting fruit

B. Kingdom shalom

C. Resourcing of pastors and urban churches

D. Witness to the world

VI. Samples of UCA Agreements (See Appendix, pp. 208-221)

VII. Suggested Reading

A. A place to begin: "Dry Wood for a Really Hot Fire: Laying the Foundation for Aggressive Urban Church Planting Movements" (*Planting Churches among the City's Poor: An Anthology of Urban Church Planting Resources,* Vol. 2, pp. 283-303)

B. A select bibliography

1. Allen, Roland. *Missionary Methods, St. Paul's or Ours?* Grand Rapids, MI: William B. Eerdmans Publishing Company, 1962.

2. Brock, Charles. *Indigenous Church Planting.* Nashville: Broadman Press, 1981.

3. Cheyney, Tom, J. David Putman and Van Sanders, eds. *Seven Steps for Planting Churches.* Alpharetta, GA: North American Mission Board, SBC, 2003.

4. Garrison, *Church Planting Movements: How God Is Redeeming a Lost World.* Midlothian, VA: WIGTake, 2004.

5. Griffith, Jim and Bill Easum. *Ten Most Common Mistakes Made by Church Starts.* Chalice Press, 2008.

6. Hesselgrave, David J. *Planting Churches Cross-Culturally: North America and Beyond,* 2nd ed. Grand Rapids, MI: Baker Book House, 2000.

7. Hiebert, Paul G. and Eloise Hiebert Meneses. *Incarnational Ministry: Planting Churches in Band, Tribal, Peasant, and Urban Societies.* Grand Rapids, MI: Baker Publishing House, 1995.

8. Keller, Tim and J. Allen Thompson. *Church Planting Manual.* Redeemer Church Planting Center, New York, 2002.

9. Logan, Robert E. *Be Fruitful and Multiply.* ChurchSmart Resources, 2006.

10. Mannoia, Kevin. *Church Planting: The Next Generation.* Indianapolis, IN: Light and Life Communication, 1994.

11. Malphurs, Aubrey. *Planting Growing Churches for the 21st Century: A Comprehensive Guide for New Churches and Those Desiring Renewal*, 2nd ed. Grand Rapids, MI: Baker Book House, 1998.

12. Rainey, Joel. *Planting Churches in the Real World.* Missional Press, 2008.

13. Roberts, Bob, Jr. *The Multiplying Church: The New Math for Starting New Churches.* Grand Rapids, MI: Zondervan, 2008.

14. Shenk, David W. and Ervin R. Stutzman. *Creating Communities of the Kingdom: New Testament Models of Church Planting.* Scottdale, PA: Herald Press, 1988.

15. Smith, Efrem. *The Post-Black and Post-White Church: Becoming the Beloved Community in a Multi-Ethnic World.* San Francisco: Jossey-Bass Publishers, 2012.

16. Smith, Efrem, and Phil Jackson. *The Hip-Hop Church: Connecting with the Movement Shaping Our Culture.* Downers Grove: InterVarsity Press, 2005.

17. Steffen, Tom. *Passing the Baton: Church Planting That Empowers.* La Habra, CA: Center for Organizational & Ministry Development, 1997.

18. Stetzer, Edward. *How to Plant a Church, A Seminary Extension Study Course.* Nashville, TN: Seminary Extension, 2001.

19. ———. *Planting Missional Churches*. Nashville, TN: B&H Publishers, 2006.

20. Towns, Elmer L. and Douglas Porter. *Churches That Multiply*. Kansas City: Beacon Hill Press. 2003.

21. Wagner, C. Peter. *Church Planting for a Greater Harvest*. Ventura: Regal Books, 1990.

The Threefold Cord of Urban Cross-Cultural Church Planting Movements

Rev. Dr. Don L. Davis

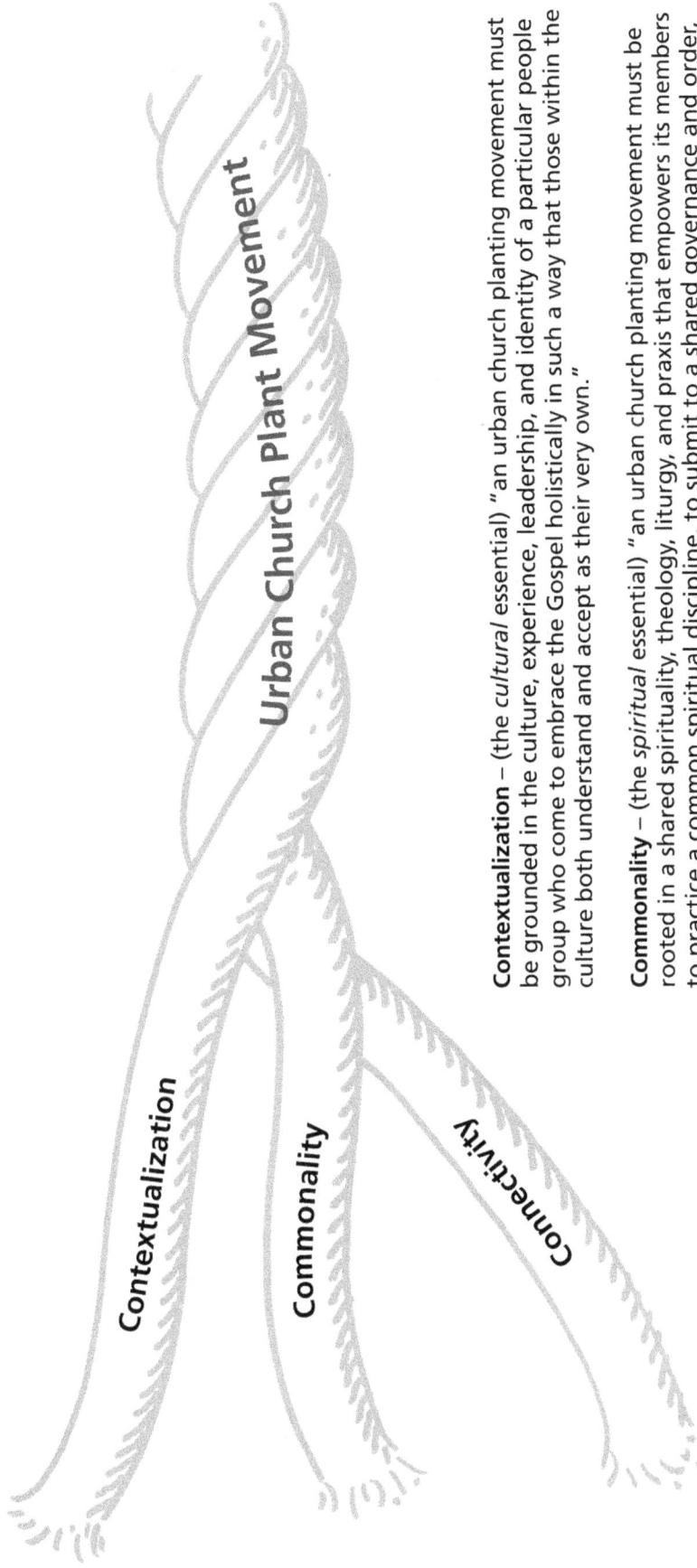

Urban Church Plant Movement

Contextualization

Commonality

Connectivity

Contextualization – (the *cultural* essential) "an urban church planting movement must be grounded in the culture, experience, leadership, and identity of a particular people group who come to embrace the Gospel holistically in such a way that those within the culture both understand and accept as their very own."

Commonality – (the *spiritual* essential) "an urban church planting movement must be rooted in a shared spirituality, theology, liturgy, and praxis that empowers its members to practice a common spiritual discipline, to submit to a shared governance and order, to recognize and affirm its unique theological and spiritual distinctives, to incorporate and confirm its members and leaders according to a common protocol, and to integrate the efforts of its congregations together into a coherent, unified movement."

Connectivity – (the *structural* essential) "an urban church planting movement must connect its leaders, members, and congregations through integrated structures that enable its congregations and leaders to gather regularly for convocation and fellowship, that combine resources and funds for cooperation and mutual support, and that provide oversight that protects and equips the members of the movement for dynamic reproduction."

Ecc. 4.12 (ESV) - *And though a man might prevail against one who is alone, two will withstand him – a threefold cord is not quickly broken.*

The Communal Context of Authentic Christian Leadership

Rev. Dr. Don L. Davis

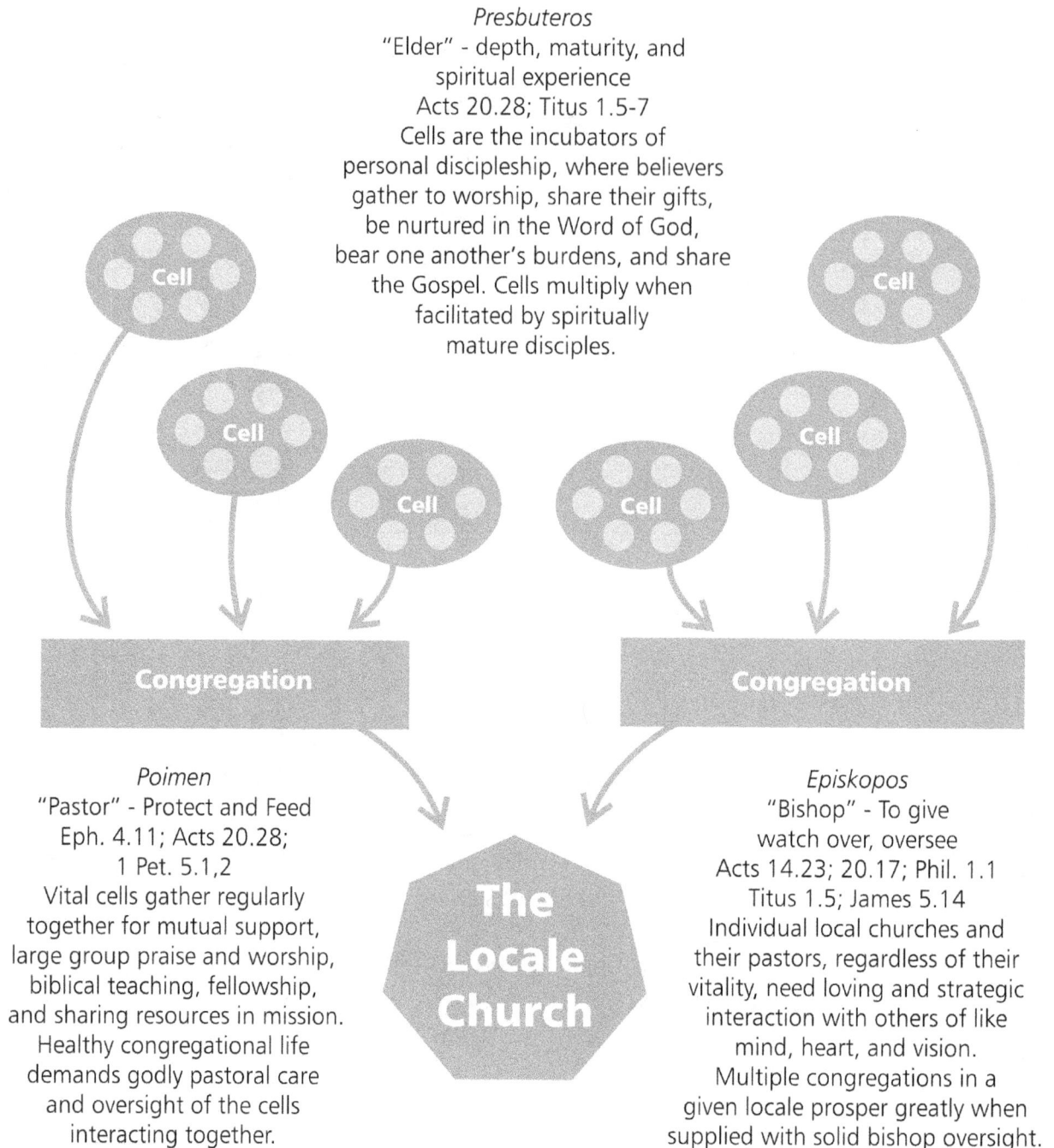

Presbuteros
"Elder" - depth, maturity, and
spiritual experience
Acts 20.28; Titus 1.5-7
Cells are the incubators of
personal discipleship, where believers
gather to worship, share their gifts,
be nurtured in the Word of God,
bear one another's burdens, and share
the Gospel. Cells multiply when
facilitated by spiritually
mature disciples.

Cell

Cell

Cell

Cell

Cell

Cell

Congregation

Congregation

The Locale Church

Poimen
"Pastor" - Protect and Feed
Eph. 4.11; Acts 20.28;
1 Pet. 5.1,2
Vital cells gather regularly
together for mutual support,
large group praise and worship,
biblical teaching, fellowship,
and sharing resources in mission.
Healthy congregational life
demands godly pastoral care
and oversight of the cells
interacting together.

Episkopos
"Bishop" - To give
watch over, oversee
Acts 14.23; 20.17; Phil. 1.1
Titus 1.5; James 5.14
Individual local churches and
their pastors, regardless of their
vitality, need loving and strategic
interaction with others of like
mind, heart, and vision.
Multiple congregations in a
given locale prosper greatly when
supplied with solid bishop oversight.

Presbuteros, "an elder" is another term for the same person as bishop or overseer . . . . The term "elder" indicates the mature spiritual experience and understanding of those so described; the term "bishop" or "overseer," indicates the character of the work undertaken. According to the divine will and appointment, as in the NT, there were to be bishops in every local church, Acts 14.23; 20.17; Phil. 1.1; Titus 1.5; James 5.14." - *Vines Complete Expository Dictionary*. Nashville: Thomas Nelson Publishers, 1996. p. 195

Church Planting Models

Rev. Dr. Don L. Davis

The following models represent a spectrum of models which have been associated with evangelical church planting. Questions are designed to help us explore the various options available to the cross-cultural urban church planter in establishing congregations among the poor. Our dialogue today hopefully will isolate some of the critical issues necessary for a church plant team to think through in order to make its selection as to what particular kind of church they ought to plant, given the culture, population, and other factors encountered in its particular mission field.

1. What is the definition of the phrase "church planting models"? Why might it be important to consider various options in planting a church among the poor in the city?

2. How would you characterize the various models (or other) which have been allowed or employed in traditional church planting? What would you consider to be its strengths and/or weaknesses, and should we use any of them in our planting of churches among the poor in the city?

    a. Founding Pastor Model – a leader moves into a community with a commitment to lead and shepherd the church that is planted.

    b. Church Split Model?! – a new church is formed due to fundamental disagreement over some issue of morality, Bible interpretation, or schism.

    c. Nucleus Model – (sometimes referred to as the "colonization" model). This model involves a central assembly commissioning a smaller nucleus from its group (usually with leadership and members already organized) to leave the larger assembly and relocate into an unreached community as a kind of ready-made nucleus of the church which is to be formed.

    d. Beachhead or Mother Church Model – a strong, central congregation determines to become a kind of sending center and nurturing headquarters for new churches planted through its oversight and auspices, in the immediate area and/or beyond.

e. Cell Church Model – once centralized assembly which considers the heart of its life and ministry to occur in the cells which are connected structurally and pastorally to the central congregation; their participation together constitutes the church.

f. Home Church Model – a church, which although similar to a cell church model, is intentionally planted with greater attention given to the authority and autonomy of the gathering of Christians who meet regularly in their respective homes.

g. Missionary Model – a church where a cross-cultural church planter seeks to plant a church among an unreached people with an intent from the beginning to help the church to be self-propagating, self-governing, and self-supporting.

3. Instead of models language, World Impact recognizes three distinct "expressions" of church planting, out of which various models can be considered and employed.

The Small Church Expression (or "house church," 20-50 people). The small (or house) church can be understood as a *small store in a shopping mall*. Needs the connections to other small churches to both survive and thrive. Small churches are able to meet virtually anywhere and can operate with a tiny footprint with little to no financial burdens. They can focus on a specific block, housing development, or network of families. This expressions allows for a strong discipleship focus of indigenous leadership development can take place in this smaller connected group.

The Community Church Expression (60-150 people) The community church is the most common expression of church, numerically speaking, in the world today. This expression can be understood as a *grocery or convenience store in a neighborhood or community*. This expression focuses on a particular geographic identity and proximity, highlighting both the, affinity, connection, and unique context of the congregation and the surrounding community. It is developed around a deep calling and connection to a particular neighborhood, and typically requires a semi-stable place to meet (e.g., a park, community center, or school). Partnership with other community churches is important.

The Mother Church Expression (200+ people) The mother church (or "hub church") represents a larger assembly of believers, and can be understood as *a Walmart Superstore or Super*

Target, a store which houses a number of select entities that supply its patrons with many choices and opportunities. This kind of church, which has both the economic and spiritual resources for multiplication, can leverage its resources and capabilities to become both a sending/empowering church which reproduces itself many times over. Ideally, a mother or hub church is a congregation that is led by clear missional intents that allow it to leverage its capabilities and gifts to become a center of compassion, mercy, and justice ministries. It can also come to serve as the nurturing headquarters for church planters and ministry starters, and can easily operate as an incubator of other effective ministries among the unreached urban poor. Such an expression usually is more rooted in a particular built-to-suit facility that allows it to leverage these kinds of capabilities.

4. What are the critical issues (e.g., culture, the tradition of the church planters, and contextualization) which ought to be factored most into selecting the appropriate model or expression for use in planting a church cross-culturally in the city?

5. Of all the things which a church planter may be aware of, what do you believe is the central element he or she must understand in order to choose the "right" option for them?

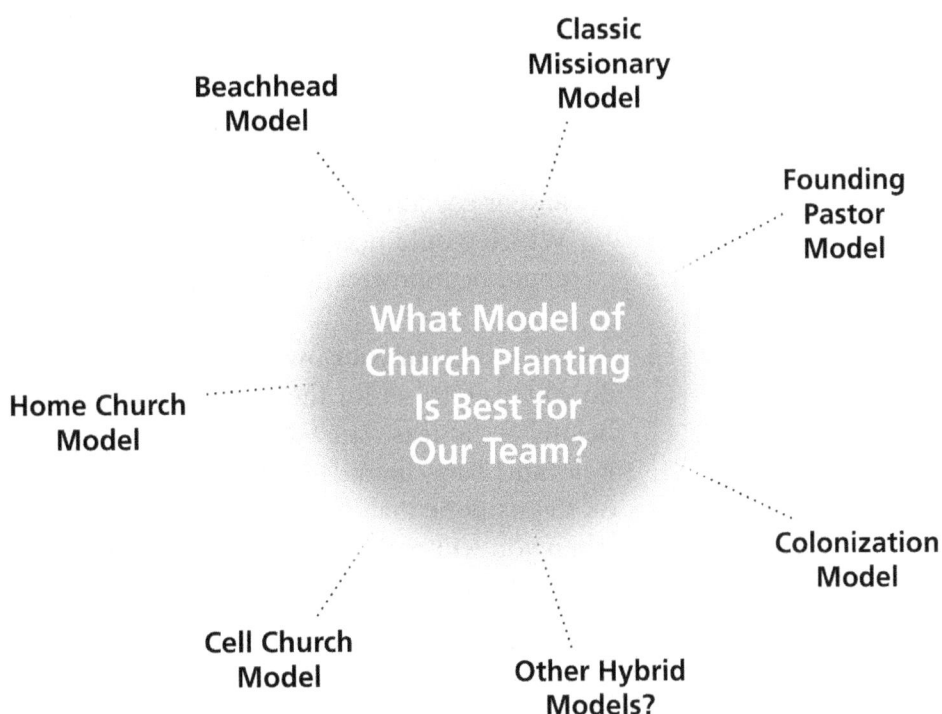

Beachhead
Model

Classic
Missionary
Model

Founding
Pastor
Model

What Model of
Church Planting
Is Best for
Our Team?

Home Church
Model

Colonization
Model

Cell Church
Model

Other Hybrid
Models?

Dean Exercise

Evangel and Movements

One hour

Your Dean Team needs to make specific plans for how you will prepare for hosting your first Evangel Dean School. Use this exercise time to continue the conversation and think through your own "Prepare" phase.

This dean's exercise is an adaptation of the Evangel School exercise found on pages 190–194 in *Ripe for Harvest: A Guidebook for Planting Healthy Churches in the City*.

Exercise Instructions

1. Open in prayer, committing your time to the Lord and seeking his wisdom (5 min).

2. Look over the Prepare Questions for Church Plant Teams on pages 191–193 in *Ripe for Harvest* (20 min).

   a. Which of the "Preparing the Church-Planting Team" questions (191–192) would you be especially concerned with if you were assessing and/or coaching an Evangel Church Plant team right now? Which would need to be addressed at the school, and which could be followed up with later on?

   b. Which of the "Preparing for the Task" (193–194) questions would you be especially concerned with if you were assessing and/or coaching an Evangel Church Plant team right now? Which would need to be addressed at the school, and which could be followed up with later on?

3. As you reflect on your own Evangel Vision and Values, what goals do you need to set for the next six months in the areas identified below? Set at least one S.M.A.R.T. (Specific, Measurable, Achievable, Relevant, Time-bound) goal for each of the following six areas. It is ok to postpone making a decision as long as you establish a goal for when you will make the decision (e.g. Make decision about where to host website for school by October 15).

    a. Recruitment

        1) Team Leaders

        2) Assessor Coaches

        3) School administration and support staff

    b. Assessment

    c. Publicity and funding

    d. Evangel and movements

    e. Field Coaches

4. Appoint a spokesperson who will present your initial goals for the next six months.

DEAN EXERCISE

Field Coaches

One hour

Your Dean Team needs to make specific plans for how you will prepare for hosting your first Evangel Dean School. Use this exercise time to continue the conversation and think through your own "Prepare" phase.

This dean's exercise is an adaptation of the Evangel School exercise found on pages 190–194 in *Ripe for Harvest: A Guidebook for Planting Healthy Churches in the City*.

Exercise Instructions

1. Open in prayer, committing your time to the Lord and seeking his wisdom (5 min).

2. Look over the Prepare Questions for Church Plant Teams on pages 191–193 in *Ripe for Harvest* (20 min).

   a. Which of the "Preparing the Church-Planting Team" questions (191–192) would you be especially concerned with if you were assessing and/or coaching an Evangel Church Plant team right now? Which would need to be addressed at the school, and which could be followed up with later on?

   b. Which of the "Preparing for the Task" (193–194) questions would you be especially concerned with if you were assessing and/or coaching an Evangel Church Plant team right now? Which would need to be addressed at the school, and which could be followed up with later on?

3. As you reflect on your own Evangel Vision and Values, what goals do you need to set for the next six months in the areas identified below? Set at least one S.M.A.R.T. (Specific, Measurable, Achievable, Relevant, Time-bound) goal for each of the following six areas. It is ok to postpone making a decision as long as you establish a goal for when you will make the decision (e.g. Make decision about where to host website for school by October 15).

Evangel School Resource Pack Information

Evangel School Resource Pack Detail

Evangel Resources Overview

Evangel Resource Pack Overview.wpd
Evangel Resources itemized list.xlsx
Evangel School Dean Protocol.xlsx

Templates and Project Resources

Communion Liturgy 2016.pdf
DelegateNameTagBlank.jpg
DelegateNameTagSample.jpg
StaffNameTagBlank.jpg
StaffNameTagSample.jpg
Team Name Table Sign Template.docx
Team Sign Template with Background.docx
Team Sign Tempalte.docx
Trifold Schedule Template 2.docx

Certificate and Fonts for Certificate

CALIFB_4.TTF
CALIFI_4.TTF
CALIFR_4.TTF
Evangel School Certificate.docx

Music Mp3s, Leadsheet PDFs, and Lyrics (PDF and Text)

Come Jesus Come
For Me to Live Is Christ
Give Glory to the Lamb
Let's Take This City for God
Praise to You
Spirit of God
The Battle Belongs to the Lord
The Church of the Living God
The Fight Is On
The Lord Is a Warrior

Graphics

Black arch sower Evangel School of UCP.jpg
Black arch sower Evangel School of UCP.png
Black arch sower Evangel School.jpg
Black arch sower Evangel School.png
color-arch new sower EVANGEL SCHOOL.jpg
Gold arch sower.png
Sower.jpg
Web Graphic - Sower Evangel School of UCP.jpg
Web Graphic - Sower Evangel School.jpg
Web Graphic - Sower-600.jpg
CoachesTableSign.jpg
Evangel School final banner.jpg
folder label.jpg
one minute sign 11x17.jpg
one minute sign 8.5x11.jpg
registration banner 1.png
registration banner 2.png
registration banner 3.jpg
RegistrationSignLarge.jpg
RegistrationSignSmall.jpg
tshirtback1.jpg
tshirtback2.jpg
tshirtback3.jpg
tshirtback4.jpg
tshirtfront1.jpg
tshirtfront2.jpg
tshirtfront3.jpg
tshirtfront4.jpg

Project Support

Minute x Minute
Project Task Chart
Project Setup
Project Breakdown
Packing Lists
Announcements
Shopping List
Draft Schedule

Videos	Time
Dr. Davis Welcome	6:00
01-Dev-Power-Praise	30:46
02-SS1-Seeing-Big-Picture-TO	3:43
03-SS1-Sem1-What-is-Church	33:03
04-SS1-Sem2-Church-plant-over	31:20
05-SS1-Sem3-Using-Wisdom-Ministry	16:13
06-SS1-TE-Establishing-context	3:49
07-SS1-TE-Define-values-vision	7:08
08-Dev-Freedom-Christ	31:34
09-SS2-Prepare-Church-TO	7:22
10-SS2-Sem1-Diff-Diff-Makes	32:23
11-SS2-Sem2-Theo-of-Poor	33:52
12-SS2-Sem3-Build-Team-Success	33:20
13-SS2-TE-Prepare-Church	3:23
14-Dev-Prayer-Walk-Talk-Faith	31:55
15-SS3-Launch-Assemble-TO	7:51
16-SS3-Sem1-Evang-Follow-Mission	32:16
17-SS3-Sem2-Christus-Victor	33:37
18-SS3-Sem3-Events-Projects	7:54
19-SS3-TE-Launch-Expand-Church	2:46
20-SS3-TE-Assem-Estab-Church	2:27
21-Dev-God-Warrior	30:10
22-SS4-Nurture-Transition-TO	9:18
23-SS4-Sem1-Effective-Discipling	33:41
24-SS4-Sem2-Discipling-Urban	33:59
25-SS4-Sem3-Preaching-Teaching	32:50
26-SS4-Sem4-Select-Credible-Criteria	33:43
27-SS4-TE-Nurture-Mature-Church	2:36
28-SS4-TE-Transition-Release-Church	2:58
29-Dev-Adapt-Win	32:51
30-SS5-Bring-It-Together-TO	3:11
31-SS5-Sem1-Importance-Review	6:40
32-SS5-TE-Bringing-It-Together	5:28
Camp Fire Stories	9:46

PowerPoints
01-Dev-Power-Praise.ppt
02-SS1-Seeing-Big-Picture-TO.ppt
03-SS1-Sem1-What-is-Church.ppt
04-SS1-Sem2-Church-plant-over.ppt
05-SS1-Sem3-Using-Wisdom-Ministry.ppt
06-SS1-TE-Establishing-context.ppt
07-SS1-TE-Define-values-vision.ppt
08-Dev-Freedom-Christ.ppt
09-SS2-Prepare-Church-TO.ppt
10-SS2-Sem1-Diff-Diff-Makes.ppt
11-SS2-Sem2-Theo-of-Poor.ppt
12-SS2-Sem3-Build-Team-Success.ppt
13-SS2-TE-Prepare-Church.ppt
14-Dev-Prayer-Walk-Talk-Faith.ppt
15-SS3-Launch-Assemble-TO.ppt
16-SS3-Sem1-Evang-Follow-Mission.ppt
17-SS3-Sem2-Christus-Victor.ppt
18-SS3-Sem3-Events-Projects.ppt
19-SS3-TE-Launch-Expand-Church.ppt
20-SS3-TE-Assem-Estab-Church.ppt
21-Dev-God-Warrior.ppt
22-SS4-Nurture-Transition-TO.ppt
23-SS4-Sem1-Effective-Discipling.ppt
24-SS4-Sem2-Discipling-Urban.ppt
25-SS4-Sem3-Preaching-Teaching.ppt
26-SS4-Sem4-Select-Credible-Criteria.ppt
27-SS4-TE-Nurture-Mature-Church.ppt
28-SS4-TE-Transition-Release-Church.ppt
29-Dev-Adapt-Win.ppt
30-SS5-Bring-It-Together-TO.ppt
31-SS5-Sem1-Importance-Review.ppt
32-SS5-TE-Bringing-It-Together.ppt
CV-01-Calling-of-God.ppt
CV-02-Kingdom-of-God.ppt
CV-03-Centrality-of-Church.ppt
CV-04-Power-of-Community.ppt
CV-05-Gods-Election-of-Humble.ppt
CV-06-Standard-of-Excellence.ppt
CV-07-Explosiveness-of-Multiplication.ppt
LetGodArise-prayer.ppt
Cmmissioning.ppt
Communion.ppt

Evangel School Resource Pack Overview

Below you will find listed some specifics about the package you just downloaded.

Links to Evangel Forms

- *Assessment Tools*: www.tumi.org/evangel

  One of our two most important resources for helping church planters and their home churches discern their call is the World Impact Planter Profile and Assessment (WIPPA) evaluation tool. You will find the "Church Planter Self-Evaluation", "Church Planter Evaluation by Pastor", and the "Church Planter Evaluation by Spouse" forms here.

- *Registering Your Upcoming Evangel School*: www.tumi.org/evangel

  Please be sure to register your school at this location 60 days prior to hosting your Evangel School.

- *Submit Evangel School Reports*: www.tumi.org/evangel (with uploads)

  Please be sure to complete this form within 15 days of hosting your Evangel School.

- *Field Coach Quarterly Report Form*: www.tumi.org/evangel

  This is the formal form to guide you in your quarterly review of your Church Plant Team.

- *Evangel Grant Applications*: www.tumi.org/evangel. If grants are available, you will find applications for them here.

Evangel Theme Verse

For I am not ashamed of the gospel, for it is the power of God for salvation to everyone who believes, to the Jew first and also to the Greek (Rom. 1.16 [ESV]).

Evangel School Gold Color

Here are the color palette codes for the Sower Gold color:

- RGB – R:247 | G:220 | B:147
- CMYK – C:4 | M:16 | Y:51 | K:0

Videos

We have 34 videos teaching all of the Devotions, Seminars, Themes and Objectives, and Team Exercises for the Evangel School. These are a part of the Evangel School Resource Pack. They are available on our TUMI Vimeo, and we have included the password here for you.

The links below will take you directly to the "album" for each session as there are multiple videos for each of the five sessions of the Evangel School.

The password for each album is located in the "video and password" file in your Evangel School Resource Pack.

The links to all the Evangel video albums are below (as well as in your Evangel School Resource Pack):

- Evangel Album (all videos): *https://vimeo.com/album/4005140*
- Evangel Session 1: *https://vimeo.com/album/4053919*
- Evangel Session 2: *https://vimeo.com/album/4053917*
- Evangel Session 3: *https://vimeo.com/album/4053921*
- Evangel Session 4: *https://vimeo.com/album/4057635*
- Evangel Session 5: *https://vimeo.com/album/4057641*

Graphics

- *Evangel and Sower Graphics*

  We have given you a host of graphics to enable you to create resources and products that you wish for your schools. There are several versions of the Evangel graphics with full title, partial title, and no title (just Sower).

- *Evangel School Banner*
  - ~ Final Print Size to: 4 x 8 feet
  - ~ There is 4-inch bleed at top and bottom for 2-inch pole pockets.
  - ~ There is 1-inch bleed on sides so printer would fold over edges and stitch.

- *Signs*

  One-minute sign: There are two versions: one can be printed on 8.5x11, the other on 11x17

  ~ one minute sign 8.5x11.jpg

  ~ one minute sign 11x17.jpg

  Evangel Registration or Web Page Headers
  (3 options to choose from)

  ~ registration banner 1.png (transparent background)

  ~ registration banner 2.png (transparent background)

  ~ registration banner 3.jpg

  Registration sign: Directions for each of these are a part of the jpg and will be trimmed by you when you produce.

  ~ Registrationsignlarge.jpg (can be printed on 11x17)

  ~ Registrationsignsmall.jpg (can be printed on 8.5x11)

T-Shirts

There are several options for t-shirts here. Each t-shirt front design or back design is separate so you can mix and match your choices. We also included sample t-shirt graphics so you can see what these t-shirt graphics will look like on a shirt.

The shirt color that we chose for the sample was selected from Gildan. (Color: "Yellow Haze"). There are sample graphics on this document but they are also included as graphic files in your package.

tshirtfront1.jpg
tshirtfront1sample.png*

tshirtfront2.jpg
tshirtfront2sample.png*

* Please note: The sample t-shirt graphic files (png) are for viewing purposes only. Give the jpg file(s) (not sample files) to the vendor who is printing your shirts.

tshirtfront3.jpg
tshirtfront3sample.png*

tshirtfront4.jpg
tshirtfront4sample.png*

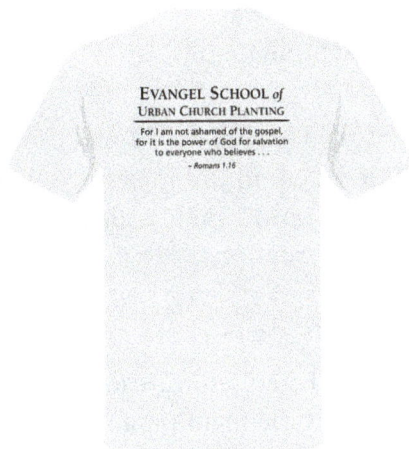

tshirtback1.jpg
tshirtback1sample.png*

tshirtback2.jpg
tshirtback2sample.png*

tshirtback3.jpg
tshirtback3sample.png*

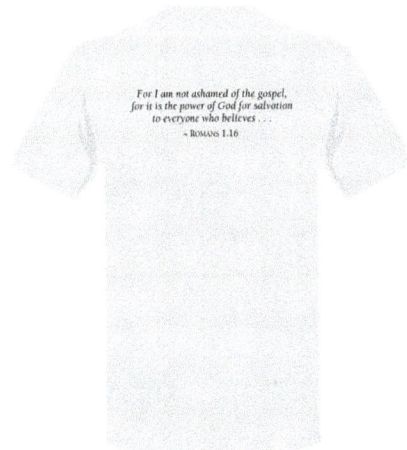

tshirtback4.jpg
tshirtback4sample.png*

Templates and Project Resources

- *Templates*

  Directions for each of these are a part of the jpg and will be trimmed by you when you produce.

  ~ DeansTableSign.jpg

  ~ CoachesTableSign.jpg

  ~ Team sign template.docx

  ~ Team sign template with Background.docx

  ~ Team name table sign template.docx

  ~ Delegatenametagblank.jpg

  ~ Delegatenametagsample.jpg

  ~ Staffnametagblank.jpg

  ~ Staffnametagsample.jpg

- *Communion Service*

  We have included a communion service PowerPoint along with a document for the Lord's Table Celebrant to follow which has some additional instructions.

- *Certificate and Fonts*

  The Certificate can be edited for each team. As you can see by the template, we put the team name on the template. We print a copy for each member of the team and the 2 Deans who are hosting the school and the two coaches for that team at the school are the ones who sign their certificate.

  ~ *Fonts*: The fonts used in this template are included in case you do not have on your computer. Load these on your computer and you will be set to print.

  ~ *Certificate Covers*: You may purchase Certificate covers on Amazon. There is a wide choice of options.

  ~ Evangel School Certficate.docx (along with 3 fonts)

- *Commissioning Service*

  At the end of Evangel School (last day) there will be a commissioning service. Please ask all of the teams to where their Evangel shirts for the service (you will need to tell them this before Saturday).

We have created a PowerPoint for you to use, a call and response time, ending with a prayer that everyone can read together.

- *For the Commissioning Service:*

  ~ We call a team up (along with their two coaches), and ask the team to face the Dean who is commissioning them.

  ~ The Dean running the commissioning leads the teams through the "call and response" of the Commissioning PowerPoint, ending with the prayer that everyone can read together.

  ~ The Dean then gives the signed certificates to the coaches and they hand out to the team (or the Deans can do if they prefer).

  ~ The Commissioning Dean then asks the team to face the audience and asks 1 of the 2 coaches to pray for the team. The Dean leading the commissioning can ask the audience to raise their hands toward the team and join the coach in prayer for the team.

  ~ Right after prayer, allow a couple of minutes to get pictures of the team together with their coaches, each team member holding up his / her certificate.

  ~ After prayer the team, coaches, and deans shake hands / hug and the team sits down.

  ~ The commissioning Dean calls up the next team and repeats.

  ~ At the end of the Commissioning Service, one of the Dean can pronounce a closing prayer over all of the teams and coaches.

- *Project Support*

  All of the files here are meant to be resources to help you think through your plan for this event.

  ~ Project Task Chart, Setup, Breakdown, Packing lists, Announcements, Shopping.xlsx: There are 6 sheets in this spreadsheet of project info that will help you plan this project out excellently

    1) Project Task Chart which lists tasks and has a place for due dates and person(s) assigned to the task.

    2) Setup List which will give you ideas as to what you may need to do to set up for your event

3) Breakdown List which details what needs to happen for some breakdown the night before the end of the school, as well as at the close of your Evangel School.

4) Packing List if you are hosting the Evangel School at a different location, here are some things to help you as you make your list of what needs to be brought with you to pull of this event.

5) Announcements ideas: as you are putting together the opening welcome and announcements for your school as well as announcements throughout, here are some ideas of things you may want to include.

6) In prepping for the school, we've started a basic shopping list of things you may need to purchase for this event.

~ Min x Min: This is a minute by minute schedule that you can edit to fit your schedule for your school.

~ Trifold Schedule Template.docx

~ Communion Liturgy: This is the document for the Lord's Table Celebrant to follow which has some additional instructions. This lines up with the Communion PowerPoint.